Is This Any Way to Run a Democratic Election?

Is This Any Way to Run a Democratic Election?

Stephen J. Wayne
Georgetown University

CQ PRESS

A Division of SAGE
Washington, D.C.

CQ Press
2300 N Street, NW, Suite 800
Washington, DC 20037

Phone: 202-729-1900; toll-free, 1-866-4CQ-PRESS (1-866-427-7737)

Web: www.cqpress.com

Cover design: Silverander Communications
Cover photos: Getty Images, Stefan Klein
Composition: C&M Digitals (P) Ltd.

♾ The paper used in this publication exceeds the requirements of the
American National Standard for Information Sciences—Permanence of Paper
for Printed Library Materials, ANSI Z39.48-1992.

Printed and bound in the United States of America

14   13   12   11   10   1   2   3   4   5

Library of Congress Cataloging-in-Publication Data

Wayne, Stephen J.
   Is this any way to run a democratic election? / Stephen J. Wayne. — 4th ed.
      p. cm.
   Includes bibliographical references and index.
   ISBN 978-1-60426-635-1 (pbk. : alk. paper)   1. Democracy—United States.
   I. Title.
   JK1726.W38 2010
   324.973—dc22
                                                                    2009049666

To my son, CPT Jared Wayne, USA

Defending democracy is a noble cause;
imposing it on others is not.

May you and your generation
keep the flame of American democracy
burning brightly in the United States.

CONTENTS

Figures

Tables

Boxes

We are a nation of critics, self-critics. As we laud our democratic system, we also complain about it. The election process in particular has been the source of much lament and critical commentary, especially in the aftermath of the controversial presidential election of 2000.

WHAT'S WRONG WITH AMERICAN ELECTORAL POLITICS?

A lot, say its critics. Their complaints are legion. The election cycle is too long, too complex, and too costly. The system is controlled by and for the few, the special interests, not the public's interest. Election laws are biased in favor of those who enacted them—the major parties and their candidates—and sometimes they have been implemented in a partisan and discriminatory manner. Money drives the process, and wealthy contributors exercise disproportionate influence over the candidates, parties, and campaigns, and on what follows from this election activity—public policy making. The news media are more interested in a good scandal than in discussing substantive policy issues and their consequences for society. Politicians are not to be trusted; they will say and do almost anything to get elected, and once elected, they are beholden to their large contributors and the special-interest groups that aided their campaigns. Moreover, incumbents have stacked the deck in favor of their own renomination and reelection, thereby undercutting two of the basic goals of a democratic electoral process—to keep public officials responsive to the people and to hold them accountable for their public policy decisions and actions.

And as if these allegations are not enough, there is the charge that election returns today do not result in winners who are compatible with one another, who are willing to compromise on the major policy issues, and who put the public's interest ahead of their own private interests. Nor does the outcome of the vote easily translate into a governing agenda and a majority coalition for achieving it. All of these charges have produced negative perceptions of the electoral process today and undoubtedly have contributed to public cynicism, apathy, and mistrust of politicians and the politics in which they engage. Something is very wrong with American electoral politics, or so its critics allege.

Are these charges correct? Is the current way the best way to run a democratic election? Have we drifted from the ideals and goals of the American political tradition? If so, how and when did we do so, and what, if anything, can be done about it? If not, why are there so many persistent complaints, and why do so many people not vote? These are some of the questions that concerned citizens should be asking about our electoral system and that public officials, party leaders, political scientists, and others should be answering.

This book is intended to help its readers address these questions and thereby participate in the debate on American electoral politics. Its aim is to explore critical and controversial issues that confront our political system today, and to do so in a reader-friendly way. *Is This Any Way to Run a Democratic Election?* looks at American democracy in theory and practice, notes where and why practices deviate from theory, and then proposes reforms to close the gap.

THE ORGANIZATION AND FEATURES OF THE BOOK

The book's first chapter discusses democratic theory in general and the democratic electoral process in particular. The next five chapters (chapters 2–6) examine key aspects of electoral politics: suffrage and turnout, representation, money, media, and political parties. Each of these factors shapes a political contest, affects its outcome, and has consequences for governing. From the environment in which elections occur, the last three chapters (chapters 7–9) turn to the electoral process itself: the nomination and general election, and their collective and individual impact on governing.

Each chapter of the book includes features intended to pique a reader's interest in electoral issues and foster critical thinking and participation. Every chapter begins with "Did you know that . . . ," an opening feature that presents interesting and sometimes disturbing facts about democratic election practices, processes, and outcomes that may not be widely known. After a discussion of the electoral dilemmas and ways to overcome them, each chapter concludes with a short summary, followed by a critical thinking section, "Now It's Your Turn." Included in this section are Discussion Questions, Topics for Debate, research-oriented exercises that encourage use of the Internet, and a listing of Internet Resources and Selected Readings.

WHAT'S NEW ABOUT THE FOURTH EDITION?

The election of 2008 was historic Americans elected their first African American president. People voted in record numbers. Each party had a competitive nomination process, with the Democrats taking six months to determine their nominee. More people made contributions to the candidates and their parties. More money was raised and spent, but money was not the principal factor determining the outcome in either the primaries or the general election.

The means by which the candidates communicated their campaigns to voters also changed. The Internet became a principal vehicle that facilitated Obama's bottom-up campaign. He used it to raise money, to gain volunteers, to mobilize crowds at his events, and to get out the vote. Social networking was key to his success. The campaign launched a text-messaging program to which one million people subscribed. When the campaign ended, the Obama organization had more than thirteen million e-mail addresses that could be reused to mobilize support for the new administration's policies and programs and potentially for the president's reelection.

The election appears to have ended partisan parity. For the first time in more than thirty years a Democratic presidential candidate received more than 50 percent of the vote, and Democrats strengthened their majorities in both houses of Congress. Women, racial and ethnic minorities, and new voters provided a substantial part of the Democratic vote, creating a dilemma for the Republicans—how to enlarge their base and appeal to the groups that voted Democratic without alienating their conservative supporters. For the Democrats the problem is how to maintain unity with such a diverse electoral coalition.

In several ways, the 2008 election challenges the premise that the electoral process in the United States is fatally flawed and that American elections cannot and do not meet the criteria for a democratic electoral system in terms of the level of participation, the representative character of the vote, the equity of resource distribution, the quantity and quality of the information available to voters, and the transformation of a winning electoral coalition into a viable governing majority. Perhaps the Obama message of optimism and change was right, that "yes, we can" improve our politics and the process by which it is conducted.

This fourth edition reexamines the democratic electoral process, factoring in the temporary or permanent changes that occurred during the 2007–2008 election cycle and the implications that those changes have for governance. It asks the same question as previous editions—*Is this any way to run a democratic election?*—but provides more nuanced answers. You be the judge!

ACKNOWLEDGMENTS

I would like to thank the people who worked on this edition at CQ Press: Charisse Kiino, Allison McKay, freelance copy editor Mary Marik, and Allyson Rudolph.

Finally, I would like to thank the reviewers of my manuscript for their thoughtful and helpful comments: Brian McQuide, University of Idaho; Dan Palazzolo, University of Richmond; and Jeffery Walz, Concordia University–Wisconsin.

Stephen J. Wayne
November 2009

Democratic Elections
What's the Problem?

Did you know that . . .

- a majority of the voting-age population does not vote in most elections in the United States?
- Bill Clinton and George W. Bush, when first elected president, each received the votes of only about one quarter of those eligible to vote; in his sizable electoral victory, Barack Obama received the votes of 33 percent of those eligible and 30 percent of voting-age adults?
- most members of Congress have no effective opposition in running for renomination, and some have no opponents in the general election?
- more than 90 percent of members of the House of Representatives and 80 percent of senators were reelected in the period from 1960 through 2008?
- no third-party presidential candidate has received any electoral votes since 1972?
- there were more ballots discarded or undercounted in New York City and Chicago in the 2000 election than there were disputed ballots in the controversial Florida presidential vote that year?
- about $5 billion was spent on federal elections in 2008?
- information about how elections are conducted in the United States is so fragmentary that the government does not know how many people were turned away at the polls, how long people stood in lines waiting to vote, how many ballots were voided or simply not counted, and how many voting machines malfunctioned?
- it took more than seven months in 2008 for officials and the courts to determine the winner of the election in Minnesota for a seat in the U.S. Senate?
- the average length of time that presidential candidates appeared on the evening news shows of the major broadcast networks in the last three elections was about seven seconds?
- more than 50 percent of candidate advertising in recent federal elections contained some negative reference to an opponent's character or policy positions?

- more than $200 million was spent on advertising during the 2008 nomination process, with the Democrats spending more than twice as much as the Republicans?
- only about one-third of the people can name the member of Congress who represents them during nonelectoral periods?

Is this any way to run a democratic election?

These facts suggest that something is terribly wrong with our electoral process. They raise serious questions about how democratic the American political system really is. They also point to the major problems within that system: low voter turnout; fraudulent, error-prone, and discriminatory voting practices; uneven and inadequate administration of elections by state and local officials; high costs and unequal resources for candidates running for office; short, compartmentalized, and negative media coverage; and contradictory, often inconclusive results. Let's take a look at some examples of these problems.

CONTEMPORARY ELECTION ISSUES

Low Voter Turnout

People fight for the right to vote when they don't have it. Americans certainly did. In 1776, British colonists, protesting taxation without representation in Parliament, declared their independence with a rhetorical flourish that underscored the people's right to alter or abolish a government that wasn't fulfilling the purpose for which it was established.

Now, more than 230 years later, in a country that prides itself on its long and successful political tradition and on its fundamental democratic values, a majority of the electorate does not vote on a regular basis. Why do so few people vote? Does it have to do with how candidates run for office, how and when elections are conducted, or whether the public perceives that elections really matter, that they make a difference in people's lives or in the country's future?

Congress considers low turnout to be a problem, a sign that the democracy is not as vigorous as it could or should be. During the last several decades, it has enacted legislation to encourage more people to vote. At the end of the 1970s, an amendment to the Federal Election Campaign Act (FECA) was passed to permit political parties to raise and spend unlimited amounts of money on building their grassroots base and getting out the vote. Yet turnout continued to decline.

During the 1980s, amendments were added to the act to broaden its applicability and facilitate minority participation in the electoral process. Yet the turnout of most population groups continued to decline.

In 1993 a "motor voter" bill, designed to make it easier for people in all fifty states to register to vote, was enacted, yet the percentage of the adult population reporting that it registered decreased in the years following the passage of the law.

In 2002, Congress enacted the Help America Vote Act, which provides money to states to computerize their voter registration lists, buy more accurate voting machines, and allow for provisional voting for people who claim that they registered but whose names do not appear on the lists of eligible voters in the precinct in which they live and vote. An additional twelve million new voters registered between 2002 and 2006.

The good news is that this growth in newly registered voters was larger than the proportionate increase in the voting-age population during this period. In 2002, 74.7 percent of the voting-age population registered to vote; by 2006, that percentage had risen to 76.6.[1] Turnout also increased in 2004 and remained high in 2008. The bad news is that still four out of ten people eligible to vote do not do so. In midterm elections, the figure is about six out of ten.[2]

The issue of nonvoting raises serious questions about the vibrancy of America's civic culture and the health of its democratic political institutions. With so many people not voting, do elections reflect the judgment of all the people or of a small and unrepresentative proportion of them? Similarly, to whom are elected officials more responsive—the entire population or the people who elected them? Do elections with low participation rates still provide an agenda for government and legitimacy for its actions? If they do not, then what does?

Fraudulent, Error-Prone, and Discriminatory Voting Practices

The Florida voting controversy in the 2000 election highlighted many of the voting problems that have plagued the U.S. electoral system since its creation. The Constitution charges the states with the conduct of federal elections. The states set most of the rules for registration, ballot access, and absentee voting; they determine the period during which voting occurs, the procedures for exercising a vote, and the manner in which votes are to be tabulated and reported. Local electoral districts within the states often designate the polling places, run the election, and provide the ballots or machines for voting. As a consequence of the decentralization of election administration, there is considerable variation in voting procedures among the states and even within them.

Political parties indirectly affect the vote by the influence they exert on elected and appointed state officials. In fact, for most of the nation's first one hundred years, the major parties actually ran the elections. They rallied their supporters, got them to the polls, and made sure they voted "correctly" by designing and distributing color-coded ballots on which only the names of their candidates appeared. They also had poll watchers observing how people voted.

Allegations of fraudulent practices, including voting by noncitizens and the deceased, casting multiple ballots in the same election, and under- and over-counting of the votes were rampant. The adoption of the secret ballot and the administration of elections by state officials were responses to these unfair, underhanded, and undemocratic election practices. The development of machines to tabulate the vote was another. But problems persisted because most state legislatures still enacted election laws and drafted legislative districts to benefit those in power.

Registration and residence requirements have been used to limit the size of the electorate. Geographic representation in one of the two legislative bodies (prior to the 1960s) gave rural areas a disproportionate advantage. In some states, the laws were administered in a discriminatory and haphazard fashion, making it more difficult for some people, particularly minorities, to vote.

Not until the 1960s did the Supreme Court and Congress address some of these issues.[3] The Court ruled that population and population alone had to be the criterion by which representation was determined: one person–one vote. The Voting Rights Act of 1965 was intended to end discriminatory practices and effectively extend the vote to all eligible citizens. Registration requirements were eased, voting hours were extended, absentee voting was facilitated, and for a time, money for party-building activities was exempted from federal contribution limits.

These laws and judicial decisions went a long way toward extending the franchise, encouraging turnout, and ending some of the practices that undercut the democratic character of U.S. elections. But they did not eliminate all of them. Nor did they improve the actual conduct of elections. After the 2000 election controversy in Florida, the U.S. Commission on Civil Rights issued a report that concluded that African Americans in that state were much more likely than white voters to be turned away from the polls.[4] Researchers at the Massachusetts Institute of Technology (MIT) and the California Institute of Technology (CalTech) deduced that between four million and six million votes for president in the 2000 election were not counted, some because of registration foul-ups, some because of voter confusion and error, and some because of faulty equipment.[5] In close elections, these undercounted voters could have made a difference, even changed the final outcome.

Problems remain today. Registration foul-ups, inadequate parking, long lines to vote, insufficient numbers of poll workers, machine malfunctions, and poor ballot designs continue to hamper the act of voting. Can an election be considered democratic if eligible voters have to overcome these hurdles? Can the results be regarded as legitimate if the votes of a sizable proportion of a state's population, enough to have changed the outcome of the election, are not correctly counted? Can the election be said to represent the will of the people if the ballots are confusing to many voters, and if some of the votes were not properly cast and thus voided? A lot of people do not think so. Six months after the Supreme Court's decision that effectively determined George W. Bush's victory in Florida and thus in the Electoral College, 26 percent of the American people indicated that they still did not regard him as the legitimate president.[6]

High Costs and Unequal Resources

Campaign finance is another issue and has been one for the last four decades. The federal election campaign finance system has broken down. From 1992 through 2002, both major parties used a loophole in the law to solicit large contributions from wealthy donors and spend hundreds of millions of dollars on behalf of their candidates for federal office.

The Bipartisan Campaign Reform Act (BCRA), enacted in 2002, was designed to end this practice, but it has not done so. Although the act prohibits national parties from accepting contributions that exceed federal limits, it has not stopped their supporters from creating nonparty groups that solicit and spend contributions not subject to the federal limits. In 2004, these groups raised and spent more than $440 million, using this money to fund surrogate campaigns on behalf of their respective parties and candidates; in 2008, they raised and spent about to $260 million.[7]

To make matters worse, each party used its access to and the facilities of its officeholders as inducements and rewards for obtaining large donations, the maximum amount allowed by law. Private telephone numbers of cabinet secretaries and congressional committee heads were made available to top contributors. As president, Bill Clinton held numerous coffee hours in the White House to encourage people to give money to the Democratic Party. He rewarded those who gave the most with trips on Air Force One, trade missions with the commerce secretary, and sleepovers in the Lincoln bedroom. Not to be outdone by his Democratic predecessors, Vice President Dick Cheney lavishly entertained the most generous GOP contributors at a gala at his official residence in April 2001. And while the practice of using government facilities has finally ended, public officials still solicit funds and reward contributors with access, appointments, and social invitations, practices that are not consistent with the basic tenets of a democratic political system.

Even without the illegal solicitations and legal circumvention of the campaign finance legislation, the amount of money required to mount an effective campaign for federal office has become astronomical, a consequence in large part of mass media advertising. Moreover, the advertising itself has distorted rather than enhanced political debate.

Is too much money being raised for and spent on election campaigns? Do those who contribute represent a cross section of Americans or do they overrepresent the most prosperous individuals and groups in society? And what do contributors, especially those who give the maximum amount, get for their money? The answer is access, influence, political appointments, and frequently the policy outcomes they desire; at least that is what the public believes.

The resources issue also affects how elections are conducted. Small electoral districts and those in poorer areas, particularly districts with high concentration of minorities, are less able to provide the facilities, services, and up-to-date equipment that facilitate voting. Lines are longer and vote counts slower and less reliable. These inequities, which can affect turnout and voting behavior, can affect overall state and national results.

Compartmentalized and Negative Media Coverage

Closely related to the issue of money is that of news coverage. For better or worse, the mass media have become the principal vehicle through which candidates for national office communicate to voters. Political parties have become much less effective intermediaries than they used to be. Reliance on the news media would not be so bad if the goals of the media were similar to those of the parties, candidates, and country, but they are not.

Although the news media are not oblivious to the need to educate the public, they also are interested in making money—the more, the better. Profit from advertising is based on the size of the viewing or listening audience. To enhance audience size, the news media present the news that they believe would be most interesting to the most people most of the time. In campaigns, the most newsworthy items tend to be the dramatic ones—the horse race, with all its color and drama; the unexpected occurrences; the screwups; and the confrontations as well as the human dimensions of a candidate's personal character and family. These subjects engage readers, viewers, and listeners but do not necessarily educate, energize, or motivate them to participate in the campaign and to vote. In fact, press compartmentalization, negativism, and spin are often blamed for low turnout and for the public's cynical attitude toward candidates, parties, and the political system.[8]

How to square the interests of largely private media with the needs of an informed and involved electorate is no easy task, nor one that Congress wishes to tackle. Not only must First Amendment protections for the press be considered, but the desires of the public for the news it wants, not necessarily the news it needs, also must be weighed in the balance.

Contradictory, Often Inconclusive Results

Another problem, less obvious but equally dangerous for a democratic political system, is that elections may not contribute to governing, but actually make it more difficult. Candidates make promises, political parties present platforms, and groups promote issues. But in a heterogeneous society, policy priorities and issue stands are likely to be diverse and even inconsistent with one another. Elections in the United States reflect this diversity far better than they mirror a popular consensus. They regularly produce mixed and incompatible results with unclear meanings and undefined mandates. Parties often share power, making the institutional divisions that much greater and more difficult to overcome. In an age of political polarization, these divisions have become more pronounced, political rhetoric has become more strident, civility among elected officials has declined, and compromises on major policy issues have been made more difficult.

Each of these problems—turnout, voting, money, and governing—points to shortcomings in the democratic electoral process in the United States, gaps between theory and practice. One goal of this book is to examine those gaps; another is to discuss ways they could be narrowed or, perhaps, eliminated. Finally, the book aims to stimulate thinking about democracy in general and democratic elections in particular.

To answer the central question—Is this any way to run a democratic election?—this chapter next examines the nature of democracy and some of the ways in which a democratic political system may be structured. The discussion then turns to the role of elections in a democracy and the criteria that elections must meet to be considered democratic. Finally, the chapter concludes with a look at the inevitable tensions within a democratic electoral system between political liberty and citizen equality, between majority rule and minority rights, and between a free press and an informed electorate.

THE NATURE OF DEMOCRACY

A **democracy** is, simply put, a government of the people. Initially used in ancient Greece, where such a system was first practiced, the term itself comes from the Greek words *demos,* meaning "people," and *kratos,* meaning "rule." In a democracy, the people rule.[9]

But which people? Everyone? Everyone who is a citizen? Every citizen older than eighteen years of age? Every eighteen-year-old citizen who is literate and mentally competent? Every eighteen-year-old, literate, and mentally competent citizen who has knowledge of the issues and can apply that knowledge to make an intelligent judgment? The list of qualifications could go on and on. Naturally, an informed electorate is desirable, but the more people excluded because they lack certain characteristics or qualifications, the less likely the electorate will reflect the general population.

And how do the people rule? By themselves? By selecting others and holding them accountable? By agreeing to a set of rules and procedures by which some are selected to perform certain public tasks, such as teaching school, maintaining law and order, or protecting the country's security?

There is no single right answer to these questions. There are many types of democracies, distinguished by *who* and *how:* by who makes the decisions and by how power is distributed.[10]

TYPES OF DEMOCRACIES

Who Makes Public Policy Decisions?

When the people themselves make public policy decisions, the democracy is said to be a **direct democracy.** A New England town meeting in which all residents participate on matters of local interest, such as where to build a new town hall or whether to recycle disposable waste, is an example of direct democracy at work. A state ballot initiative on which voters indicate their preferences on a range of issues, such as legalized gambling, same-sex marriage, or public benefits for illegal immigrants or new residents, is another example of direct democracy. When George W. Bush, as a managing partner of the Texas Rangers, helped convince voters of Arlington, Texas, to support a special tax to pay for two-thirds of the cost of a new baseball stadium, he was engaging in direct democracy, as were Californians in 2008 when they voted in favor of a state constitutional amendment that recognized marriage as only between a man and a woman.

In a direct democracy there is true collective decision making. Obviously, in a country as large and diverse as the United States, such a system in which all citizens had the opportunity to vote on most major policy issues would be impractical and undesirable for the nation as a whole.[11] There would be too many people with limited information and understanding of the issues participating in too many public policy decisions. As a consequence, most democracies are by necessity **representative democracies,** in which people choose others to represent them in government, to formulate and implement public policy, and sometimes even to adjudicate it.[12]

A basic goal of representative government is to be responsive to the needs and interests of the people who elected that government. How can these needs and interests be identified? One way is through elections. Although elections aren't the only means by which the public views find expression and can influence public policy, they are the most decisive and popular method for doing so. They also tend to be the fairest way in which public choice can be exercised. That's why elections are such a critical component of a democratic political system. They are a mechanism through which the citizenry expresses its desires and by which it can evaluate the performance of those in office. Elections link government to the governed.

How Is Power Distributed?

Another way to categorize democracies is according to how they distribute power. In a **popular,** or **plebiscitary, democracy,** the people exercise considerable influence over the selection of government officials and the policies they pursue. Such a system provides opportunities for the populace to initiate policy issues and vote on them directly as well as to elect candidates and, if necessary, to remove them from office. Ballot access is easy, there are few impediments to voting, and the people have the last word.

In a **pluralistic democracy,** a wide variety of groups—from political parties to nonparty groups with economic interests (such as business, labor, and the professions) to those motivated by social and political (ideological and issue-oriented) beliefs—compete for influence. They do so in accordance with their own interests and beliefs, using their own resources to gain and maintain public support. James Madison argued in *The Federalist,* No. 10, that such factions in society were inevitable and that one of the merits of the Constitution that was being debated for ratification was that it made it difficult for any one faction to dominate the government.[13]

A third model is an **elitist democracy,** in which power is concentrated in fewer hands than in a pluralistic system. There is more hierarchy, and more discretion is exercised by those in power. However, to maintain its democratic character, the system requires that there be competition between elites in elections and in governing.

In all three systems, government officials remain accountable to those who elected them. Whatever the form of democratic government, it rests directly or indirectly on popular consent. Elections anchor government to its popular base. Without elections, a democratic political system cannot exist.

ELECTIONS AND DEMOCRACY

Elections tie citizens to their government. They provide a mechanism by which the people can choose those government officials—legislators, top executives, and, in some cases, judges—who make, implement, and adjudicate public policy. Elections are also a means by which the public can hold these officials accountable for their actions and keep them responsive to the public's needs, interests, and desires.

To make decisions on who makes public policy and to evaluate how well they do so, voters need information about the beliefs, positions, and proposals of the candidates and their parties. The mass media are a conduit for such information. Without a free press reporting the election news, the electorate would either have to gather and analyze its own information or be dependent on those with a vested interest for doing so—candidates, parties, and interest groups. Naturally, those with an interest in the election outcome would be inclined to release information that puts themselves and their interests in the best possible light. The public needs alternative sources that are credible and objective; diverse and independent news media are most likely to meet such informational goals, but a government-controlled press or one that is influenced by a small group of individuals or corporations is not.

In choosing the people who will run the government, elections directly or indirectly provide direction to that government. They establish the agenda—the promises and policy positions of the winners—that guides public officials, and they help build coalitions that facilitate governing.

Elections also confer legitimacy on government and what it does. By giving citizens an opportunity to select public officials and influence their policy agendas, elections contribute to the ongoing support for the policy decisions and administrative actions that follow. Whether people agree with a particular policy or not, they are more likely to accept it as valid and lawful if they perceive that those who made it were selected in a fair and honest way and make their decisions according to an established set of rules and procedures. They also will be more likely to accept the policy if they know that they will have other opportunities down the road to express their opinions, participate in a political campaign, and vote for the candidates of their choice. Similarly, people will respect and abide by the decisions of elected officials, even approving their performance in office when they do not like them personally, as long as they consider their election to be legitimate. Take President Clinton, for example. His job approval exceeded his personal favorability throughout his second term and especially after his affair with White House intern Monica Lewinsky became public.[14]

Criteria for Democratic Elections

For elections to be consistent with the basic tenets of a democratic political system, they must be "free, fair, and frequent."[15] The principle of inclusiveness should apply. Adult citizens must be eligible to vote, have the opportunity to do so, and must be able to exercise their right without fear or coercion. The votes must be weighted equally in determining the winner. The results of the election must be accepted as official and binding for a limited period of time, after which another election must occur. Without the guarantee of a future election, it would be difficult to hold those in office accountable for their actions.

Let's explore these essential criteria: political equality, universal suffrage, meaningful choice, and the free flow of information about the candidates, issues, and their parties.[16] **Political equality** is essential. It is a basic building block for a democracy. There can be no classes or ranks, no individuals or groups whose positions elevate them to a higher status. As Thomas Jefferson put it in the Declaration of Independence, "All men are created equal."[17] If everyone is equal, then all should have the opportunity to exercise an equal voice in the running of the political system. At the very least, this means that the principle of one person–one vote must apply to all elections unless otherwise specified by the Constitution. It also means that all votes count equally, that no individual, group, region, or jurisdiction should gain extra representation or exercise extra influence. Translated into election terminology, equality requires **universal suffrage,** the right of all adult citizens to be able to vote.

Unless all adult citizens have an opportunity to participate in the electoral process, the election results cannot be said to reflect the views of the entire country. The exclusion of any group of citizens because of any characteristic other than those directly related to their capacity to exercise an informed and intelligent vote (such as being literate and having the mental capacity to make an intelligent voting decision) naturally weakens the representative nature of the system. The more people excluded, for whatever reason, the less the government can be said to rest on the consent of the governed.

Not only must adult citizens be given the opportunity to vote, but also the voting decision must be made freely. And that decision has to represent a **meaningful choice.** Contestation is important. If there were only one candidate for an office or if all the candidates had equal qualifications and voiced essentially the same views, then there would be grounds for claiming that the voters did not have a meaningful choice.

To choose is to select from among diverse alternatives. But how diverse should they be? A choice among candidates who differ widely in their beliefs, particularly if the views of some of them are extreme, may amount to no real choice at all for most people. If the major parties were to agree on the same candidate and the only other candidate is unknown to most voters, the choice for most voters would not be meaningful. In other words, the choices should lie within the broad parameters of public acceptability yet be distinctive enough for voters to distinguish between them and assess them on the basis of their own values, attitudes, and opinions.

Related to making a meaningful choice is the **free flow of information and ideas.** At the very least, there should be alternative sources of information, not just from the candidates, the parties, the government, or a dominant group that controls the news media. Unless there is ample information and discussion within the public arena, people will have difficulty understanding the issues, much less determining which candidates are most qualified and merit support.

A free press is essential. Few, if any, subjects, issues, or questions should be off limits. Few, if any, arguments should be precluded, no matter how unpopular they may be. That is why the allegation of a candidate being unpatriotic, if that candidate expresses opposition to government policy, undercuts the very fabric of a democratic electoral process. The objective must be the creation of an environment in which voters can make informed judgments based on an enlightened understanding of the issues.[18] That objective can only be accomplished in a society in which free and broad expression is encouraged and protected.

Democratic Electoral Systems

The number of people elected, the way winners are determined, and the size and shape of electoral districts may vary within the country as well as among countries. In the United States, the United Kingdom, and some other democratic nations, public officials are elected on the basis of **plurality rule in single-member districts.** Simply put, this means that the candidate who receives the most votes for a particular office within an electoral district wins. Unless rules specify otherwise, the winner need not receive a majority of the vote; a simple plurality is usually sufficient. If there is a majority requirement, however, and no candidate receives more than half the votes in the initial balloting, there is usually a runoff election between the top two vote getters in the first round of voting.[19]

The U.S. Supreme Court has ruled that all legislative districts must be equal in population to ensure that the one person–one vote principle prevails. The exceptions are the Senate, in which each state, regardless of its population, has two senators, and the Electoral College, in which each state is entitled to electors equal in number to its congressional delegation.[20]

The main advantage of a plurality voting system is that it is simple and direct. The winner is easily and usually quickly determined, and the elected representative is accountable to the entire district. Responsibility, in other words, can be pinpointed.

The principal disadvantage of such a voting system is that those in the minority are less likely to be represented by a candidate of their choice. Their views and interests may not be adequately considered when public policy decisions are made. Moreover, plurality voting tends to enlarge the advantage of the majority if that majority is equally dispersed across the entire electoral area.[21] What happens is that those in the majority tend to vote for candidates who have similar demographic and attitudinal characteristics. Overcoming this voting behavior requires that minorities constitute a large proportion of the voters within the electoral district, at least 40 percent according to David Epstein and Sharyn O'Halloran.[22]

To improve minority representation in Congress, the U.S. Department of Justice, citing the 1982 Voting Rights Act and several Supreme Court decisions, pressured states to create legislative districts in which minority groups, such as African Americans and Hispanics, constitute the voting majority. However, the Supreme Court subsequently declared that race could not be the *primary* factor for determining the boundaries of these districts, once again putting minority groups at a disadvantage in the U.S. system of plurality voting in single-member districts.

There is another way, however, to achieve broader representation: Institute a system of **proportional voting,** in which the winners are determined in proportion to the vote that they or their party receives. In some democratic countries, such as Canada and Israel, parties run slates of candidates in districts. Similarly, in the presidential nomination process in the United States, there may be proportional voting. Democratic Party rules require it, and Republican Party rules permit it.

The principal advantage of proportional voting is that it provides a fairer and more accurate representation of minorities in the government. A disadvantage is that majoritarian sentiment is more difficult to discern. Such sentiment, often referred to as political or policy consensus, must be constructed after the election by those who have been elected rather than by the electorate in the votes they have cast.

Proportional voting also increases the likelihood of a multiparty government in which coalitions among competing parties may be necessary to achieve an operating majority. Multiparty coalitions, however, are apt to be more fragile and less able to agree on public policy than a government composed of a single party. Moreover, it is more difficult to assign credit or blame for what the government does in the case of a multiparty coalition than with a single party.

In a plurality system, coalition building occurs primarily within the major parties, not between them. Each of the parties tries to reach a broad cross section of the electorate. In doing so, they have to balance diverse and often conflicting interests. Thus the major parties in a plurality system are apt to be more heterogeneous and, conversely, in a proportional voting system more homogeneous.

As the plurality-proportional voting dichotomy suggests, election procedures and rules are not neutral. They benefit some at the expense of others. These clashes of interests create ongoing tensions within a democratic electoral process. They are what politics is all about, temporarily resolving tension on an issue by issue basis.

TENSIONS WITHIN A DEMOCRATIC ELECTORAL SYSTEM

The problem of obtaining a fair election outcome underlies the natural tensions in a democratic political system between political liberty and equality, between majority rule and minority rights, and between a free press and an informed electorate.

Liberty versus Equality

If a democracy is based on the consent of the governed, then the ability to give that consent and, if need be, to take it away is essential. That's why political liberty is so important. It is the freedom to decide for oneself and act on the basis of that decision. Take that freedom away, and a democratic political system cannot exist.

In the electoral process, liberty requires the right to vote as one chooses, not to vote if one chooses, and in either case, to make the voting decision freely and without duress. It is the right to exercise personal choice within the framework of the political system. Accessible voting places, guidance in voting, and casting a secret ballot help protect that right.

Freedom to support the candidate of one's choice, however, can undermine the equity principle. A conflict is created when certain people have more resources at their disposal than others to use in campaigns. Should individuals and groups be free to spend as much money as they want to promote their ideas and beliefs, or should spending be limited to ensure that every citizen has a more equal opportunity to affect the outcome of the vote?

Proponents of unlimited expenditures cite the constitutional protection of free speech and the right of people to spend their money as they see fit. Opponents argue that elected officials are more likely to be responsive to large donors than to average citizens. Moreover, they claim that the advantage of the wealthy extends past the election to governing and to the public policy that government makes.[23]

A related issue pertains to participation itself, personally getting involved. For a variety of reasons, those with a higher income and more education participate at a higher rate than do those with less income and education.[24] Their higher rate of participation magnifies their influence on the election results and on the decisions made by elected public officials.

There are many forms of participation, from the simple act of voting, to working for a candidate (ringing doorbells, handing out literature, sending e-mail or text messaging, coordinating events, and the like), to contributing money to a candidate's campaign and spending money to promote one's own views, which may or may not coincide with those of a particular candidate. Placing no restrictions on these activities allows those with the interest, time, resources, and will to do more and, as a result, to potentially exercise greater influence. At what point should a line be drawn between voluntary actions of citizens in the electoral process, which should be encouraged, and the activities that give an unfair advantage to those with superior resources at their disposal?

Majority Rule versus Minority Rights

Plurality voting decisions seem to be a pretty straightforward criterion for a democratic society. If every vote is equal, those with the most votes should win. The problem, as we have already mentioned, is that plurality voting systems overrepresent the majority, whereas proportional systems give more representation to minorities.

Many factors affect the majority-minority relationship: the ways the boundaries of electoral districts are drawn and the number of people elected within them, how the ballot is organized, whether candidates are listed by office or by party, and even where, when, and for how long voting occurs. If registration is difficult, voting places few and inaccessible, the hours for voting too short, or the ballot too complicated and confusing, then turnout will be lower; those in power will more likely remain in power; and those who benefit under the current arrangement will continue to do so.

Representation of groups within the society also can be affected by ballot access. In 1992 and 1996, Ross Perot's Reform Party spent millions of dollars and used hundreds of volunteers and paid workers just to obtain the necessary signatures for its candidates to appear on all fifty state ballots. The Reform and Green Parties did this as well, albeit less successfully, in more recent presidential elections. But for the Republican and Democratic candidates, ballot access is automatic. They have a built-in advantage. Is that fair?

The majority-minority issue extends to government as well. Should majority rule be restricted so that minorities are better protected when public policy decisions are made? James Madison thought so. Fearing that the "tyranny of the majority" could deny minorities their basic rights, he argued successfully for a divided government that separates institutions representing differing constituencies so that no single group can easily dominate. But in the process, Madison and his colleagues at the Constitutional Convention created a system that has enabled powerful minorities to exercise a tyranny of their own, preventing change and thereby thwarting the desires of the majority or plurality in violation of a basic precept of democratic theory.

A Free Press versus an Informed Electorate

The framers of the Bill of Rights believed that a free press is essential. In a government based on the consent of the governed, those in office must be held accountable for their decisions and actions. Similarly, the qualifications, promises, and positions of candidates for elective office must be evaluated by the electorate.

The public cannot assess candidates running for office or the performance of those in office unless they have the necessary information to do so. The problem is that most sources for such information—the candidates, their parties, interest groups, policy-oriented think tanks, even government officials—have a stake in the outcome that affects the information they present and how they present it. Although information from stakeholders in the election is still valuable, it must be assessed with the interests of the source in mind.

Here's where a free press comes in. For some of the same reasons that we select others to represent us in government, we also depend on others to inform us about politics and government, to help us sort out what's going on and make informed judgments about it. That's the role of the news media—to be a watchdog, to provide the information they believe we need to know or would be interested in knowing. Anticipating that the press will perform this role is itself an incentive for those running for office not to lie, although they are still prone to exaggerate their claims. It is also a motivation for those holding office to stay attuned to public opinion and not to behave in a manner that would draw unfavorable attention and admonishment.

A free press is unfettered but not necessarily neutral. News reporters describe the campaign as they see it. Naturally, their perceptions are influenced by their own political beliefs, their journalistic needs, and their personal feelings about the candidates and issues. To the extent that many in the news media share similar political and professional orientations, their reporting of the campaign reflects a pack mentality, a collective reading and interpretation of events.[25] This journalistic outlook colors the public's understanding and its evaluation of the candidates and parties. It gives the electorate a jaundiced view that highlights the dramatic and human elements of the campaign, usually at the expense of a detailed debate over substantive issues.

What can be done about the media's orientation and perceived bias? Restricting press coverage is not only impractical but also violates the First Amendment's protection of freedom of the press. Relying on the candidates to monitor the coverage they receive seems equally impractical given their vested interest in favorable coverage. Nor can the government take on a supervisory role over political communication in a campaign, especially in light of the number of incumbents who seek reelection. How, then, can citizens obtain the information they need, particularly as it relates to policy issues and their impact on society—information that many consider essential for voters to make an informed judgment based on an enlightened understanding of the issues?

SUMMARY: DEMOCRATIC ELECTION DILEMMAS IN A NUTSHELL

In theory, a representative democracy is a government of the people, by some of them, and for all of them. It is connected to the people through elections of the people's representatives. One democratic dilemma is how to provide citizens with equal opportunities to affect the electoral and governmental processes without reducing their freedom to pursue their own interests and utilize their own resources as they see fit. Another dilemma is how to provide electoral mechanisms that are efficient and representative, effective and accountable, dynamic and deliberative—a tall order, to be sure!

To meet these criteria, citizens must be accorded universal suffrage and equal voting power. They must be free to vote, given the opportunity to do so, have a meaningful choice, and be able to obtain timely information about the parties, candidates, and issues that is sufficient to make informed judgments on election day.

In practice, contemporary elections fall short of meeting these criteria. There is universal suffrage in theory, but large-scale nonvoting in practice. There are many choices of candidates and some of policy initiatives as well, but a lot of people still complain that their choices are unsatisfactory because they are too narrow, too broad, or all distasteful.

All votes count equally, but all groups do not benefit equally from current electoral procedures and practices. Ethnic and racial minorities, in particular, seem to be disproportionately disadvantaged by plurality voting in single-member districts. Wealthy people have the advantage that their superior resources provide. Finally, the United States has a free press but, in the view of much of the electorate, neither an objective nor a responsible one. Complaints that the media are too powerful, too judgmental, and too negative are regularly reported in survey and anecdotal research.[26] That much of the electorate is underinformed and underinvolved has been attributed in large part to the press's penchant for emphasizing the most entertaining news, as well as to inefficient and ineffective grassroots operations by party and nonparty groups and personal attacks by the candidates against each other. But from the perspective of the mass media, driven by audience size, a very competitive news environment, and conventions of contemporary journalism, interesting and exciting news is what the public wants, so they provide it.

The disjunctions between democratic theory and practice arise from many sources: the manner in which the electorate can and does participate in elections; the ways in which elections are structured and conducted and the manner in which representatives are chosen; the structure of the party system and the candidate orientation of electoral politics; the laws governing financial contributions and expenditures; press coverage, particularly its emphasis on the contest, its orientation toward personal character issues, and its general negativity; the parties' methods for selecting their nominees; the ways campaigns are run, appeals communicated, and images created; and finally, incompatible outcomes, unclear meanings, and vacuous mandates.

Now It's Your Turn

Discussion Questions

1. How nearly universal must suffrage be for the popular will to be asserted?
2. Can elections be structured to reflect both majority sentiment and minority views at the same time?
3. What current electoral issues pit individual liberty against political equality?
4. To what extent is the democratic goal of an informed electorate that makes enlightened judgments on election day realistic, and to what extent is it necessary?
5. Can the news media serve the informational needs of the electorate and the profit motives of media owners simultaneously?
6. What are the most serious problems that threaten the democratic character of the American electoral system?

Topics for Debate

Challenge or defend the following statements:

1. It is possible to have political liberty and citizen equality simultaneously.
2. If the majority always rules, then the rights and interests of the minority are always going to be threatened.
3. A press that is both free and fair is a contradiction in terms.
4. To make sure that voters can make informed judgments, they should be required to know the principal candidates and their major issue positions before being allowed to vote.
5. A democratic government cannot exist without a democratic electoral process.

Exercises

1. How democratic is the constitutionally prescribed electoral process?
   a. Answer this question by first examining what the Constitution requires and allows for national elections, noting its democratic and nondemocratic features.
   b. To the best of your knowledge, have the nondemocratic features of American elections been changed by amendment, law, or practice? If so, how and why; if not, why not?

    c. Is the electoral system becoming more or less democratic today, and are the changes that have occurred in the electoral process good or bad for the country as a whole? Give examples to support your view.

    d. What aspects of the last presidential election reflect positively or negatively on the democratic character of the U.S. electoral system? Do you anticipate that the same positive or negative aspects will be apparent in the next election?

2. Advocates of democracy have urged that the electoral system be made as democratic as possible to achieve the ideal of a government of, by, and for the people. Others are reluctant to change a system that has worked so well for so long and has become so large a part of America's political tradition. What do you think? Would more democracy be better served if the system were changed, or would it actually impede the functioning of the electoral and governing systems? Might too much democracy be a bad thing? If you had to choose between liberty and equality or between majority rule and minority rights, how would you choose and why?

INTERNET RESOURCES

The Internet is a rich and immediately available source of information on campaigns and elections. Here are some of the best generic sources for all kinds of information. Most of them contain links to the news media, public interest groups, ongoing political campaigns, polling organizations, and appropriate government agencies. In addition, you may access the Congressional Quarterly's Web site, www.cq.com, for links to other sites of interest to students of American government.

Media Sites on Politics and Elections

- CNN: www.cnn.com
- C-SPAN: www.cspan.org
- FOX: www.foxnews.com
- Los Angeles Times: www.latimes.com
- National Public Radio: www.npr.org
- New York Times: www.nytimes.com
- Politico: www.politico.com
- Washington Post: www.washingtonpost.com

Government Sites on the Electoral System

- Census Bureau: www.census.gov/compendia/statab/
  Publishes the yearly *Statistical Abstract*, which contains information on registration, turnout, and voting results in recent federal elections.

- Election Assistance Commission: www.eac.gov
  Established by the Help America Vote Act, the commission provides information on how to register and vote, state and federal election laws, and surveys of who registers and who votes.
- Federal Election Commission: www.fec.gov
  Provides easily accessible data on campaign finance activities filed by candidates and compiled in tabular form by analysts at the FEC.
- Library of Congress: http://thomas.loc.gov
  Provides access to Congress, its committees, members, legislative process, rules, and schedules, as well as reports on campaigns and elections.
- National Archives and Records Administration: www.archives. gov/federal-register/electoral-college/
  Contains official statistics about past presidential elections, the Electoral College, election laws, and presidential documents.
- White House: www.whitehouse.gov
  Contains not only information on presidential and vice presidential activities, speeches, press releases, and official business, but also links to all other parts of the government.

SELECTED READINGS

American Political Science Association Task Force on Inequality and American Democracy. "American Democracy in an Age of Rising Inequality." *Perspectives on Politics* 2 (December 2004): 651–666.

Barber, Benjamin R. *A Passion for Democracy.* Princeton: Princeton University Press, 1998.

Bartels, Larry M. *Unequal Democracy: The Political Economy of the New Gilded Age.* Princeton: Princeton University Press, 2008.

Dahl, Robert A. *Democracy and Its Critics.* New Haven: Yale University Press, 1989.

———. *How Democratic Is the American Constitution?* New Haven: Yale University Press, 2001.

———. *A Preface to Democratic Theory.* Chicago: University of Chicago Press, 1956.

Diamond, Larry. *Developing Democracy.* Baltimore: Johns Hopkins University Press, 1999.

Downs, Anthony. *An Economic Theory of Democracy.* New York: Harper and Row, 1957.

Dryzek, John. *Discursive Democracy.* Cambridge: Cambridge University Press, 1990.

Held, David. *Models of Democracy.* Cambridge: Polity Press, 1996.

Hirst, Paul. *Representative Democracy and Its Limits.* Cambridge: Polity Press, 1990.

Schmitter, Philippe, and Terry Karl. "What Democracy Is . . . And Is Not." *Journal of Democracy* 2 (Fall 1991): 75–88.

Stout, Jeffrey. *Democracy and Tradition.* Princeton: Princeton University Press, 2004.

Tilly, Charles. *Democracy.* Cambridge: Cambridge University Press, 2007.

Thompson, Dennis. *Just Elections: Creating a Fair Electoral Process in the United States.* Chicago: University of Chicago Press, 2002.

Tocqueville, Alexis de. *Democracy in America.* New York: HarperCollins, 1988.

Warren, Mark, ed. *Democracy and Trust.* New York: Cambridge University Press, 1999.

Welch, Susan. "The Impact of At-Large Elections on the Representation of Blacks and Hispanics." *Journal of Politics* 52 (1990): 1050–1076.

Young, Iris Marion. *Inclusion and Democracy.* New York: Oxford University Press, 2000.

NOTES

1. Election Assistance Commission, "The Impact of the National Voter Registration Act of 1993 on the Administration of Elections for Federal Office, 2005–2006," June 30, 2007, 1, www.eac.gov/program-areas/research-resources-and-reports/completed-research-and-reports/national-voter-registration-act-studies.

2. Michael McDonald, "Voter Turnout: The Numbers Prove that 2004 May Signal More Voter Interest," *Milwaukee Journal Sentinel,* November 27, 2004, http://elections.gmu.edu/Turnout_Materials.html.

3. In the past the Court had stayed out of controversies over legislative districting by contending that they involved political and therefore nonjusticiable issues. In other words, they were not subject to judicial review.

4. U.S. Commission on Civil Rights, "Voting Irregularities in Florida During the 2000 Presidential Election," June 2001, http://www.usccr.gov/pubs/vote2000/report/main.htm. Florida state officials and Republican members of the commission criticized the conclusions of the report, asserting that there was no evidence that the disproportionate disfranchisement of African American voters resulted from discriminatory behavior of state and county election officials.

5. Massachusetts Institute of Technology and California Institute of Technology, "Voting: What Is and What Could Be," July 17, 2001.

6. Gallup Poll, "Seven out of 10 Americans Accept Bush as Legitimate President," July 17, 2001, http://www.gallup.com/poll/4687/Seven-Americans-Accept-Bush-Legitimate-President.aspx.

7. Center for Responsive Politics, "527s: Advocacy Group Spending in the 2008 Elections," www.opensecrets.org/527s/527cmtes.php?level=E&cycle=2008.

8. For example, see Stephen Ansolabehere and Shanto Iyengar, *Going Negative: How Political Advertisements Shrink and Polarize the Electorate* (New York: Free Press, 1995); and Thomas E. Patterson, *Out of Order* (New York: Knopf, 1993).

9. For a good basic discussion of democracy, see Robert A. Dahl, *On Democracy* (New Haven: Yale University Press, 1998). Dahl has written extensively on this subject. Two of his other well-known works on democratic theory are *A Preface to Democratic Theory* (Chicago: University of Chicago Press, 1956) and *Democracy and Its Critics* (New Haven: Yale University Press, 1989).

10. An excellent discussion of types of democratic systems appears in David Held, *Models of Democracy* (Cambridge: Polity Press, 1996).

11. Former Alaska senator Mike Gravel, one of the Democrats running for the party's 2008 presidential nomination, proposed a national ballot initiative in which voters would cast votes on major policy issues. Gravel's proposal and candidacy received little media attention and public support, however.

12. In many of the southern states, judges are elected in partisan or nonpartisan elections. In other states, they are appointed by the governor, legislature, or special commission, in some cases later subject to an up or down vote by the electorate. At the federal level, judges are nominated by the president and appointed with the advice and consent of the Senate. Federal judges serve during good behavior for life.

13. James Madison, *The Federalist,* No. 10.

14. Gallup Poll, "Presidential Approval Ratings—Bill Clinton," 1993–2001, www.gallup.com/poll/116584/Presidential-Approval-Ratings-Bill-Clinton.aspx.

15. Robert Dahl, "What Political Institutions Does Large-Scale Democracy Require?" *Political Science Quarterly* 120 (Summer 2005): 188.

16. For a classic discussion of the fundamental principles of democracy, see James W. Prothro and Charles M. Grigg, "Fundamental Principles of Democracy," *Journal of Politics* 22 (May 1960): 276–294.

17. President Obama restated Jefferson's words in his inaugural address: "The time has come to reaffirm our enduring spirit; to choose our better history; to carry forward that precious gift, that noble idea passed on from generation to generation: the God-given promise that all are equal, all are free, and all deserve a chance to pursue their full measure of happiness." Barack Obama, "President Barack Obama's Inaugural Address," January 20, 2009, www.whitehouse.gov/blog/inaugural-address/.

18. Dahl, "What Political Institutions," 196.

19. Several southern states, such as Louisiana and Georgia, require runoffs if the winning candidate does not receive more than half the total vote.

20. The exception is the District of Columbia, which has no voting representation in Congress but was given three electoral votes by the Twenty-third Amendment to the Constitution. The number of electoral votes was determined on the basis of what the District's representation would have been if it had been a state at the time of the ratification of the amendment in 1961.

21. Dahl, *On Democracy,* 132–134.

22. David Epstein and Sharyn O'Halloran, "Measuring the Electoral and Policy Impact of Majority-Minority Voting Districts," *American Journal of Political Science* 43 (April 1999):

367-395. A more recent study by Zoltan L. Hajnal found that African Americans are more likely than other groups to cast votes for losing candidates; see "Who Loses in American Democracy? A Count of Votes Demonstrates the Limited Representation of African Americans," *American Political Science Review* 103 (February 2009): 37-57.

23. Sidney Verba, Kay Lehman Schlozman, and Henry E. Brady, *Voice and Equality: Civic Voluntarism in American Politics* (Cambridge: Harvard University Press, 1995), 512.

24. Ibid., 511–533.

25. S. Robert Lichter, Stanley Rothman, and Linda S. Lichter claim in their book *The Media Elite* (Bethesda, Md.: Adler and Adler, 1986) that most national correspondents are liberal in ideology and Democratic in political allegiance.

26. *Striking the Balance: Audience Interests, Business Pressures, and Journalists' Values* (Washington, D.C.: Pew Research Center for the People and the Press, 1999); Pew Research Center for the People and the Press, "Big Doubts about News Media's Values: Public Votes for Continuity and Change in 2000," February 25, 1999; and Pew Research Center for the People and the Press, "High Marks for the Campaign, A High Bar for Obama," November 13, 2008.

Popular Base of American Electoral Politics
Suffrage and Turnout

Did you know that . . .

- less than one-fifth of adults living in the United States were eligible to vote in the first election held under the Constitution?
- by 1800, about one-third of those eligible actually voted—practically all of them adult white males?
- Congress almost refused to allow Wyoming to enter the Union in 1890 because its state constitution allowed women to vote?
- the United States has a lower rate of voting than do most European democracies?
- despite the fact that most Americans believe that voting is a civic responsibility, 28 percent report that they vote only part of the time, seldom, or not at all?
- at the beginning of the twentieth century, three out of four eligible voters cast ballots in the presidential election; at the end of that century, only two out of four did so?
- Hispanics, the fastest-growing group in the population, turn out at lower rates than do most other minority groups?
- election day is not and never has been a U.S. national holiday?
- about 30 percent of the voters in the 2008 election cast their ballots before the campaigns ended?
- the people who do vote are disproportionately better educated and have higher incomes than those who don't vote?
- nonvoters are less informed, less partisan, and less trustful of government than are voters?

Is this any way to run a democratic election?

To be democratic, an electoral system must allow all adult citizens to vote and to have their votes count equally.[1] Such a system also should encourage people to vote and facilitate their doing so. To what extent do U.S. elections meet these democratic goals? To what extent do they achieve participatory democracy in theory and in practice?

This chapter will answer these two questions that underlie the popular foundation of American democracy. It begins with a historic overview of suffrage and turnout and then turns to the reasons why people do not vote, the factors that influence those who do, and the difference turnout makes for a democratic political process and public policy outcomes. Proposals for increasing voter turnout are then assessed in light of contemporary trends in the American electoral system.

SUFFRAGE IN AMERICAN ELECTIONS

A participatory democracy was not what the framers had in mind when they drafted the Constitution. Most of the delegates who attended the Philadelphia convention neither desired nor encouraged large-scale public involvement in politics. The relatively low level of education most people had at the time, poor communications within and between the newly independent states, and the distrust that pervaded relations among the people of the thirteen states led the delegates at the Constitutional Convention to design a government that would be responsive to various segments of the society but not necessarily to the popular mood of the moment.

Who should vote was a contentious issue in 1787. Not wanting to derail the Constitution's ratification by imposing conditions on suffrage to which some states might object, the framers decided not to decide who should be allowed to vote. They left the matter to the individual states, subject to any restrictions Congress might later establish.

Expanding the Right to Vote

Initially, most state constitutions limited suffrage to white male citizens twenty-one years of age and older who owned property and were Christians. Gradually, these restrictions were eliminated. By the 1830s, most states had removed religion and property ownership as conditions for voting, thereby enfranchising about 80 percent of adult white males.[2]

In some northern states, African American males also were allowed to vote. The vast concentration of African Americans was in the South, however, and not until after the Civil War were they granted suffrage. The Fifteenth Amendment, ratified in 1870, removed race and color as qualifications for voting. In theory, it enfranchised all African American males who were citizens. In practice, only those who lived in the North and in border states could easily vote. A series of institutional devices, such as poll taxes, literacy tests, and restrictive primaries in which only Caucasians could participate (so-called white primaries), effectively combined with social pressure to prevent African Americans in the South from voting for another hundred years.[3]

Women, too, were denied the right to vote. Wyoming was the first territory to grant women equal voting rights with men in 1869, and it was the first state to do so after being admitted to the Union in 1890. Congress actually tried to compel Wyoming to rescind women's suffrage as a condition for entering the Union, but the Wyoming legislature refused, declaring, "We will remain out of the Union 100 years rather than come in without the women."[4] Congress relented. Only a few other states, primarily in the West, followed Wyoming's lead. By 1904, only four states permitted women to vote.[5]

The almost exclusive authority that states exercised to determine eligibility began to break down after the Civil War. During the next hundred years, Congress essentially nationalized the right to vote. A series of constitutional amendments and statutes limited the states' power to restrict suffrage. First, the Fifteenth Amendment (1871) prevented states from discriminating against otherwise eligible citizens on the basis of race, color, or previous condition of servitude. The Seventeenth Amendment (1913) required all states to elect their senators by popular vote. The Nineteenth Amendment (1920) prohibited gender from being used as a qualification for voting, and the Twenty-fourth Amendment (1964) precluded states from denying the vote for federal officials to residents who failed to pay a poll tax or any other tax.[6] The most recent constitutional restriction on the states, the Twenty-sixth Amendment (1971), forbade them from setting an age older than eighteen years as a condition for voting.

These constitutional strictures have been supplemented by legislation that also has limited state discretion on suffrage. The 1964 Civil Rights Act prevented a literacy test from being required for any citizen with a sixth-grade education from an accredited school in the United States or its territories. The 1965 Voting Rights Act authorized the federal government to send examiners to register voters in any legislative district in which 50 percent or more of the eligible adult population was not registered to vote. Amendments to this law further precluded states from imposing a residence requirement of more than thirty days for voting in any presidential election. The 1993 motor-voter bill requires states to make registration material available at their motor vehicle and social services offices, as well as at military recruitment centers, thereby enabling residents to register at these offices or by mail when they apply for or renew their driver's license, receive state health or welfare benefits, or enlist in the armed services.

Together, these constitutional amendments and statutes have established nearly universal suffrage, a policy that most Americans support. Prior to the enactment of the Twenty-sixth Amendment, 70 percent of the population favored lowering the voting age to eighteen.[7] Since 1944, a majority of Americans have favored eliminating the Electoral College and using a direct popular vote to select the president.[8]

Limiting the Right to Vote

The only state restrictions that remain in place are those that prevent otherwise qualified citizens from voting because they are or have been in jail or a mental institution. The jail and felony restrictions disfranchise between 4.5 and 5 million Americans.[9] Of this number about 1.4 million are African American males, approximately 13 percent of all African American men. In states that permanently disfranchise felons, that percentage rises to about 25 percent.[10] To help rectify this problem, the National Commission on Federal Election Reform has recommended that voting rights be restored to convicted felons who have served their time in jail.[11] About half the states that prohibited felons and ex-felons from voting prior to 2000 have since changed their laws to permit people who have served their sentences (and in some cases, completed their probation periods) to vote; ten states continue to disfranchise felons and those who have been dishonorably discharged from the military on a temporary or permanent basis.[12]

Since the 2000 election, there also have been allegations that minority voters, especially those who live in low-income areas, are much more likely than others to be prevented from voting or to have their votes voided for not completing the ballot properly. A report by the U.S. Commission on Civil Rights after the controversial 2000 Florida election condemned officials of that state for their unequal treatment of African American voters. The commission noted that 54 percent of the disqualified ballots were cast by African Americans, a group that constituted only 11 percent of Florida's electorate at the time.[13]

Another study, this one prepared for Democrats on the House Governmental Reform Committee, found that in the country as a whole, 4 percent of all ballots cast in low-income districts were not counted, compared with 1.2 percent in higher-income districts.[14] Whether the differential in disqualified votes is a consequence of discriminatory behavior by state election officials, better voting machines and shorter lines in more affluent areas, or simply more errors made by less-educated voters remains a subject of considerable controversy. Voting irregularities and fraudulent voting practices also were alleged in both 2004 and 2008. During the 2008 election, Republicans charged that an organization that supported Barack Obama, the Association of Community Organizations for Reform Now (ACORN), fraudulently registered voters. Although the Obama campaign paid $800,000 to that group to help get out the vote in the presidential election, it denied involvement in any illegal registrations and attributed them to overzealous organizers working for ACORN.[15]

Even though universal suffrage has been established in the United States, the costs of voting are not uniform among the population. They may be higher for single parents, higher for parents with young children, higher for the elderly and infirm, and higher for low-wage earners who work two or more jobs to make ends meet. They also may be higher for those who have to travel greater distances to vote. Generally speaking, people who fall into the "high-cost" category tend to be those with lower incomes. This fact introduces an economic bias into the voting electorate.

Some people may lack the skills to read the ballot and comprehend the differences among candidates and their parties; they may not be able to cope with the registration requirements, understand ballot initiatives, or know how to cast their ballots properly. Punching out the chad in Florida was a problem in 2000 that led to many untabulated vote cards. People with physical disabilities may have difficulty getting to the polls, especially if the elections are held in facilities inaccessible to the handicapped. Obtaining absentee ballots also may be a problem, particularly in states that require proof of out-of-state business or disabled status before issuing such a ballot, although the number of states with such a requirement has decreased.

VARIATIONS IN VOTER TURNOUT

Although suffrage has been extended to most citizens, many do not exercise their right much of the time (see Figure 2.1). In the 1996 presidential election, a majority of the adult population (51 percent) did *not* vote; in 2000, a bare majority did. Turnouts in 2004 and 2008 were higher. In 2004, turnout was 55.4 percent of the voting-age population (VAP) and 60.7 percent of the

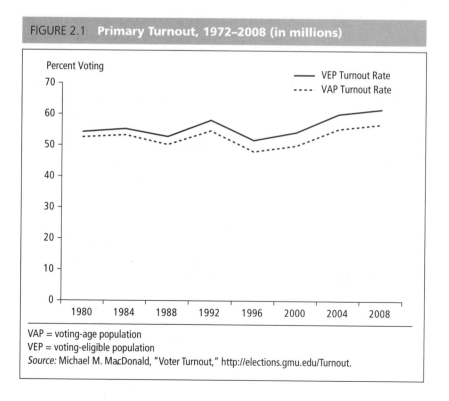

FIGURE 2.1 **Primary Turnout, 1972–2008 (in millions)**

VAP = voting-age population
VEP = voting-eligible population
Source: Michael M. MacDonald, "Voter Turnout," http://elections.gmu.edu/Turnout.

voting-eligible population (VEP), which excludes noncitizens, incarcerated individuals, ex-felons, and others precluded by state law from voting; in 2008, VAP went up to 56.9 percent and VEP to 62.3.[16]

Types of Elections

In nonpresidential years, the proportion of the population voting is even lower, usually in the range of 30 to 40 percent for congressional elections, and much lower than that in off-year elections for state and local officials. In 2002, the percentage for the VEP was 40.5 and that for the VAP was 36.3; in 2006 the percentages were 41.3 and 37.1, respectively.[17] Put another way, about 60 percent of eligible voters failed to vote.

Turnout in primaries is less than in the general election. In 2004, turnout in the primaries averaged 15 percent of the voting-age population although it was higher in the more competitive states that held their contests before the presidential nominees had been effectively determined.[18] In 2008, turnout during the parties' presidential nomination process increased significantly. With spirited contests in both parties, approximately 59 million people voted, 42.2 percent of registered voters, 32.5 percent of eligible voters, and 26.8 percent of the voting-age population.[19]

Historical Trends

Voter turnout in the United States has fluctuated considerably. After 1800, the development of the party system provided the incentive and organizational mechanism to expand the proportion of the population who voted. Turnout rose, ranging from 25 to 50 percent of those eligible between 1800 and 1828, with the higher rates in elections in which the parties were most competitive. But the competition didn't last long. One of the parties, the Federalists, ran its last presidential candidate in 1816 and effectively disintegrated after that. With the advent of one-party dominance, turnout began to decline.

By the mid-1820s, however, factions within the Democratic-Republican Party led to a more competitive political environment and, ultimately, to the reemergence of a two-party system. As that system evolved, the parties tried to get more people involved and out to vote; they succeeded by popularizing election campaigns.[20] Beginning in the 1840s, rallies, oratory, and parades brought out the faithful and the curious alike, thereby contributing to higher turnout.[21]

The new party activism continued in nonelectoral periods as well. Patronage jobs, political influence, and even a little monetary aid were given to loyal supporters, who were expected to return the favor on election day. This expectation was reinforced by the parties' oversight of the voting process. Precinct captains got out the voters, the parties printed their own color-coded ballots that contained only the names of their candidates, and poll watchers recorded who voted and how.[22]

As a consequence of these activities, turnout soared; in some elections in the second half of the nineteenth century, more than 80 percent of eligible voters reportedly voted. However, corruption and fraudulent voting practices were also rampant. Multiple voting, ballot stuffing, vote tampering, and irregularities in tallying the vote led states to print their own ballots and monitor election activities more closely in and around the areas where people voted. In addition, registration procedures were instituted to ensure that only those who were eligible could vote.

Although these reforms were designed to protect the integrity of the electoral process, they also made the act of voting more difficult. People had to register first, sometimes well in advance of the election, and do so at places and times designated by the states. Some states also enacted poll taxes to pay for the cost of the election. These taxes were particularly onerous for low-income voters.

That wasn't the worst of it, however. The taxes and literacy tests were implemented in a discriminatory manner by election officials, primarily in the South. They became barriers to prevent African Americans, as well as many poor whites, from voting.

Decreasing competition between the political parties in the South following the Civil War also contributed to lower turnout. The South became a one-party region, dominated by the Democrats. Because the winner of that party's nomination was a prohibitive favorite to win the general election, there was less incentive for southerners to vote. The Republicans also gained sufficient strength to dominate in the Northeast with much the same depressing effect on turnout.

On top of all this, both parties seemed determined to establish as many safe congressional seats as possible for their candidates. The adoption of the seniority rule in selecting the chairs of standing committees in Congress provided added incentive for state parties to protect their congressional incumbents who had risen to positions of power by "creative" districting that effectively secured their seats.

Although a reform movement at the end of the nineteenth century gave more power to rank-and-file voters through the introduction of presidential primaries in many of the states, it did not increase the rate of turnout. And by the end of World War I, this reform movement had all but dissipated. States reverted to nomination procedures that facilitated control by party leaders. With the exception of the 1928 presidential election, turnout throughout the 1920s was less than 50 percent of those eligible to vote.

The realignment of political parties in the 1930s, and especially the appeal of Franklin D. Roosevelt's Democratic Party to those on the lower rungs of the socioeconomic ladder (blue-collar workers, poor farmers, and racial and ethnic minorities), reenergized the electorate, contributing to a larger proportion of the population voting, especially in presidential elections, for the next thirty years. Turnout, however, did not return to the levels it reached in the second half of the nineteenth century.

By the end of the 1960s, it was again on the decline. The civil rights movement and the Vietnam War created divisions within the majority party, the Democrats, marking the beginning of a trend of less intense partisan allegiances among supporters of that party. Technological advances in communication, particularly the advent of television campaigning, increased the candidate-centeredness of elections, weakened party organizations, and led to a decline in partisan loyalties. Television, however, proved to be a less effective way to mobilize voters than personal contact by party workers and volunteers.

The decreasing turnout levels ended at the close of the twentieth century. Since then, partisan parity during much of this period has resulted in closer elections; partisan identification has strengthened; partisan voting patterns have emerged; and the parties, using new communication technologies to reach more people and target more messages more directly to voters, have placed greater emphasis on grassroots organizing and turnout campaigns. Voter registration has become easier, absentee ballots are more readily available, and early voting periods have been established by more and more states. Each of these factors has contributed to the increases in the proportion of the electorate voting in the twenty-first century.

INFLUENCES ON VOTING

More people claim they vote than actually do. They do so because most citizens consider voting a civic responsibility. According to national surveys conducted by the Pew Research Center for the People and the Press, almost 90 percent of those surveyed agreed with the statement "I feel it is my duty as a citizen to always vote."[23] More than 60 percent also said that they feel guilty when they do not do so.[24] So most people say they always or nearly always vote.

Why People Do Not Vote: Excuses Real and Concocted

Despite the widespread belief that voting is an important responsibility of citizenship, a substantial portion of the population does not vote. Many lack the motivation to do so. Today, a majority of people still subscribe to the proposition that "most elected officials do not really care about what people like me think."[25] They don't see what difference it makes to them who wins the election. Nor do they see their votes mattering all that much, although in Florida in the 2000 presidential election, in the 2004 governor's election in the state of Washington, in the 2008 Minnesota contest for U.S. senator, and in several of the congressional midterm elections in recent years, a small number of votes could have changed the outcome.

People are cynical. They distrust politicians. They most often cite candidate dishonesty and untruthfulness, a lack of pertinent information, and negative campaigning as reasons for not voting.[26] However, when negativity is examined within the context of other factors, such as the level of mistrust people bring to the election, it seems to be a less important influence on nonvoting.[27] Much depends on how campaign news and ads are viewed and by whom. For example, if the negativity seems appropriate, such as opposition to a popular issue, it actually may increase turnout. But if the negativity seems excessive or inappropriate, such as mudslinging or harsh and vindictive personal ads, it can adversely affect turnout and even boomerang against the candidate who uses such tactics.[28]

People give a myriad of other reasons or excuses for not voting. Some say that they are too busy trying to earn a living, raise a family, or meet other day-to-day responsibilities. And perhaps they are. Some people may be conflicted, unable to decide among competing candidates, parties, and policy alternatives. Their decision not to vote may be a considered choice, a protest about the candidates, the parties, or their public policy positions: the candidates may not seem appealing, qualified, or sufficiently different from one another. They make take positions with which people strongly disagree. The issues may not seem relevant to people in the conduct of their everyday lives.

Other reasons for not voting have to do with election rules and procedures, particularly registration requirements. Despite enactment of the motor-voter law, some people still find registration difficult or inconvenient and either fail to register or fail to do so on time. Others are prevented from voting because their registrations are not properly recorded, they come to the wrong precinct to vote, or their registration is challenged when they get to the polls. The study conducted by MIT and CalTech, mentioned in Chapter 1, estimated that three million people were not able to cast valid ballots in 2000 because of registration mishaps of one type or another. This is in addition to the four to six million individuals whose votes were not counted.[29]

To help rectify this problem, Congress enacted the Help America Vote Act in 2002 to provide for provisional voting when registration disputes occur. A person claiming to be registered but whose name does not appear on the precinct voting list may cast a provisional vote that will be accepted if the registration issue is resolved in the voter's favor.

Rules and procedures, designed to maintain the integrity of a democratic voting system, place burdens on potential voters. As previously mentioned, finding the time, physically getting to the polls, understanding the intricacies of the ballot, and even knowing how to vote—which lever to push, hole to punch, or box to check—all are factors that discourage some people from voting or disqualify others whose votes were cast improperly.

The controversy over the "butterfly" ballot in Palm Beach County, Florida, in the 2000 election is a case in point. Under Florida's election law at that time, individual counties were responsible for the design of the ballots, the monitoring of elections, and the tabulation of votes. In Palm Beach County, a Democratic election official designed an easy-to-read ballot on which the names of all the candidates appeared on a single punch card. To fit everything on one side of the card, the ballot contained two columns of names but only one column of "chads," the perforated holes that voters were supposed to punch out (see Figure 2.2). Some voters were confused and punched the chads for the wrong candidates; other voters punched two chads, automatically

FIGURE 2.2   2000 Presidential Election Ballot Used in Palm Beach County, Florida

OFFICIAL BALLOT, GENERAL ELECTION
PALM BEACH COUNTY, FLORIDA
NOVEMBER 7, 2000

**ELECTORS
FOR PRESIDENT
AND
VICE PRESIDENT**

(A vote for the candidates will
actually be a vote for their electors.)

(Vote for Group)

(REPUBLICAN)
GEORGE W. BUSH - PRESIDENT
DICK CHENEY - VICE PRESIDENT

(DEMOCRATIC)
AL GORE - PRESIDENT
JOE LIEBERMAN - VICE PRESIDENT

(LIBERTARIAN)
HARRY BROWNE - PRESIDENT
ART OLIVIER - VICE PRESIDENT

(GREEN)
RALPH NADER - PRESIDENT
WINONA LaDUKE - VICE PRESIDENT

(SOCIALIST WORKERS)
JANES HARRIS - PRESIDENT
MARGARET TROWE - VICE PRESIDENT

(NATURAL LAW)
JOHN HAGELIN - PRESIDENT
NAT GOLDHABER - VICE PRESIDENT

OFFICIAL BALLOT, GENERAL ELECTION
PALM BEACH COUNTY, FLORIDA
NOVEMBER 7, 2000

(REFORM)
PAT BUCHANAN - PRESIDENT
EZOLA FOSTER - VICE PRESIDENT

(SOCIALIST)
DAVID McREYNOLDS - PRESIDENT
MARY CAL HOLLIS - VICE PRESIDENT

(CONSTITUTION)
HOWARD PHILLIPS - PRESIDENT
J. CURTIS FRAZIER - VICE PRESIDENT

(WORKERS WORLD)
MONICA MOOREHEAD - PRESIDENT
GLORIA LaRIVA - VICE PRESIDENT

WRITE-IN CANDIDATE
To vote for a write-in candidate, follow the
directions on the long stub of your ballot card.

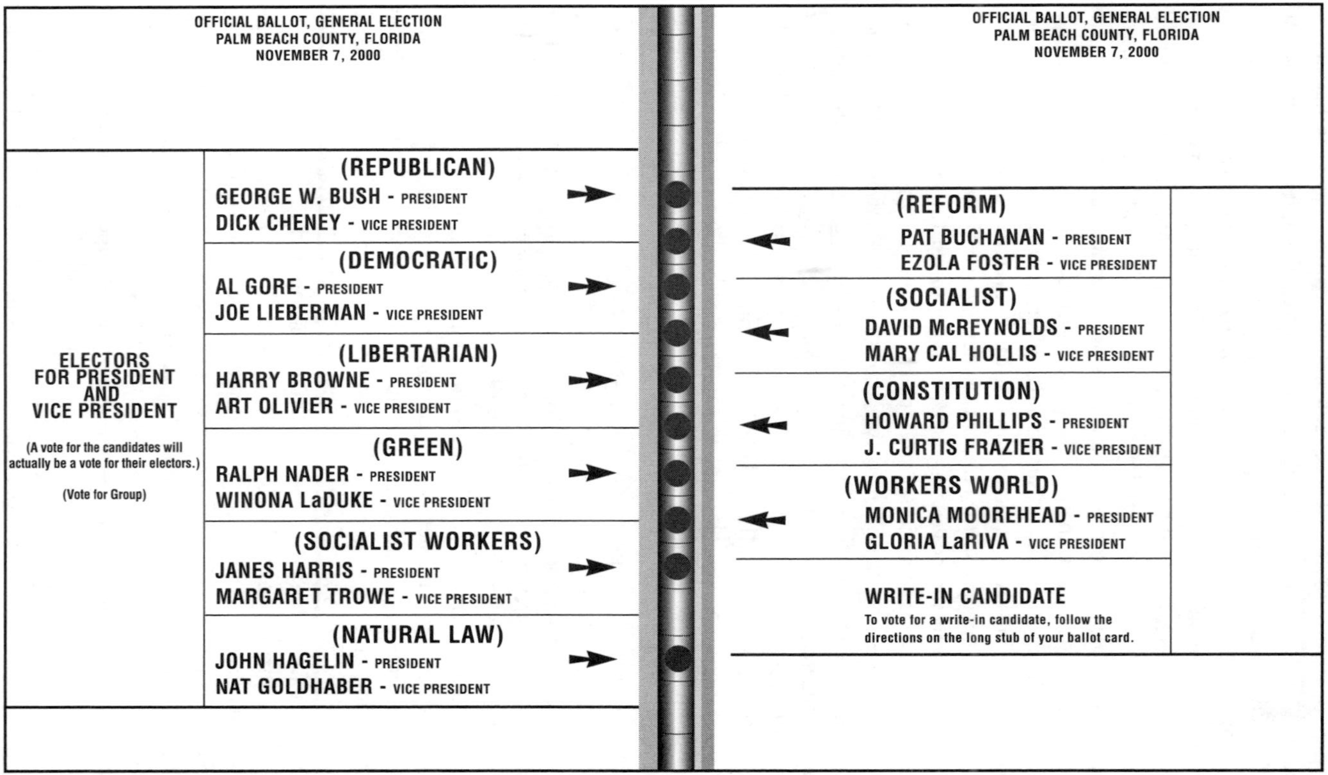

Source: The Washington Post, October 23, 2001, www.thewashingtonpost.com.

voiding their ballots. Additionally, some voters did not punch out the chads completely, leaving them dimpled or hanging. The voting machines undercounted ballots with chads that were not completely removed.[30]

Finally, the competitiveness of the election and the campaigns of the candidates also affect turnout. More competitive elections attract a larger vote for obvious reasons. They are also more likely to generate better-funded and more vigorous campaigns, which in turn should turn out more voters. In presidential elections, the battleground states that both presidential campaigns target have higher turnout levels than do states that do not receive as much candidate attention (see Table 2.1).[31]

Why People Do Vote

Political Attitudes. Personal feelings and beliefs are important in motivating people to vote. Interest in the election, concern over the outcome, and feelings of civic responsibility are factors that affect how regularly people vote. Naturally, those who feel more strongly about the election and have more interest in it are more likely to participate in the campaign and vote than those who do not have these feelings or interest.

TABLE 2.1 **Voter Turnout in the Battleground States, 2000–2008 (percentages)**			
	Percentage		
State	2000	2004	2008
Florida	57.5	64.7	68.0
Iowa	63.2	70.6	70.2
Michigan	60.5	67.1	69.4
Minnesota	70.1	78.8	78.5
Missouri	58.2	66.1	68.1
Ohio	57.8	67.9	67.6
Oregon	65.9	72.6	68.5
Pennsylvania	54.1	62.6	64.2
Washington	61.4	67.5	67.7
Wisconsin	67.6	75.3	72.9
U.S. average	55.3	60.7	62.3

Note: Figures based on the total number of ballots cast by eligible voters.

Source: Michael P. McDonald, "General Election Turnout Rates," http://elections.gmu.edu/Turnout_ 2008G.html.

Identification with a political party is another motivation for voting. The more intense a person's partisan affiliation, the more likely that person will be to vote. From the late 1960s through the 1980s, partisan attitudes weakened while the proportion of the population claiming to be independent increased. These factors contributed to declining turnout during this period.

Political efficacy, the belief that one's vote really matters, declined during this period, which also reduced voting, more so than did the weakening of partisan identities according to three political scientists, Paul R. Abramson, John H. Aldrich, and David W. Rhode, who study voting behavior.[32] People became more cynical and less trusting of government and those who ran it. Many felt that government was less sensitive to their needs, run for special interests by politicians who will say and do practically anything to get elected and reelected. The perception that public officials were more interested in serving their own needs than the needs of their constituents fueled the belief that it just doesn't matter all that much who wins.[33]

Social and Economic Factors. Several social and economic variables, such as education, income, and age, also correlate with turnout as well as with one another. Of these factors, education is the most important. The greater a person's education, the more likely it is that person will vote.[34] Higher learning develops the cognitive skills necessary to process information and to make informed judgments. It provides the skills to maneuver through the intricacies of the electoral process: meeting the registration requirements, obtaining absentee ballots, and understanding the ballot and how to mark it correctly.

Education also affects personal success. It increases a person's stake in the system, interest in an election, and concern over the outcome. Because the lesson that voting is a civic responsibility is usually learned in the classroom, schooling can contribute to a more highly developed sense of civic responsibility.

Education, income level, and occupational status tend to correlate with one another. College-educated people have better connections, more skills, and greater knowledge; as a consequence, they have more opportunities to earn more money than those who lack these resources. Individuals with higher incomes and more professional jobs also have higher rates of voter turnout. According to the American National Election Studies, only about half of those in the lowest income bracket reported that they voted in the 2004 presidential election compared with almost 90 percent in the top income bracket.[35] In midterm elections the differential is even greater.

Income differentials are even more evident in other forms of electoral activity, such as volunteering to help a campaign and, especially, contributing money. Naturally, the large donors tend to be the most affluent citizens.

Age is another factor that contributes to voting. Older citizens turn out in higher numbers than those who are younger. They do so because they have more interest in the election, more concern over the outcome and how it might affect them, and, in some cases, more time to become involved. In addition,

TABLE 2.2 **People Who Claim They Almost Always Vote**

	2007	2009
Total	45	51
Race		
White	49	53
Black	46	59
Hispanic	25	35
Partisan identity		
Republican	56	62
Democrat	48	56
Independent	38	43
Age		
18–29	25	36
30–49	40	46
50–64	52	60
65+	68	65
Education		
College graduate	58	62
Some college	49	56
High school graduate or less	36	42
Household income		
$100,000 or more	54	59
$75,000–$99,999	56	60
$50,000–$74,999	50	55
$30,000–$49,999	45	53
Less than $30,000	34	39

Source: Pew Research Center for the People and the Press, "Independents Take Center Stage in Obama Era," May 21, 2009, http://people-press.org/report/?pageid=1523.

older people tend to have greater economic interests and ties to the community in which they live, two other reasons for participating. For many of them, too, voting is habitual. Table 2.2 shows a demographic breakdown of people who have indicated to pollsters that they almost always vote.

With education and income levels rising since the end of World War II, one would have expected turnout to increase during most of this period. It did not do so, however. Between the 1960s and the 1990s, turnout declined. Most scholars believe that the decline would have been more severe had not education and income levels risen.[36]

What then explains the decline in turnout during this period? A growing number of political scientists see rising inequality as a principal culprit. The gap among income groups in the United States has widened, not only between the rich and poor, but also between the rich and the middle class. Professors Joe Soss and Lawrence R. Jacobs describe this gap:

> In a perfectly egalitarian society, each fifth of the population would receive 20 percent of a country's income. Today, the most affluent fifth of Americans receive about 48 percent of the total family income, a sum that is approximately double the proportion received by each of the two quintiles immediately below them (approximately 22.9 percent and 15.3 percent, respectively) and more than fourfold greater than the bottom two quintiles, which each received less than 10 of total family income.[37]

The disparity in incomes has contributed to living patterns segregated on the basis of income in which residents of the wealthier communities have more incentives to vote—more education, more political awareness, and more civic responsibility—while those who live in the poorest communities have fewer incentives to do so.[38]

The differences in participation among groups along economic and social lines have also been affected by organizational change. Special-interest groups, structured on the basis of industries, professions, and beliefs, have proliferated while mass-mobilization groups such as labor unions have declined. According to Soss and Jacobs, these social changes have encouraged political parties and their nominees to focus their turnout efforts among the people who would be most likely to vote, thereby enlarging the participation gap between the advantaged and disadvantaged.[39] The gap was evident in recent elections. Turnout percentages increase as income levels get higher.

Situational Variables. The electoral environment also contributes to or detracts from voting. In addition to the level of competition between the parties and their nominees, the state of the economy, the saliency of issues, and the political climate all affect turnout and voting behavior. The more people are upset with the current state of affairs, the more likely they will vote. Bad economic conditions tend to bring out more people than do good conditions. Similarly, issues that directly affect significant portions of the population are more likely to generate turnout than those that are theoretical or not of immediate concern. Naturally, the attractiveness of the candidates, the scope and impact of their appeals, the excitement of the campaign, coverage by the news media, and personal and social networking are also factors, individually and collectively, that can result in a larger proportion of the population voting.

In 2004, concern with international and domestic terrorism combined with social issues, such as same-sex marriage, motivated more people to vote. The Republican campaign highlighted these issues to mobilize a larger-than-usual vote. In 2008, broad dissatisfaction with the Bush administration over the war in Iraq, the abrogation of civil liberties, the sharp rise in the costs of energy, and, especially, mushrooming economic problems—declining property values; increasing mortgage foreclosures; the credit crisis; the failure of major investments firms, banks, and a major insurer; and increasing unemployment—all led to a higher turnout.

The resonance and hopefulness of Barack Obama's campaign message, "yes, we can"; the effective use of the Internet by his campaign operatives to raise money, gain volunteers, get out voters; the expanded efforts of his campaign in the normally red (Republican) states; and the excitement that his candidacy generated for Democrats and independents, particularly for younger voters and African Americans, all worked to stimulate a larger vote.

CONSEQUENCES OF NOT VOTING

Does it matter that so many of those eligible to vote do not do so? Most observers believe that it does, even though they concede that the outcome of most elections and the policies of newly elected officials would probably be the same even if a greater number of nonvoters participated. Postelection surveys of voters and nonvoters show little difference in their candidate selections, policy preferences, and political attitudes.[40] The findings suggest that nonvoters in retrospect and after the election say that they support the candidates in roughly the same proportion as do voters. Moreover, the policy positions of voters and nonvoters are also similar.[41] Although nonvoters do tend to be slightly more liberal than voters, the ideological differences between them do not appear to be great enough to have a major impact on public policy.[42]

If the results of the election probably wouldn't change with more people voting, then what's the big fuss about nonvoting?[43] The answer lies in the link that voting forges between citizens and their elected representatives. Nonvoting weakens that link; it creates a representational gap between the general public and the voting electorate.

Unequal Representation and Turnout

The demographic differences between voters and nonvoters have produced an electorate that is not representative of the general population. It has also resulted in class bias in voting as well as in other aspects of electoral activity, such as contributing money to the candidates and parties, attending rallies, and volunteering time.

Those who are most disadvantaged, who have the least education and the lowest incomes, and who need a change in conditions the most actually participate the least. Those who are the most advantaged by having high incomes and more education and who benefit from existing conditions and presumably from public policy as it stands vote more regularly. These trends in who votes work to reinforce, even to perpetuate, the status quo and have contributed to unequal representation in government.

The tendency of higher-income, well-connected, older Americans to get more involved in politics and to vote more often has naturally encouraged candidates seeking office to address those voters' issues, be they taxes, health care costs, or the security of pension plans, rather than issues in which the poor and the young might have more interest and concern, such as obtaining health care coverage, the availability of government subsidies for housing, or overcrowding in prisons. If the issues are geared to those who vote, then it follows that elected officials are more likely to make policy decisions that reflect the interests and desires of those who elected them rather than those who voted against them or stood on the sidelines.

Research by prominent political scientists provides empirical evidence that political activity enhances representation.[44] In other words, those who are more active and tend to vote more regularly tend to reap the benefits of their participation in the political process. They select like-minded individuals, communicate their beliefs and desires to them, and use the threat to defeat them in the next election to persuade their representatives to support their interests.[45] It is more likely that the policy issues of these activists will be addressed, and probably in a manner that works to their economic or social self-interests.

Having the will and resources to affect political activity allows the advantaged to maintain and even extend their advantage. The American Political Science Association's Task Force on Inequality and American Democracy put it this way:

> The privileged participate more than others and are increasingly well organized to press their demands on government. Public officials, in turn, are much more responsive to the privileged than to average citizens and the least affluent. Citizens with lower or moderate incomes speak with a whisper that is lost on the ears of inattentive government officials, while the advantaged roar with a clarity and consistency that policy-makers readily hear and routinely follow. The scourge of overt discrimination against African-Americans and women has been replaced by a more subtle but potent threat—the growing concentration of the country's wealth and income in the hands of the few.[46]

In short, economic inequality extends political inequality, which in turn is reflected in public policy decisions. It is a vicious cycle, one that is difficult to break. To do so would require that the disadvantaged organize and increase their level of participation and that the advantaged share more equitably the benefits they receive.

In addition to income gaps, turnout differentials among political parties and ethnic, racial, and gender groups also affect their representation throughout the political system in elections, governance, and public policy. In the 1980s and for most of the 1990s, Republican turnout exceeded that of the Democrats, giving Republicans more legislative influence than they would have had if everyone eligible had voted. In 2006 and 2008, Democratic turnout was higher than Republican turnout. Increasing turnout for women has led to greater demographic representation for this group although not nearly in proportion to its percentage within the electorate.

In contrast, Hispanics, the largest and most rapidly growing ethnic group in America, constitute about 15 percent of the population but only 8 percent of the 2008 electorate. Naturally, that differential has resulted in fewer national and state legislators to look out for that group's needs in education, social services, employment opportunities, and immigration. African Americans, about 12.5 percent of the population, made up 13 percent of the 2008 electorate. It remains to be seen whether the increase in African American turnout in 2008 will result in more political and policy influence for this racial group.

Increased Difficulties Governing

In addition to representational issues, variations in turnout can produce other problems for a democratic electoral process. Low turnout can make the meaning of the election less clear, the claim of a public mandate more problematic, and the task of fulfilling campaign pledges and promises more difficult. It also can have a negative impact on building and maintaining a majority coalition for governing. If fewer people vote, the proportion of the population who will be initially supportive of the newly elected government will be smaller, and those in elective positions may find it more difficult to gain support for their policies and legitimacy for their actions.

Low turnout can also become a policy issue. One of the cornerstones of U.S. foreign policy since the end of World War II has been the promotion of and support for democratic institutions and processes around the world. The failure of so many Americans to vote undercuts the credibility of this policy goal. Compare voter turnout in the United States with turnouts in other democratic countries, as shown in Table 2.3. Since 1945, the average turnout in western Europe has been 77 percent of the voting-age population; it has been consistently lower in the United States, even as a percentage of registered voters.[47]

Some scholars actually see benefit in having a significant proportion of the electorate not voting on a regular basis. They claim that lack of interest and inactivity enhances the quality of those who participate, mutes political conflict, promotes social stability, and implicitly provides support for public policy decisions by not challenging those decisions or holding policymakers accountable.[48] In this sense, apathy can be viewed as satisfaction with existing conditions; otherwise, it is argued, people would be more likely to protest in the

TABLE 2.3 International Voter Turnout in Selected Countries

Country	Year	Type of voting system	Type of election	Turnout of registered voters (percentage)	Required to be on voting lists: yes (Y) or no (N); Registration: voluntary (V) or compulsory (C) voting	Rest day (R) or workday (W)
Argentina	2007	Proportional	Presidential	71.8	Y / C	R
Australia	2007	Other/ two rounds	Parliamentary	95.2 / 94.8	Y / C	R
Austria	2004	Proportional	Presidential	70.8	Y / V	R
Belgium	2007	Proportional	Parliamentary	91.1	Y / C	R
Brazil	2006	Proportional	Parliamentary	83.2	Y / C	R
Canada	2008	Winner Take all	Parliamentary	59.5	N / V	W
Chile	2008	Proportional	Presidential	70.8 / 87.1	Y / C	R
Czech Rep.	2005/6	Proportional	Parliamentary	31.1 / 29.8	Y / C	W
Denmark	2007	Proportional	Parliamentary	86.6	Y / V	W
Finland	2007	Proportional	Presidential	68.3	Y / V	B`
France	2007	Two rounds	Presidential / parliamentary	83.8; 84.0 / 60.4; 60.0	Y / V	R
Germany	2005	Proportional	Parliamentary	77.7	Y / V	R
Greece	2007	Proportional	Parliamentary	74.1	Y / C	R
India	2004	Winner Take all	Parliamentary	57.7	Y / V	B`
Iran	2008	Proportional	Parliamentary	50.9	N / V	R

Country	Year	Electoral System	Election Type	Turnout		
Iraq	2005	Two rounds	Parliamentary	79.6	N / V	W
Ireland	2007	Winner take all	Parliamentary	67.0	N / V	W
Israel	2009	Proportional	Parliamentary	64.7	Y / V	W
Japan	2007	Other	Parliamentary	58.6	Y / V	R
Pakistan	2008	Winner take all	Parliamentary	44.5	N / V	W
Poland	2007	Proportional	Parliamentary	58.3	Y / V	R
Rumania	2008	Proportional	Parliamentary	39.2	Y / V	R
Russia	2007	Proportional	Parliamentary	63.7	Y / V	R
South Africa	2009	Proportional all	Parliamentary	77.3	N / V	R
South Korea	2007	Winner take all	Presidential	62.9	Y / V	R
Spain	2008	Proportional	Parliamentary	76.0 / 75.3	Y / V	W
Switzerland	2007	Other	Parliamentary	48.3	Y / V	R
United States	2006	Winner take all	Legislative	41.3	N / V	W
	2008	Winner take all	Presidential	62.3	N / V	W

B* = Election conducted over more than one day.

Sources: International Foundation for Electoral Systems, "Electionguide.org: Voter Turnout," www.electionguide.org; Michael M. MacDonald, "2008 General Election Turnout Rates," United States Elections Project, George Mason University, http://elections.gmu.edu/Turnout_2008G.html; International Institute for Democracy and Electoral Assistance, "Voter Turnout," www.idea.int/vt/index.cfm.

streets and at the ballot box. Those who support this position point to the fact that bad times and discontent normally bring out a larger vote than do good times and public contentment.[49]

Most democratic theorists, however, do not subscribe to the belief that apathy is a positive social trait. Rather, they see it as an illness, a symptom of discontent within the political system by a significant segment of the population.[50]

POSSIBLE SOLUTIONS TO THE NONVOTING PROBLEM

Change the Electoral System

Although they are not required to do so, most states have established single-member legislative districts in which the candidate with the most votes wins. A few states require the winner to receive a majority of the total vote; in most states, however, a plurality is sufficient to win.

A winner-take-all voting system is easy to understand, consistent with the one person-one vote principle, and fair so long as all adult citizens have the right to vote. But such a system does not necessarily encourage voting *unless the election is competitive;* and most elections in the United States are not. If the winner takes all, the losers and the people who voted for them get nothing. Thus, for those in the minority, whose views are not likely to prevail and whose candidates are not likely to win, what is the incentive to vote? Being a good citizen and fulfilling a civic responsibility is not a sufficient motivation for a significant proportion of the eligible population. Having influence on election outcomes and on the resulting governance and public policy is a motivation, however. Thus, one way to encourage more people to vote is to make elections more competitive; another is to change the system itself so that more people vote for the winners.

Elections are not competitive for two major reasons: one relates to the drafting of the districts and the other to the candidates running for office. The party in power drafts legislative districts in such a way as to maximize its competitive advantage, a practice is known as gerrymandering.[51] Thus, most districts in terms of their population base clearly favor one or the other of the major parties, hardly an incentive for opponents of that party to get out and vote. The second factor that discourages turnout is the advantage that incumbents have when they run for reelection. Their name recognition, fund-raising abilities, services and other tangible benefits they can provide constituents plus experienced office staff and campaign operatives help them gain renomination and reelection by sizable margins. These margins discourage quality challengers.

Reversing these noncompetitive aspects of elections would require those in power to reduce or eliminate their political advantage, an action that they are unlikely to undertake voluntarily. In the interests of promoting more democratic elections, a few states have established nonpartisan legislative or judicial commissions to redraw their electoral districts to maximize competition.[52]

A few more have tried to limit the advantage of incumbency by enacting more equitable campaign finance laws and by establishing term limits. Both of these legal and constitutional reforms have engendered considerable political opposition within the states as well as legal challenges, however. The Supreme Court has held that limiting congressional terms by statute violates the Constitution because it adds an additional qualification to the three constitutional qualifications that currently exist for holding national office.[53]

The alternative is to change the electoral structure itself from single-member to multimember districts and change the voting from winner-take-all to proportional voting. Such a change would increase the incentives for more candidates to run and more parties to compete. It would give voters more choices in the election, likely provide them with more responsive public officials after the election, and thus enable more people to influence government and public policy. All of these factors should encourage more people to turn out to vote.

But power within the political and governmental systems would also be more dispersed; majority coalitions more difficult to build and maintain; government possibly less stable; public policy less innovative; and accountability more difficult to pinpoint. These changes would also run counter to the American political tradition, one that has received considerable support over the years. Opposition to changing the way Americans select their president has prevented a modification of the Electoral College despite the election of three nonplurality winners, the controversial vote in Florida in 2000, and numerous other problems (see Chapter 3).

Lower the Costs of Voting

What can be done about the problem of nonvoting? Describing the problem, the reasons people give for not voting, and the factors that influence turnout is easier than solving the problem of a sizable proportion of the eligible population not voting. Congress has dealt with the issue in two ways. First, it has enacted laws—for example, the motor-voter bill that was designed to make registration easier, more accessible, and less time-consuming—to remove or ease legal hurdles to voting. Congress hoped that the proportion of the population who did not vote because they were not registered would decrease—perhaps by as much as 8 or 9 percent.[54] It has not done so by this amount, although the number of people registered has increased, as has turnout in the twenty-first century.

The Help America Vote Act (passed in 2002) was designed to improve the accuracy of registration lists and vote tabulation methods as well as provide better oversight of the decisions state and local electoral officials make on election day. The intent of the law was avoiding election controversies, thereby boosting the legitimacy of elections among various population groups that may have perceived discrimination, and maximizing voter turnout. Although turnout has improved, many problems still remain.

Professor Heather Gerken, an election expert at Yale Law School, describes the electoral system in the United States as "clunky at best and dysfunctional at worst:"

> Ballots are discarded. Poll workers are poorly trained. Registration lists work badly. Lines can be too long. Machines malfunction. Partisan officials change the rules of the game to help themselves and hurt their enemies. Election administrators cannot agree on what constitutes a best practice, or even whether there is any such thing. Authority is decentralized, so it's hard to know who's to blame when a problem occurs. Most experts agree that the system we use to run our elections is chronically underfunded, often poorly run, and sometimes administered in a partisan fashion.[55]

Aware of the difficulties of enacting more legislation to better fund elections, train election officials, and reduce partisan influence, Gerken suggests that states and localities calculate how democratic their election systems actually are with the use of a democracy index based on three criteria: voter registration (the extent to which every eligible voter who wants to register can do so), voting (the extent to which every registered voter who wants to cast a vote can do so), and vote tabulation (the accurate counting of every ballot that is properly cast). Gerken believes that the system needs to be convenient for citizens and that they need to have their votes tabulated in a timely and accurate manner.[56]

Implementing a democracy index would not require additional national legislation, although it might require greater funding, both public and private, to collect the data necessary for election officials to calculate their democracy score. Gerken is counting on the competitive instincts of states and local election officials and the people they represent; she sees bragging power and pride in being more democratic than other states and communities as the primary motivating factor that will improve the conduct of elections and involve the general public in those efforts. She may be right. While Barack Obama and Hillary Clinton were competing for the Democratic Party's presidential nomination, both introduced legislation in the Senate that would help turn Gerken's idea into reality; major public policy foundations have also expressed interest in the proposal.[57]

What else can Congress and the states do to reduce the personal costs of voting, costs measured in time, effort, and perhaps lost wages? One way to make it easier for people to find the time to vote is to hold elections on days that are not workdays for most people, for example, on a holiday or a Sunday. The United States is one of the few democracies that still conducts elections on a workday (see Table 2.3). Although employers are required by law to give their employees time to vote, and not penalize them financially for doing so, some people still find it difficult to take the time off.

Making election day a holiday would make it easier for more people to vote. However, there would be opposition to such a proposal. Some businesses would lose money by being closed or forced to pay employees extra for working on a holiday. Schools would be closed, thereby increasing the burden on single parents. And some people employed in essential or recreational services, such as police, fire, hospital, or even restaurant employees, would still have to work.

A second and somewhat less costly alternative would be to combine election day and Veterans Day, a proposal made by the Federal Election Commission in 2001. However, veterans groups might object to partisan politics replacing the raison d'être for a holiday that memorializes those who fought and died in defense of their country.

Instead of being held on a holiday, elections could be held on a Sunday, as they are in many European countries. But Sunday elections would compete with religious services, recreational activities, and family events.[58] Besides, many people work on Sundays or are otherwise engaged (especially during the professional football season). Under the circumstances, it is not clear whether turnout would increase all that much if elections were held on a Sunday or whether the American people would support such a change. Turnout could conceivably decrease.

As we have already noted, many states have extended the time people have for voting. Most keep their voting places open for at least twelve hours; some allow their citizens to vote up to twenty-one days before the election. Others permit "no-fault" absentee ballots so that people can vote by mail without having to certify that they will be out of the state at the time of the election. Oregon has gone even further. In 1998, voters in that state approved a ballot initiative that requires voting by mail ballot. Voting over the Internet also may be a possibility in the not-so-distant future if the security and integrity of the voting system can be protected.[59]

Increase the Costs of Not Voting

The most far-reaching and controversial proposal for increasing the proportion of the population who votes is simply to require voting as an obligation of citizenship and fine those who fail to do so. After all, there are other citizen obligations mandated by law that have penalties for noncompliance, obligations such as reporting for selective service, paying income taxes, and serving on juries. Should voting be treated any differently from these other citizen responsibilities? For several democratic countries, the answer is no. Australia, Belgium, and more recently South Africa have mandatory voting systems, and their turnouts are 90 percent or more (see Table 2.3).

Requiring all citizens to vote would convert equality in theory to near-equality in practice. Moreover, it would reduce the distinction between the electorate and the population. Government officials would have to be more responsive to the entire adult population rather than to just a portion of their electoral constituency. With mandatory voting, the poor, less educated, less informed, and less partisan would be better represented than they are today.

But mandatory voting also could result in less informed and perhaps less intelligent electoral decisions. It could reduce the quality of the electorate's judgment. Besides, there would undoubtedly be strong opposition to such a proposal. Some argue that mandatory voting would prevent people from protesting the choices they have by boycotting the election. Others claim that mandatory voting is undemocratic, that a democracy that prides itself on personal liberty should allow its citizens to decide whether or not they wish to vote.

Enhance the Incentives for Voting

With individual choice a value and voting a basic right, those interested in expanding participation have suggested other ways to encourage more people to participate in elections. These include engaging in media campaigns in which prominent citizens urge others to get involved; better civic education in schools and communities, in which the responsibilities of citizenship are stressed; and bipartisan informational campaigns by parties and nonpartisan groups that would tell people why they should get out and vote. These so-called bipartisan efforts have themselves become controversial, however, because they have been used by political parties and nonparty groups to further their own political agendas and circumvent campaign finance regulations.

More effective grassroots organizing seems to have gotten more people to vote, but such an expenditure of time, money, and effort by the political parties cannot be legislated by Congress or the states. More competitive elections also should improve turnout, but the parties have little motivation for decreasing their number of safe seats. Holding fewer elections might boost turnout as well, but such a proposal would require longer terms of office, a proposition that a cynical and distrustful public is unlikely to support. Gaining better representation for those in the minority in electoral districts might encourage more people to vote, but achieving this representation would probably involve a fundamental change in the electoral system from single-member districts and plurality voting to multimember districts and proportional voting. Such a proposal is unlikely to be supported by a majority of the American people.

Other ideas include shortening the election cycle, limiting negative campaigning, instituting voluntary codes of conduct for candidates, and providing more and better information about the candidates and their positions. But such changes might run up against the First Amendment protections of freedom of speech and of the press, and they are thus not likely to be legislated by Congress or upheld by the federal judiciary.

The bottom line is that citizens' beliefs about politics and government need to conform to their actual behavior if voter turnout is going to be significantly increased. There's no easy way to accomplish this objective. The scandals in the Clinton and Bush administrations, the campaign finance issues of soft money and independent expenses, and the concentration of presidential campaigns in a relatively few states have for the most part intensified, not alle-viated, public cynicism and mistrust of politicians. In short, nonvoting remains an attitudinal problem, one that is not likely to go away soon.

Getting people to the polls is only part of the problem; getting them to vote properly and getting officials to count those votes accurately is another one. Voting procedures need to be simplified, and the tabulation of votes needs to be improved. Suggestions include eliminating confusing ballot designs, replacing aging voting machines and punch cards with optical scan equipment, allowing voters who accidentally spoil their ballots to get new ones, and having enough election officials on hand to explain how to vote to those who have difficulty doing so.

SUMMARY: SUFFRAGE AND TURNOUT DILEMMAS IN A NUTSHELL

The U.S. electoral system wasn't designed to be a participatory democracy, but it has become one. In theory, today there is universal suffrage; in practice, most people do not vote regularly. In theory, every adult citizen has an equal oppor-tunity to participate; in practice, those with greater resources are in a better position to do so. In fact, their educational and economic advantages are both motivations for and consequences of voting. In theory, elected officials are sup-posed to be responsive to all the people; in practice, they tend to be more acces-sible and responsive to those who elected them, and even if that were not the case, the public perceives it to be, and that perception creates an appearance of inequality.

Although low turnout is thought to be undesirable in and for a demo-cratic political system, the remedies lawmakers have proposed and instituted to deal with the problem have not worked nearly as well as their sponsors had hoped. Removing the institutional barriers to voting should have increased substantially the proportion of the electorate who votes, but with the exception of African Americans living in the South, it hasn't done so. The emphasis on grassroots organizing, especially the use of new communication technologies, has helped increase voter turnout as have more competitive elections and more money raised and spent in them. But the increase in private funding has also undercut public financing of presidential elections, giving an advantage to wealthy candidates and those who have the ability to raise large amounts of money. It has also contributed to the public perception that money influences election outcomes.

The problem of nonvoting has resisted easy solutions. It is as much an attitude problem as anything else. Changing attitudes is difficult. Legislation alone cannot do so. It will require a major effort by those in and outside of government to reconstitute the civic culture and reestablish trust between the voters and their elected officials. There are no easy and quick fixes for the root causes of the nonvoting, public alienation and cynicism, mistrust of politicians and public officials, and the haphazard way in which elections are conducted in the states and local precincts.

Now It's Your Turn

Discussion Questions

1. Can the public's will be expressed in an election if all adults—or most—do not vote?
2. Should voting be an obligation of citizenship? If so, should that obligation be enforced by penalties for those who do not meet it by not voting?
3. Should people with little interest in the election and information about it be encouraged (or even entitled) to vote?
4. Should registration be made automatic for citizens in the states in which they officially reside?
5. Should electoral systems, voting rules, and the administration of elections for national officials continue to be set by the states and counties or should the federal government do so?
6. Should election day be a holiday or a nonworkday, such as Sunday, or should voting be extended for a longer period of time?

Topics for Debate

Challenge or defend the following statements:

1. Universal suffrage is neither necessary nor desirable.
2. Nonvoting is really not a major problem for American democracy.
3. Literacy tests should be instituted in a nondiscriminatory manner to ensure that people have sufficient information about the candidates and issues to make an informed judgment.
4. States should permit external voting via mail, the Internet, or telephone.
5. The right to vote should not be abridged by conviction for a crime or during periods of incarceration.
6. Truly competitive elections should be required in a democratic political system.

Exercises

1. Rock the Vote, a public interest organization dedicated to increasing voter turnout, particularly among younger citizens, ran a public relations campaign during the 2008 presidential election to increase electoral awareness, to provide potential voters with more information about the candidates and their campaigns, and, most important, to get more people registered to vote. It plans to run another educational campaign during the

next election. If that organization asked you for advice on such a campaign, what would you say?

    a. To whom should it direct its campaign?

    b. What should its principal appeals be, and how should they be articulated to achieve maximum impact?

    c. Should the content of those appeals change over the course of the campaign?

    d. What should be the principal means of communication?

    e. In addition to a public appeal, what else could the group do to enhance its educational efforts and achieve its principal objectives?

2. The National Commission on Federal Election Reform has proposed making election day a national holiday, establishing statewide systems of voter registration, replacing punch cards with ballots that can be optically scanned, and banning election-night predictions on the major networks until voting is completed within the continental United States. Assess these recommendations on the basis of

    a. their likelihood of increasing voter turnout;

    b. their costs to the governments that run the elections and to individuals who vote in them;

    c. their benefit to the major parties, third parties, and independent candidates;

    d. their constitutionality.

On the basis of your assessment, indicate which (if any) of the recommendations of the commission you support and which (if any) you oppose.

INTERNET RESOURCES

- Common Cause: www.commoncause.org
  Public interest group concerned with electoral reform, media and democracy, and accountability in government.
- Election Assistance Commission: www.eac.gov
  Created by the Help America Vote Act, this national commission allows people to download a national voter registration form and provides information on where to send it. It also collects useful data on registration and turnout.
- Fair Vote: www.fairvote.org
  Organization devoted to making American elections more democratic by constitutional and legislative reforms.
- League of Women Voters: www.lwv.org
  Established public interest group that publishes books and pamphlets on election activities, including information about the candidates and ballot initiatives. The league also lobbies Congress for campaign reform.

- Project Vote Smart: www.vote-smart.org
  Another public interest group dedicated to educating the electorate, particularly younger voters, on the issues, the candidates, and the records of public officials. The group distributes free tool kits for citizens and lots of information online.
- Public Citizen: www.citizen.org
  Public interest group started by citizen-activist Ralph Nader that is concerned with the rules and procedures that govern elections in the United States, openness of government, and accountability of those in office.
- Rock the Vote: www.rockthevote.org
  Getting people to register and vote is the primary goal of this public interest organization. Its Web site provides a short form that can be used to begin the registration process. Rock the Vote will even remind those who registered through its site to vote on election day.
- Vote 411.org: www.dnet.org
  Public affairs organization, sponsored by the League of Women Voters, that provides a range of information on candidates and issues.

SELECTED READINGS

American Political Science Association Task Force on Inequality and American Democracy. "American Democracy in an Age of Rising Inequality." *Perspectives on Politics* 2 (December 2004): 651–666.

Bennett, Stephen Earl, and David Resnick. "The Implications of Nonvoting for Democracy in the United States." *American Journal of Political Science* 34 (1990): 771–803.

Burnham, Walter D. "The Turnout Problem." In *Elections American Style*, edited by A. James Reichley. Washington, D.C.: Brookings Institution, 1987.

Conway, M. Margaret. *Political Participation in the United States*, 3rd ed. Washington, D.C.: CQ Press, 1999.

Crigler, Ann N., Marion R. Just, and Edward J. McCaffery, eds. *Rethinking the Vote: The Politics and Prospects of American Electoral Reform*. New York: Oxford University Press, 2004.

Gerken, Heather K. *The Democracy Index: Why Our Election System is Failing and How to Fix It*. Princeton: Princeton University Press, 2009.

Gilens, Martin. "Inequality and Democratic Responsiveness." *Public Opinion Quarterly* 69 (December 2005): 778–796.

Jacobs, Lawrence R., and Theda Skocpol, eds. *Inequality and American Democracy: What We Know and What We Need to Learn*. New York: Russell Sage Foundation, 2005.

Leighley, Jan E. *Strength in Numbers? The Political Mobilization of Racial and Ethnic Minorities.* Princeton: Princeton University Press, 2001.

McDonald, Michael P. "The Return of the Voter: Turnout in the 2008 Presidential Election." *The Forum* 6, no. 4 (2008): article 4.

McDonald, Michael P., and Samuel Popkin. "The Myth of the Vanishing Voter." *American Political Science Review* 95 (December 2001): 963–974.

Overton, Spencer. *Stealing Democracy: The New Politics of Voter Suppression.* New York: Norton, 2006.

Pew Research Center for the People and the Press. *Deconstructing Distrust.* Washington, D.C.: Pew Research Center for the People and the Press, 1998.

Piven, Frances Fox, and Richard A. Cloward. *Why Americans Don't Vote.* New York: Pantheon, 1988.

Rosenstone, Steven J., and John Mark Hansen. *Mobilization, Participation, and Democracy in America.* New York: Macmillan, 1993.

Schlozman, Kay Lehman. "Citizen Participation in America: What Do We Know? Why Do We Care?" In *Political Science: The State of the Discipline,* edited by Ira Katznelson and Helen V. Milner. New York: W.W. Norton, 2002.

Soss, Joe, and Lawrence R. Jacobs. "The Place of Inequality: Non-participation in the American Polity." *Political Science Quarterly* 124 (Spring 2009): 99–125.

Teixeira, Ruy A. *The Disappearing American Voter.* Washington, D.C.: Brookings Institution, 1992.

Verba, Sidney, Kay Lehman Schlozman, and Henry E. Brady. *Voice and Equality: Civic Voluntarism in American Politics.* Cambridge: Harvard University Press, 1995.

Wolfinger, Raymond E., and Jonathan Hoffman. "Registering and Voting with Motor Voter." *PS: Political Science and Politics* 34 (March 2001): 85–92.

Wolfinger, Raymond E., and Steven J. Rosenstone. *Who Votes?* New Haven: Yale University Press, 1980.

NOTES

1. Noncitizens, such as legal and illegal immigrants who are residents of the United States, also have a stake in the system. They have common interests, needs, and obligations, including the payment of taxes on income earned in the United States. They are not afforded voting rights, however, until they become naturalized citizens. For people who entered the country illegally, it is often difficult to meet the legal requirements for citizenship and voting.

2. For an excellent study of turnout since the beginning of the Republic, see Walter Dean Burnham, "The Turnout Problem," in *Elections American Style,* ed. A. James Reichley (Washington, D.C.: Brookings Institution, 1987), 97–133.

3. In every southern state, a majority of African Americans was *not* eligible to vote until the mid- to late 1960s. Earl Black and Merle Black, *The Vital South: How Presidents Are Elected* (Cambridge: Harvard University Press, 1992), 217.

4. Susan Welch et al., *American Government,* 3rd ed. (St. Paul, Minn.: West, 1990), 196.

5. Michael X. Delli Carpini and Ester R. Fuchs, "The Year of the Woman? Candidates, Voters, and the 1992 Elections," *Political Science Quarterly* 108 (Spring 1993): 30.

6. Two years later, the Supreme Court extended this prohibition to the election of state and local officials. It did so through its interpretation of the Fourteenth Amendment's equal protection clause, which holds that every person's vote should be equal: one person–one vote.

7. Benjamin I. Page and Robert Y. Shapiro, *The Rational Public: Fifty Years of Trends in Americans' Policy Preferences* (Chicago: University of Chicago Press, 1992), 166.

8. Frank Newport, "Americans Support Proposal to Eliminate Electoral College System," Gallup Poll, January 5, 2001, www.gallup.com/poll/2140/americans-support-proposal-eliminate-electoral-college-system.aspx; Darren K. Carlson, "Public Flunks Electoral College System," Gallup Poll, November 2, 2004, www.gallup.com/poll/13918/public-flunks-electoral-college-system.aspx.

9. NAACP Legal Defense and Educational Fund, "Democracy for All: Ending Felon Disfranchisement," n.d., www.naacpldf.org/content/pdf/felon_free/Felon_Disfranchisement_Q&A.pdf.

10. Michael P. McDonald, "Every Eligible Voter Counts: Correctly Measuring American Turnout Rates," n.d., www.brookings.edu/views/Papers/20040909mcdonald.pdf.

11. Janelle Carter, "Election Panel Submits Report to Bush," Associated Press, July 31, 2000.

12. American Civil Liberties Union, "Voting Rights for People with Criminal Records: 2008 State Legislative and Policy Changes," 2008, www.aclu.org/votingrights/exoffenders/statelegispolicy 2008.html#nt.

13. U.S. Commission on Civil Rights, as reported in Robert E. Pierre and Peter Slevin, "Florida Vote Rife with Disparities, Study Says," *Washington Post,* June 5, 2001, sec. A.

14. Associated Press, "Votes of Poor More Likely Uncounted," July 9, 2001.

15. Robert F. Kennedy Jr. alleged in "Was the 2004 Election Stolen?" *Rolling Stone,* June 1, 2006, www.rollingstone.com/news/story/10432334/%20was_the_2004_election_stolen, that President George W. Bush's victory in 2004 was fraudulent. Kennedy cited numerous irregularities ranging from absentee ballots not received to Democratic registration materials being destroyed to more than one million ballots voided. He also claimed that 350,000 Democratic voters in Ohio were prevented from casting their ballots or having them counted. This number would have been sufficient to reverse the official results in that state. Other irregularities also were reported. In the governor's race in the state of Washington, a race that was decided by 129 votes, it was alleged that ineligible ex-felons voted as well as people who voted in the name of deceased persons. In Wisconsin, one hundred people were alleged to have voted twice. See "Building Confidence in U.S. Elections," *Report of the Commission on Federal Election Reform,* September 2005, 4.

16. Michael P. McDonald, "2004 General Election Turnout Rates," http://elections.gmu.edu/Turnout_2004G.html; Michael P. McDonald, "2008 General Election Turnout Rates," http://elections.gmu.edu/Turnout_2008G.html.

17. Michael P. McDonald, "2002 General Election Turnout Rates," http://elections.gmu.edu/Turnout_2002G.html; Michael P. McDonald, "2006 General Election Turnout Rates," http://elections.gmu.edu/Turnout_2006G.html.

18. Rhodes Cook, "Democratic Primary Turnout: Comparing 2004 with Previous Highs," www.rhodescook.com/primary.analysis.html; Chris Cillizza and Zachery A. Goldfarb, "Primary Turnout Low," *Washington Post,* October 8, 2006, sec. A.

19. Stephen J. Wayne, "When Democracy Works: The 2008 Presidential Nominations," in *Winning the Presidency*, ed. William J. Crotty (Boulder, Colo.: Paradigm Publishers, 2009), 50.

20. Frances Fox Piven and Richard A. Cloward argue that ethnic and religious identities reinforced partisan loyalties to mobilize the vote, particularly among the working class. Similarly, sectional issues and party competitiveness also contributed to the high turnout in the nineteenth century; see their book *Why Americans Don't Vote* (New York: Pantheon, 1988), 26–29.

21. Keith Melder, *Hail to the Candidate* (Washington, D.C.: Smithsonian Institution Press, 1992), 69–100; Gil Troy, *See How They Ran* (New York: Free Press, 1991), 20–30.

22. The influx of immigrants, first predominantly from northern Europe during the period from 1840 to 1860, and later from southern Europe from 1880 to 1910, provided fertile ground for parties to recruit new partisans by providing them with social services and other benefits in exchange for their votes.

23. Pew Research Center for the People and the Press, "Independents Take Center Stage in Obama Era," May 21, 2009, http://people-press.org/report/517/political-values-and-core-attitudes.

24. Ibid.

25. Ibid.

26. Princeton Survey Research Associates, national survey conducted from October 21 to November 2, 1996.

27. Martin P. Wattenberg and Craig Leonard Brians, "Negative Campaign Advertising: Demobilizer or Mobilizer?" *American Political Science Review* 93 (December 1999): 891–899.

28. Steven Finkel and John Greer, "A Spot Check: Casting Doubt on the Demobilizing Effect of Attack Advertising," *American Journal of Political Science* 42 (April 1998): 573–595; Kim Fridkin Kahn and Patrick J. Kenny, "Do Negative Campaigns Mobilize or Suppress Turnout?" *American Political Science Review* 93 (December 1999): 877–889.

29. Massachusetts Institute of Technology and California Institute of Technology, "Voting: What Is and What Could Be," July 17, 2001; MIT, "Caltech-MIT Team Finds 4–6 Million Votes Lost in the 2000 Election; Nationwide Reforms Outlined in Report," News release, July 16, 2001, http://web.mit.edu/newsoffice/2001/voting2.html.

30. For a detailed discussion of the problems, politics, and consequences of the presidential vote in Florida in 2000, see Charles L. Zelden, *Bush v. Gore: Exposing the Hidden Crisis in American Democracy* (Lawrence: University Press of Kansas, 2008).

31. Martin P. Wattenberg, "Getting Out the Vote," *Public Perspective* (January/February 2001): 16–17.

32. Paul R. Abramson, John H. Aldrich, and David W. Rohde, *Change and Continuity in the 2004 Elections* (Washington, D.C.: CQ Press, 2006), 100.

33. Pew Research Center for the People and the Press has conducted polls over the past decade that show declining trust and confidence in government. These results were collected in *Deconstructing Distrust*, which Pew published in 1998 and updated in "Public Votes for Continuity and Change in 2000," February 25, 1999. Another contemporary survey, "Expecting More Say: The American Public on Its Role in Government Decisionmaking," this by the Center on Policy Attitudes and issued on May 10, 1999, found strong support (74.5 percent) for the proposition that "the government is pretty much run by a few big interests looking out for themselves."

34. Raymond E. Wolfinger and Steven J. Rosenstone, *Who Votes?* (New Haven: Yale University Press, 1980), 13–26.

35. American National Election Studies, "Voter Turnout, 1948–2004," www.electionstudies.org/nesguide/toptable/tab6a_2.htm. There may also be a genetic component to voting; see James

H. Fowler and Christopher T. Dawes, "Two Genes Predict Voter Turnout," *Journal of Politics* 7 (July 2008): 579–594.

36. Abramson, Aldrich, and Rohde, *Change and Continuity,* 95.

37. Joe Soss and Lawrence R. Jacobs, "The Place of Inequality: Non-participation in the American Polity," *Political Science Quarterly* 124 (Spring 2009): 101.

38. Ibid., 122.

39. Ibid., 121–122.

40. Ruy A. Teixeira, *The Disappearing American Voter* (Washington, D.C.: Brookings Institution, 1992), 95.

41. Stephen Earl Bennett and David Resnick, "The Implications of Nonvoting for Democracy in the United States," *American Journal of Political Science* 34 (1990): 771–802; and Michael M. Gant and William Lyons, "Democratic Theory, Nonvoting, and Public Policy," *American Politics Quarterly* 21 (1993): 183–204.

42. Teixeira, *The Disappearing American Voter,* 100.

43. Thomas E. Cavanaugh argues that elections have to be close and that the likely nonvoters who do cast ballots have to be disproportionately favorable to one candidate for the outcome to be changed; see "When Turnout Matters: Mobilization and Conversion as Determinants of Election Outcomes," in *Political Participation and American Democracy,* ed. William J. Crotty (New York: Greenwood Press, 1991), 89–112.

44. Sidney Verba, Kay Lehman Schlozman, and Henry E. Brady, *Voice and Equality: Civic Voluntarism in American Politics* (Cambridge: Harvard University Press, 1995).

45. John D. Griffin and Brian Newman, "Are Voters Better Represented?" *Journal of Politics* 67 (November 2005): 1206–1227.

46. Task Force on Inequality and American Democracy of the American Political Science Association, "American Democracy in an Age of Rising Inequality," 2004, 1, www.apsanet .org/imgtest/taskforcereport.pdf.

47. International Institute for Democracy and Electoral Assistance, "Voter Turnout," November 2006, www.idea.int/vt/findings.cfm.

48. This argument was advanced by Bernard Berelson, Paul F. Lazerfeld, and William McPhee in their book *Voting* (Chicago: University of Chicago Press, 1954); see also Lester Milbrath, *Political Participation* (Chicago: Rand McNally, 1965).

49. Blame tends to be greater than credit. Political scientists have found that people seem more motivated to turn out to vote during bad times than during good ones. See Howard Bloom and H. Douglas Price, "Voter Response to Short Run Economic Conditions: The Asymmetric Effects of Prosperity and Recession," *American Political Science Review* 69 (1975): 1240–1254; and Morris P. Fiorina, "Economic Retrospective Voting in National Elections: A Microanalysis," *American Journal of Political Science* 22 (1978): 426–433.

50. See "Why Don't Americans Trust the Government," *Washington Post,* Kaiser Family Foundation, and Harvard University, 1996; and *Deconstructing Distrust* (Washington, D.C.: Pew Research Center for the People and the Press, 1998).

51. The term gerrymander owes its origin to the creative districting in the state of Massachusetts following the enactment of the Constitution. Governor Elbridge Gerry and his supporters created a legislative district in the western part of the state that looked like a salamander. A Massachusetts newspaper, critical of the political motives that shaped the district lines, called it a gerrymander, and the term stuck.

52. Iowa and Colorado have done so.

53. The three qualifications are age, residence, and U.S. citizenship. The Supreme Court decided that state-imposed term limits add a fourth qualification that can be accomplished only by a constitutional amendment.

54. Teixeira, *The Disappearing American Voter,* 106–147; and Wolfinger and Rosenstone, *Who Votes?* 73.

55. Heather K. Gerken, *The Democracy Index: Why Our Election System Is Failing and How to Fix It* (Princeton: Princeton University Press, 2009), 1.

56. Ibid., 28–29.

57. Ibid., ix.

58. Moreover, churches are often polling and voting stations in the United States.

59. Another change that might facilitate voting would be to redesign the form and shape of the ballot. Some states still use a party-column ballot, in which all of a party's candidates are listed together below the party's label. Partisans have no difficulty discerning their candidates. The office-column ballot, on which candidates are listed by the position for which they are running, may confuse people not familiar with the names of all the candidates. In addition, ballots also may contain complex policy initiatives on which voters are asked to decide quickly so as not to delay those waiting in line to vote.

chapter 3

How Representative Are American Elections?

Did you know that . . .

- the constitutional system was designed to protect the rights of minorities, and the electoral system has evolved to reflect the influence of majorities (or at least pluralities)?
- drawing the shape of a legislative district to advance the party in power is an old American tradition that goes back more than two hundred years?
- for most of U.S. history, the Supreme Court regarded the drafting of legislative districts as a political, not a judicial, issue and thus stayed away from this type of representational question?
- the redrafting of congressional districts to gain more representation for African American and Latino voters in the 1990s contributed to increasing the number of conservative Republican members of Congress?
- most democracies automatically register their citizens who reach voting age and the United States does not?
- the Electoral College was originally designed to ensure that the most qualified, not necessarily the most popular, candidates were selected as president and vice president?
- fifteen states currently have laws that place limits on the number of terms their state legislative representatives can serve?
- women make up 52 percent of the electorate but only 17 percent of Congress and 24 percent of state legislators?
- most members of the House of Representative usually face no opposition for renomination?
- in the twenty-first century, more than 3 out of 4 members of the House of Representatives have won reelection by 60 percent or more of the vote?
- most groups that are less well represented in government support a stronger role for government than do those that are better represented?

Is this any way to run a democratic election?

I n a representative democracy, all citizens are entitled to have their interests represented. Is the U.S. electoral system, in which candidates are chosen by plurality vote in single-member districts, fair and equitable for all groups in the society? Many people say no. They claim that the system overrepresents the majority and underrepresents the minority.

This chapter addresses the issue of representation. It examines how the electoral system affects the representative character of government. Beginning with a discussion of the concept of representation, the chapter then turns to the relationship between the structure of elections and the type of representation that this structure produces. Those who have benefited from this representational struggle and those who have not are identified and their attitudes toward government and public policy outcomes discussed. The chapter also explores the necessity and desirability of imposing legal qualifications for office and their effect on a democratic electoral process.

THE CONCEPT OF REPRESENTATION

The concept of representation is central to the democratic belief that government should reflect the values and policy preferences of its citizens. This belief became the principal justification for the American Revolution. "Taxation without representation is tyranny!" was the rallying cry of those who wanted their representational rights as English citizens restored.

Although the issue for the colonists was their lack of representation in Parliament, for the framers it was devising a system that would permit diverse representation but not reflect every mood of the people, much less convert those moods into public policy. By overlapping constituencies between the federal government and the states and within the federal government itself, the delegates at the Constitutional Convention hoped to achieve both state and popular representation without domination by a single interest, region, or group. To do so, they designed a system in which parts of the polity were better and more effectively represented than was the polity as a whole. Their artful constitutional framework has shaped the representational character of the American electoral system ever since, as have the structure and administration of elections and the creation and evolution of the two major political parties.

The Constitution gave the states the authority to determine how their representatives would be chosen. Most used their discretion to create institutions that paralleled those of the national government in which representatives were chosen from clearly defined geographic areas. Within these areas, voters selected candidates directly by popular vote or indirectly by voting for state legislators who in turn selected the state's senators and presidential electors.

How the election was to be conducted, voter eligibility determined, and candidates chosen was left to the states to decide. The Constitution specifies only a few qualifications for federal office: a minimum age, a geographic residence requirement at the time of election, citizenship for a specified number of years, and, in the case of the president, being both native born and a fourteen-year resident of the United States before the election. The Constitution also prohibits religious tests as a condition for holding public office.

Types of Representation

In choosing their representatives, the states selected candidates from their pool of eligible voters: initially, white, male Christians who owned property. Most elected officials were better educated than the average male citizen and usually prominent within their communities. As the country became more diverse and as suffrage expanded, so too did the acceptable qualifications for being elected to office. However, what qualifications were deemed acceptable changed much more slowly than did the composition of the electorate. Even today, most of the initial dominant characteristics still prevail: white, male, with above-average education and income.

Herein is part of the representational dilemma for the United States. If one purpose of representation is to reflect the needs and interests of the society as a whole, then how can a government dominated by white males provide fair and equal representation?

Many say that it cannot. They argue that only a person who shares the characteristics of a particular constituency can effectively represent it. Knowing how it feels to live in the constituency; having interests and needs similar to those of the people who reside there; and sharing the values, political beliefs, and perceptions of these residents are keys to effective representation. Taken to its obvious conclusion, this argument contends that the best representative for most people most of the time is a person who resembles themselves demographically, attitudinally, and politically.

It follows that the composition of government also should reflect the composition of society if the government is to be representative of that society. In other words, if a particular group, such as African Americans, constitutes a certain proportion of the voting-age population, about 13 percent, then that group should constitute a similar proportion of the government. When Bill Clinton promised in his 1992 campaign to appoint an administration as diverse as America, he was subscribing to this tenet of equal and fair representation for all.[1]

Getting their fair share has become a goal of underrepresented groups and a hot-button political issue for them. Not only do the underrepresented want their needs addressed, their interests satisfied, and their values incorporated into policy decisions, but they also want to be represented by people like themselves. They see representation as a symbol of acceptance and equality.

In addition to **descriptive representation**, or how well the government reflects the composition of society, there is also the issue of **substantive**

representation, which is how well public policy decisions reflect the values, interests, and desires of the various groups that comprise the American population. Whereas descriptive representation is reflected in the "who" of government (the people in office), substantive representation is reflected in the "what" of government (public policy and its impact). The distinction between these two types of representation arises in part because it is possible for a person who reflects the demographic characteristics of a particular group to hold beliefs that don't reflect the dominant sentiment of that group. To use a few extreme examples, do the beliefs and decisions of Justice Clarence Thomas or former secretary of state Condoleezza Rice better reflect those of the African American community than do those of Justice Ruth Bader Ginsburg or the late senator Ted Kennedy of Massachusetts?

Although substantive representation is more difficult to evaluate than descriptive representation, it is every bit as important. Not only do people want to see their own reflection in government, they also want that government to be responsive to their needs and interests.

Roles of Representatives

How to achieve equitable representation is an important issue; what role representatives should play in office is another. People want their representatives to serve their constituency and the nation. But serving both may be difficult if the interests of the constituency and nation diverge. For example, members of Congress have increasingly earmarked special projects for their districts while complaining about the amount of government spending. They provide short-term fixes for their constituents' needs that exacerbate longer-term problems for the country. During 2009, the House of Representatives enacted a bill to reduce pollution by taxing manufacturers that failed to meet the new energy emission standards. To gain sufficient support for the legislation, the bill's sponsors and party leaders agreed to exempt from the bill's provisions for a period of eight years any industries dependent on coal and oil. The exemption, designed to reduce costs, also reduced the environmental impact of the legislation. Specific constituencies gained at the expense of the country's meeting its air quality goals.

There are other representational issues: disagreements among constituents as well as differences in the intensity of their feelings and disagreements between constituents and their elected representatives. How should an elected representative act if these differences persist?

There are basically two schools of thought about what the representative's proper role should be.[2] The democratic school perceives the representative as a **delegate** of the people and, as such, duty bound to discern and reflect the majority opinion. If there is a consensus, the representative should follow it; if there isn't one, then a representative may be able to exercise more personal discretion in deciding what to do, particularly if that representative has the information and expertise to make an informed judgment.

The other representational role is that of a **trustee,** a person charged with using the information and expertise at his or her disposal to make the best possible decision. Edmund Burke, a British politician and scholar, defended this approach in a speech to the people of Bristol who elected him to Parliament:

> Parliament is not a congress of ambassadors from different and hostile interests, which interests each must maintain, as an agent and advocate, against other agents and advocates; but Parliament is a deliberative assembly of one nation, with one interest, that of the whole—where not local prejudices ought to guide, but the general good, resulting from the general reason of the whole. You choose a member, indeed; but when you have chosen him he is not a member of Bristol, but he is a member of Parliament.[3]

Those who favor a trustee role believe that the public has neither the desire, the ability, nor the knowledge to focus on policy matters, much less make good policy decisions. This is why they elect representatives to make those decisions for them. Representatives have greater interest and desire (as indicated by their candidacy) in public policy making and, it is hoped, more knowledge and ability to do the job effectively. Moreover, this school of thought sees legislative institutions as deliberative bodies in which internal debate should affect a representative's policy judgments.

The American people are ambiguous about the role they want their representatives to play. They prefer leaders to followers, but they also want their leaders to stay in touch with popular sentiment. They expect their elected officials to look out for their interests, but they also think that their representatives are too sensitive to special interests, and they believe that most members of Congress are too parochial for the good of the country, but they keep reelecting most of them anyway.

People think that elected officials would make better decisions if they did what most of the people want, but they do not believe that officials do so most of the time.[4] Moreover, they are also skeptical of public opinion polls as accurate measures of public opinion. Most people do not understand how a poll of about one thousand people can accurately measure the sentiment of an entire country.[5] Their skepticism about polling extends to the motivation that prompts officials to rely on them. More people believe that those in government use polls to stay popular and get reelected rather than because they want to give the public a say in what the government does.[6]

Contemporary political developments have been pushing elected representatives closer to their constituents than in the past. Candidates for office make representational promises that they are expected to fulfill. Failure to do so is frequently the subject of media attention and can become a campaign issue if the incumbent stands for reelection. Getting reelected is believed to be a primary motivation for elected officials when they make policy judgments.

Legislative and executive officials are devoting more staff, more time, and more resources to servicing constituency needs. Members of Congress have received greater allowances for home travel, and even the legislative calendar has been adjusted to permit representatives to spend more time in their home districts.

Nonetheless, the use of public opinion polls and focus groups to dig more deeply into the opinions and attitudes of the populace; the development of rapid and easy communication by telephone, fax, e-mail, and text messaging; and the growth and professionalization of interest groups have all kept public officials more closely in touch with their constituents than they were in the past. Similarly, the expansion of local news programming has allowed constituents to become better informed about the behavior of their representatives and has created the perception among public officials that their words and actions are increasingly visible to the folks back home or the clientele they serve. Frequent elections keep these officials accountable. All of these linkage mechanisms are consistent with a democratic political system, although the low level of public information and the absence of dominant constituency opinions on many issues give officials considerable discretion when deciding on public policy.

THE STRUCTURE OF ELECTIONS AND THE UNDERREPRESENTATION OF MINORITIES

How elections are structured shapes the representative character of the American political system—particularly its descriptive representation. The boundaries of legislative districts, the number of officials selected within them, and the procedure by which the winner is determined all affect the character of representation.

As noted in Chapter 2, the structure, rules, and procedures of elections aren't neutral. Plurality voting in single-member districts disproportionately benefits those in the majority. It also benefits the two major parties at the expense of third parties and independent candidates. Similarly, the way the Electoral College operates today favors the large, competitive states and groups within them.

Plurality Voting in Single-Member Districts

The Constitution does not prescribe single-member legislative districts. What it does require is a reapportionment, every ten years, of the members of the House of Representatives on the basis of the national census. States gain or lose seats depending on how their proportion of the population compares with that of the country as a whole. There is one proviso, however, that every state must have at least one representative in the House.

As mentioned in the previous chapter, the single-member-district system has generally prevailed since the Constitution was ratified. In such a system, the state drafts the boundaries of its legislative districts; each district is represented by one legislator, elected on the basis of the popular vote within the district.

A voting system in which the candidate with the most votes wins favors those in the majority, both candidates and parties. It does so within each district as well as cumulatively among the districts within the state. It is difficult for a minority group to gain representation unless it constitutes a majority or near majority within a district or state.

The best evidence to support the proposition that a system that results in plurality winners from single-member districts adversely affects minority groups is the composition of legislative bodies today.

Take Congress, for example. Table 3.1 shows the percentages of African Americans, Latinos, and Asian Americans elected to Congress since 1985. Although African Americans constitute 12.8 percent of the voting-age population; Latinos, 15.1 percent (and growing); and Asian Americans, 4.4 percent, these groups have traditionally been underrepresented in Congress, although more so in the past than at present.[7]

Not only has the underrepresentation of minority groups become a political issue, but it also has become a legal one because the Fourteenth Amendment requires that states not deny their citizens equal protection of the laws. Equal protection, in turn, implies equal influence on and representation within the body that makes the laws.

Not until the 1960s, however, did the judiciary begin to address constitutional issues associated with minority representation. In 1962 the Supreme Court decided in the case of *Baker v. Carr* (369 U.S. 186) that malapportioned state legislatures may violate the equal protection clause of the Fourteenth Amendment. The Court's judgment that legislative districting can be a judicial matter, not simply a political one, opened the floodgates to lawsuits by those who believed that the size and shape of their districts discriminated against them and denied them equal representation.

In cases arising from these lawsuits, the Supreme Court ruled that all districts that elect representatives, except for those for the U.S. Senate and the Electoral College, had to be apportioned on the basis of population according to the one person–one vote principle.[8] Additionally, the Court said that the size of congressional districts within a state cannot vary very much, no more than one-half of 1 percent.[9]

The configuration of districts, however, wasn't subject to judicial scrutiny until 1986, when the Supreme Court ruled in the case of *Davis v. Bandemer* (478 U.S. 109) that partisan gerrymandering, the drafting of legislative district boundaries to benefit the party in power, could also become a constitutional issue if people were denied equal representation, that is, if the drafting was done in a discriminatory fashion.

By the 1980s, the battle over representation had spread to all institutions of the national government. Congress got involved when it amended the Voting Rights Act in 1982 to encourage states to create districts in which racial

TABLE 3.1	**Minority Members of Congress, 1985–2009 (percentages)**		
Congress/Year	African Americans	Hispanics	Asian Americans
	House of Representatives		
99th/1985	4.4	2.5	1.1
100th/1987	5.1	2.5	1.4
101st/1989	5.3	2.5	1.4
102nd/1991	5.7	2.3	1.1
103rd/1993	8.7	3.9	1.6
104th/1995	9.0	4.1	1.6
105th/1997	8.5	4.1	1.4
106th/1999	9.0	4.4	1.6
107th/2001	8.3	4.4	1.6
108th/2003	8.5	5.3	1.1
109th/2005	9.1	5.3	1.1
110th/2007	9.1	5.7	1.4
111th/2009	9.0	5.7	1.6
	Senate		
99th/1985	0	0	2
100th/1987	0	0	2
101st/1989	0	0	3
102nd/1991	0	0	2
103rd/1993	1	0	2
104th/1995	1	0	2
105th/1997	1	0	2
106th/1999	0	0	2
107th/2001	0	0	2
108th/2003	1	0	2
109th/2005	1	2	2
110th/2007	1	3	2
111th/2009	1	2	3

Source: U.S. Census Bureau, Statistical Abstract of the United States: 2009, Table 390; Members of Congress: Selected Characteristics, 1985–2007, www.census.gov/prod/2008pubs/09statab/election.pdf; and updated by author.

and ethnic minorities were in the majority. Subsequently, the Justice Department pressured the states to follow the dictates of the legislation after the 1990 census and legislative reapportionment was completed.

The redrafting of state congressional districts resulted in an increase in minority representation in Congress (see Table 3.1), but it also contributed to a more Republican, more conservative Congress for the next decade. Most of the newly crafted districts were in the South and Southwest. Because African Americans and Hispanics are predominantly Democratic, concentrating them in so-called majority-minority districts resulted in "whiter" districts in other parts of the state that benefited the Republicans at the expense of the Democrats.

The gain in GOP seats helped the Republicans win control of Congress in 1994 and allowed them to institute their more conservative policy agenda, which was opposed by the minority groups that the voting rights legislation was designed to help. Thus, in effect, the establishment of more districts in which a minority within the state became a majority within the district improved the descriptive representation for these minority groups but adversely affected their substantive representation.[10]

Legal challenges to these new minority districts were quickly initiated by Democrats and others who believed that they amounted to racial gerrymandering. A divided Supreme Court agreed. By a majority of only one, the Court held that race could not be a primary factor in drafting the boundaries of legislative districts.[11] The Court's decision was seen as a major setback for those desiring greater minority representation of elected officials.

Not only does minority underrepresentation contribute to a racial and ethnic bias, it also reinforces economic inequality within the political system given the lower levels of income and higher levels of unemployment among people in the two largest minority groups, African Americans and Hispanics. As noted in the previous chapter, economic inequality is evident in elections as well as pressures on government and public policy outcomes.

In short, single-member districts with winner-take-all voting work to favor the demographic and partisan majorities in those districts. Aspiring politicians have to run on the Democratic or Republican labels if they are to have a reasonable chance of being elected in competitive districts. In noncompetitive ones, where the primary is effectively equivalent to the general election, they have to vie for the nomination of the dominant party.

Sometimes, to improve their chances, Democratic and Republican candidates in the general election seek a third-party endorsement to get an extra line on the ballot and garner support from those who do not identify with either of the major parties. But rarely does a candidate who is endorsed only by a third party, or who runs as an independent, win. In the twenty-first century, there have been only a very few members of Congress who have been elected as independents, and all but one had a major party affiliation before declaring themselves independent.

Improving Minority Representation

What can be done to improve demographic and partisan minority representation? There are several answers, but none of them affords much immediate hope of rectifying the representational problem for certain groups. The principal structural change that would contribute to minority representation would be to create multimember districts and use a proportional system of voting in which candidates are chosen roughly in proportion to the vote they or their parties receive.[12]

Many countries, especially those with a parliamentary form of government such as Brazil, Israel, and Spain, have such voting systems. Others, such as Italy, Japan, and Mexico, mix proportional and plurality voting systems for their legislative representatives. (Table 3.2 lists the electoral systems of several other democratic countries.)

Some of the states in the United States use proportional voting in multimember districts to choose state legislators, city council members, and school board members. The principal advantage of proportional voting is that demographic and partisan minorities can gain representation roughly in proportion to their strength within the electorate. And as we noted in Chapter 2, it also encourages turnout. When the outcome of the election is decided by the proportion of the vote that parties or candidates receive, parties, campaign organizations, and nonparty groups try to maximize their vote; in noncompetitive, single-member districts, they do not necessarily do so if the outcome is predictable.

There are other benefits of multimember districts and proportional voting. Gerrymandering is eliminated; public debate is extended; and voters have greater choice. The governing coalitions formed after the election represent a wider variety and usually a larger number of voters. Such representation tends to broaden public support for legislative policy outcomes.

On the negative side, a proportional election might require more complicated voting instructions and more complex ballots. It could also make it easier for candidates and parties with extreme political views to gain a platform and even a voice in government. In Israel, which has a proportional representation system, the small religious parties, some of which have strong fundamentalist beliefs, exercise disproportional influence because their support has been necessary to form a governing majority.

Another disadvantage of a proportional system is that it is much less likely that one party will constitute a legislative majority. The absence of a majority forces the leader of the party with the most seats to try to form a governing coalition with other parties. A multiparty coalition is more fragile than a coalition composed of a single party. A vote against the government on a major issue frequently topples the governing coalition and either forces new elections or requires a new person to try to form a viable government. Pragmatism is the order of the day, and political compromise a necessity. It is also harder to pinpoint accountability in a multiparty government.

TABLE 3.2 Electoral Systems of Selected Democratic Countries

Country	System of representation
Australia	Single-member districts (SMD), but uses proportional representation (PR) for senate elections
Austria	Proportional representation
Belgium	Proportional representation
Canada	Single-member districts
Czech Republic	Proportional representation
France	Single-member districts
Germany	Combination of SMD and PR
Greece	Proportional representation
Ireland	Proportional representation
Israel	Proportional representation
Italy	Combination of SMD and PR
Japan	Combination of SMD and PR
Korea (Rep. of)	Combination of SMD and PR
Mexico	Combination of SMD and PR
Romania	Proportional representation
South Africa	Proportional representation
Spain	Proportional representation
Sweden	Proportional representation
United Kingdom	Single-member districts
United States	Single-member districts

Source: Data from "Voting in Major Democracies." Copyright © 1999 The Center for Voting and Democracy, http://fairvote.org/library/geog/europe/systems.htm.

The other way to achieve fairer and more equal representation for minorities is to eliminate the allegiances and attitudes (some consider them biases and prejudices) that favor the majority. Although Barack Obama's election as president suggests that race may no longer be the inhibiting factor it once was in American national politics, bias remains. Polling done before the 2008 presidential election suggests that ethnicity, sexual orientation, and some religions and antireligious beliefs may still prevent otherwise qualified candidates from being elected. Major attitudinal change within the population takes time, usually several generations, and judging by the demographic composition of elected public officials the United States has some way to go.[13]

AMERICAN POLITICS AND THE UNDERREPRESENTATION OF WOMEN

Women outnumber men in the U.S. population today, composing almost 52 percent of the voting-age population. They are also a majority of the electorate, although that is of more recent origin. Women won the right to vote in 1919, but it took another sixty years for them to vote in equal proportion to men. Today, the proportion of women voting is slightly higher than that of men. Yet women represent a substantially lower proportion of members of Congress and of state legislative and top executive officials than do men. Why?

For most of the nation's existence, men dominated politics, and that domination, to some extent, still exists. Incumbency advantage in elections reinforces this domination. It will take time for women to gain the electoral positions or professional status from which they can more successfully seek office. Moreover, women still take time off from their careers, far more often than do men, to raise a family, and are disadvantaged politically for doing so. Women have also been hurt by the persistence of gender stereotypes that they are weaker and more emotional and less rational than men—stereotypes that lack empirical verification but that conflict with public images of successful political leadership.

A proportional voting system would probably help women gain greater representation in government. A study by the National Civic Review found gender balance improves when multiple candidates are chosen in electoral districts.[14] In the presidential nomination process, Democratic Party rules require proportional voting and gender balance; Republican rules permit both, with the result that women constitute about half the delegates at Democratic nominating conventions and between 40 and 45 percent at recent Republican conventions.

Table 3.3 lists the gains women have made since 1975 in Congress, top state executive positions, and state legislatures; it also indicates that they have a way to go to achieve gender equality. The fact that women constitute a majority of the electorate, turn out to vote at a slightly higher rate than men, and are more likely to support women candidates suggests that the gap will continue to decline for the foreseeable future.

THE ELECTORAL COLLEGE SYSTEM AND THE OVERREPRESENTATION OF LARGE COMPETITIVE STATES

The Electoral College system also creates a representational bias. Initially designed as a dual compromise between the large and small states and between proponents of a federal structure and of a more centralized national government, it provided an alternative to the other methods considered for choosing the president: legislative selection or a direct popular vote. The framers did not want Congress to select the president because they feared that would jeopardize

TABLE 3.3 **Women in Elective Office, 1975–2009 (percentages rounded)**

Level of office	Year																	
	1975	'77	'79	'81	'83	'85	'87	'89	'91	'93	'95	'97	'99	2001	'03	'05	'07	'09
Congress	4	4	3	4	4	5	5	5	6	10	10	11	12	14	14	16	15	17
Statewide executive	10	10	11	11	11	14	14	14	18	22	26	25	28	28	26	26	24	24
State legislature	8	9	10	12	13	15	16	17	18	21	21	22	22	22	22	23	24	24

Source: Center for Women and Politics, Eagleton Institute of Politics, Rutgers University, www.cawp.rutgers.edu/fast_facts/index.php.

the executive's independence. Nor did they want the people to do so because they lacked faith in the average person's judgment and in the states' ability to conduct fair and honest elections. Moreover, the delegates at the·Constitutional Convention wanted a leader, not a demagogue, a person selected on the basis of personal qualifications, not popular appeal. Finally, they hoped that their electoral system, which had electors voting at the same time in their respective states, would limit the potential for cabal, intrigue, and group dominance over the election outcome. Given the state of communications and transportation in 1787, distance provided safety, or so the framers thought.

According to the original plan, states would be allocated electors in proportion to their congressional representation in the House and Senate, thereby giving some advantage to the smallest states because of their equal representation in the Senate, an advantage that remains in place today. Wyoming, the least populous state, has a population that is less than 1.5 percent of California's, but Wyoming has 5.6 percent of California's electoral votes. Other inequities result from the apportionment of House seats. Montana's population is twice that of Wyoming's, yet both states have the same representation in the Electoral College.

The original plan also allowed the states to choose their electors in any manner they saw fit. In the first election, in which ten states participated, half of them had their legislatures select the electors and the others chose them in some form of popular vote. The Constitution stated that after the electors were selected they would meet in their respective states and vote for two people, at least one of whom could not be an inhabitant of their state.

The person with the most votes would be president, provided the plurality winner had a majority;[15] the person with the second-highest number of votes would be vice president. In this way the framers hoped to ensure that the two most qualified people would be chosen for the top two offices.

The system worked according to the original design for the first two elections in 1788 and 1792. Washington was the unanimous choice of the electors, but there was no consensus on the other candidate. John Adams, the eventual second choice, benefited from some informal caucusing prior to the vote.

Partisanship and Winner-Take-All Voting

The development of the party system in the mid-1790s transformed voting in the Electoral College. Instead of making an independent judgment, each elector began to exercise a partisan one. Electors became partisan agents. Selected on the basis of their loyalty to a party, they were expected to vote for its candidates. And with a very few exceptions, they have. Since 1787, there have been only 11 "faithless electors" (out of a total of 21,915) who did not vote for their party's nominee as was expected. None of these errant votes affected the elections' results.[16]

In the early part of the nineteenth century, there was a movement in many of the states to directly elect the electors. In 1800, ten of the fifteen states had their legislatures choose the electors. By 1832, all but South Carolina elected them by popular vote. That state began to do so in 1864.

The popular selection of electors made the Electoral College more democratic than it had been and was intended to be. However, the movement of states to a winner-take-all system, in which partisan slates of electors competed against one another, created a plurality-rule scenario. It also created advantages for some states and disadvantages for others.

The large states, whose electoral votes are magnified by winner-take-all voting, benefit the most. Within these states, groups that are geographically concentrated and unified in their voting behavior also are helped because they can exercise an influence disproportionate to their numbers. Moreover, these groups tend to get candidates to focus on their issues and the positions they favor: Iranians living in California want to maintain pressure on the Iranian government to conduct free and fair elections and allow political protests; Jews in New York want to continue economic and military aid for Israel; and Hispanics in the Southwest are concerned about immigrant rights and a guest worker program. The list goes on.

If the large states were equally competitive, the electoral system would encourage candidates to concentrate their campaigns in these states. The seven largest states combined have 36 percent of the entire electoral vote. But some of these states are not as competitive as some of the middle-size and smaller ones. And in this age of polling and targeting, candidates concentrate their campaigns, advertising, and voter mobilization efforts in states that are the most competitive.[17] At the beginning of an election cycle, this can be as many as one-third of the states; by the end of the cycle, that number is usually reduced to single digits. In the last three presidential elections, the major battleground states that received the most attention and campaign activities were Florida, Michigan, Ohio, and Pennsylvania. In 2008, The Center for Voting and

Democracy reported that 57 percent of all the major party campaign events between September 5 and election day occurred in only four states, representing just 17 percent of the nation's eligible voters; more than half the advertising occurred in these same states. Fifteen states, having a little more than one-third of the population, received 98 percent of all campaign expenditures during the last six weeks of the 2008 campaign.[18]

Concentrated campaigning makes strategic sense, but it also undercuts the democratic and national character of presidential elections. It undermines the democratic process by discouraging turnout in the states not considered battleground states and by neglecting or downplaying the issues and interests of people who live in those states. It makes a mockery of the only national election in the United States for the only nationally elected public officials, the president and vice president. If that election were truly national, then the campaigns should be national as well, and the parties should devote their efforts to getting all eligible voters out to vote, not just focus on those in the key, competitive states. Moreover, to create or sustain a national agenda, a national mandate, and a national coalition for governing, it is necessary to think about issues in national terms; make national appeals; and mount a national campaign with candidate appearances, advertising, and grassroots activities held across the country rather than concentrated in only a few states.

In addition to the unequal representation in the Electoral College, made worse by the general ticket system that produces a winner-take-all outcome in forty-eight of the fifty states and the District of Columbia, the Electoral College system also can produce an undemocratic result. Three times in American history, in 1876, 1888, and 2000, the winning candidate did not receive a plurality of the popular vote.[19] Many more times, the shift of a relatively small number of votes in a few states would have changed the outcome of the election.

The most likely situation in which the candidate with the most popular votes would lose in the Electoral College is that of very close competition between the major parties, along with a strong third-party candidate who captures sufficient electoral votes to deny the leading candidate a majority. The elections of 1968, 1992, and 2004 could have produced such a scenario but did not. The election of 2000 did: there were six states (Florida, New Hampshire, Iowa, New Mexico, Oregon, and Wisconsin) in which the winning candidate's margin of victory was less than the votes that third-party candidates Ralph Nader and Pat Buchanan received. According to the Voter News Survey exit poll, 47 percent of Nader voters said they would have voted for Gore, 21 percent for Bush, and 30 percent indicated that they would not have voted at all. Had Nader not run, Gore would have won Florida and the presidency.

If the Electoral College provides unequal representation to the states, if this system encourages the candidates to mount highly concentrated campaigns in only a few of the states, and if the election can result in an undemocratic outcome, then why keep it?

Supporters contend that it has worked reasonably well. It has been decisive and reflective of the popular vote most of the time, even enlarging the winning candidate's margin of victory in the Electoral College. They claim that the system reflects the country's federal structure, requires the winner to have support across the country, protects concentrated minorities, and compartmentalizes and thereby reduces the impact of fraudulent voting practices and vote-counting errors.

Opponents note that the system has not worked as the framers intended since the two-party system developed, and has produced three nonplurality winners and close calls in several other elections. They contend that it was never based on the principle of federalism, nor would its demise affect the federal character of the United States, and that its benefits to any one group are offset by the disadvantages to other groups, including other minorities, thereby undermining the principle of equal protection of the laws.

Nor do its opponents perceive the electoral system as more likely to contain the evils of cabal, intrigue, and voter fraud. On the contrary, they argue, the more complex the electoral system, the more likely it is to be subject to deals among the electors and those who support them; the smaller the electoral unit, the more likely a dispute over relatively few votes could make a difference. They point to Florida in 2000 as an example. In the national popular vote, Gore won about 540,000; in Florida, the final tally gave Bush a 537-vote victory. Which of these two situations, the national vote or the Florida vote, is more likely to result in controversy?

Reforming the Electoral College System

What are the options? Most Americans favor a direct popular vote. Gallup polls preceding the 2000 and 2004 presidential elections report that a majority of the population supports a constitutional amendment to elect the president by direct popular vote.[20] There is a partisan cleavage in the support for this reform, with 73 percent of Democrats and 66 percent of independents in favor but only 46 percent of Republicans.[21]

In 1969, the House of Representatives voted for a constitutional amendment to directly elect the president, but the Senate did not follow suit. In 1979, fifty-one Senators supported a joint resolution for a direct popular vote, not the two-thirds necessary for a constitutional amendment. Since then, members of Congress have repeatedly introduced direct election amendments, but to no avail.

The tradition of the Electoral College, the reluctance of states that are advantaged to change it, and the Republican Party's hesitancy, based in part on philosophy and in part on the increasing number of Hispanics coming into the electorate and their current inclination to vote Democratic, have thus far prevented a direct election amendment from being passed by Congress and put to the states for a vote. Even in the aftermath of the controversial 2000 election, Florida vote, and Supreme Court decision, Congress, controlled by the Republicans, did not even hold public hearings on the matter.

Congress's reluctance to address the issue, combined with the increasing public dissatisfaction with the Electoral College and the way campaigns are conducted within it, have prompted a variety of citizen proposals for changing the current system. One of the most innovative is a state-based plan for electing the president by a national popular vote. States would enter into an interstate compact in which they would agree to join together to pass identical laws that awarded all of their electoral votes to the presidential candidate who received the most popular votes in the country as a whole. The compact would not take effect, however, until it was agreed to by enough states to cast a majority of the electoral votes, thereby ensuring that the candidates with the most popular votes would win in the Electoral College.[22] The practical merits of this proposal are that it does not necessitate a constitutional amendment, which is unlikely at this time, and would continue to allow the states to retain the authority for determining their electors and how they voted. By October 2009 only five states with a total of 68 electoral votes had agreed to join the compact.

A direct election of the president and vice president would certainly be consistent with a democratic election process; it would encourage turnout across the country, not just in the battleground states; it would prevent a discrepancy between the popular vote and the electoral vote; and it would force the candidates to campaign in population centers, appeal to urban-suburban interests, and provide a national agenda and more justification for claiming a national mandate.

Critics, however, see a direct, popular vote, particularly a close one, as more likely to nationalize and thereby aggravate such problems as voter (in) eligibility, possible vote fraud, and ballot tabulation errors like the ones in Florida in 2000. A national election would probably cost more than the focused presidential campaigns of the late twentieth and early twenty-first centuries. Less-populated rural areas, particularly in the mountain states and the Midwest, might be neglected. An election decided primarily by voters concentrated on the Atlantic and Pacific coasts would not provide the geographic balance and reflect the federal character as much as the current system does.

Finally, a plurality winner might not receive a majority of the total vote as the Electoral College requires today. In seven out of the twenty-five elections in the twentieth century and one out of three in the twenty-first century, the winner did not receive 50 percent of the popular vote. One way to deal with this problem is to have a runoff election between the top two candidates if neither receives a majority;[23] another is to have Congress select the winner from the top two vote-getters; a third alternative would be to elect the plurality winner if that candidate received at least 40 percent of the total vote. Only Abraham Lincoln in 1860 fell below this percentage. In a four-candidate contest, he received 39.8 percent of the vote.

Other proposals, such as allocating a state's electoral votes in proportion to the popular vote that the candidates received in that state, have been advanced. Known as the **proportional plan,** such a voting system would more closely reflect the diversity of views across the country and encourage turnout among the population, but it also might result in a proliferation of votes among different candidates and parties, thereby making it more difficult for any one of them to get a majority. Third-party and independent candidates would exercise more influence under a proportional voting system. Moreover, unless all the states move to such a system those that allocate their electoral votes in proportion to their popular votes would be disadvantaged. Candidates would not concentrate their efforts on proportional voting states because the payoff in electoral votes would be much smaller than in winner-take-all states—a principal reason that Colorado voters rejected a proportional voting initiative in 2004.

Another option, known as the **district plan,** currently is used in the states of Maine and Nebraska. This option gives two at-large electoral votes to the candidate who wins the popular vote in the state and one electoral vote to the candidate who wins the vote in each legislative district in the state. In the 2008 election, one district in Nebraska voted for Obama while the other two and the state overall voted for McCain. The district plan would produce closer presidential elections than the current system, but it also might align the presidential election more closely to that of Congress, particularly the House of Representatives. Moreover, the uncompetitive nature of most congressional districts would not provide incentives for candidates to campaign in these less-competitive districts unless the overall state vote was competitive. Table 3.4 lists the Electoral College vote since 1960 under the present system and the vote that would have resulted if each of the other systems had been employed on a national level. The results of only one of these elections would have changed. Under both the proportional and the district systems, Nixon probably would have defeated Kennedy in 1960.[24] In 1976 Carter and Ford would have tied under the district plan, but a Democratic Congress probably would have selected Carter anyway. In 2000 Bush wins in every voting system except direct election.

Despite the results in 2000, the present Electoral College system, with its winner-take-all voting in forty-eight of the fifty states, has tended to enlarge the winning candidate's margin of victory, thereby giving the victor a larger mandate for governing than that candidate would have received from a direct popular vote. However, acting on the basis of such a mandate can be hazardous as President George W. Bush discovered in 2005 when his second-term domestic agenda priorities of Social Security privatization and immigration reform met with public and congressional opposition. The current system also has compartmentalized voting problems, although in 2000 that compartmentalization extended the indecisive outcome for five weeks.

PUBLIC OPINION, REPRESENTATION, AND POLICY OUTCOMES

Representational inequalities have contributed to public policy outcomes that favor those who are already economically and educationally advantaged.

TABLE 3.4 Voting for President, 1956–2008: Four Methods for Aggregating the Votes

Year	Candidates	Electoral College	Proportional plan	District plan	Direct election
1956	Eisenhower	457.0	296.7	411.0	57.4
	Stevenson	73.0	227.2	120.0	42.0
	Others	1.0	7.1	0	0.6
1960	Nixon	219.0	266.1	278.0	49.5
	Kennedy	303.0	265.6	245.0	49.8
	Byrd	15.0	5.3	14.0	0.7
1964	Goldwater	52.0	213.6	72.0	38.5
	Johnson	486.0	320.0	466.0	61.0
	Others	0	3.9	0	0.5
1968	Nixon	301.0	231.5	289.0	43.2
	Humphrey	191.0	225.4	192.0	42.7
	Wallace	46.0	78.8	57.0	13.5
	Others	0	2.3	0	0.6
1972	Nixon	520.0	330.3	474.0	60.7
	McGovern	17.0	197.5	64.0	37.5
	Others	1.0	10.0	0	1.8
1976	Ford	240.0	258.0	269.0	48.0
	Carter	297.0	269.7	269.0	50.1
	Others	1.0	10.2	0	1.9
1980	Reagan	489.0	272.9	396.0	50.7
	Carter	49.0	220.9	142.0	41.0
	Anderson	0	35.3	0	6.6
	Others	0	8.9	0	1.7
1984	Reagan	525.0	317.6	468.0	58.8
	Mondale	13.0	216.6	70.0	40.6
	Others	0	3.8	0	0
1988	Bush	426.0	287.8	379.0	53.4
	Dukakis	111.0	244.7	159.0	45.6
	Others	1.0	5.5	0	1.0
1992	Bush	168.0	203.3	214.0	37.5
	Clinton	370.0	231.6	324.0	43.0

TABLE 3.4	**Voting for President, 1956–2008: Four Methods for Aggregating the Votes** (continued)				

Year	Candidates	Electoral College	Proportional plan	District plan	Direct election
	Perot	0	101.8	0	18.9
	Others	0	1.3	0	0.6
1996	Clinton	379.0	262.0	345.0	49.2
	Dole	159.0	219.9	193.0	40.7
	Perot	0	48.8	0	8.4
	Others	0	7.3	0	1.7
2000	Bush	271.0	260.3	288.0	47.9
	Gore	266.0*	260.0	250.0	48.4
	Others	0	17.7	0	3.7
2004	Bush	286.0	275.2	317.0	50.7
	Kerry	251.0†	258.3	221.0	48.3
	Others	0	4.5	0	1.0
2008	Obama	365	283.4	301	52.9
	McCain	173	246.9	237	45.7
	Other	0	8.5	0	1.4

*One Democratic elector in the District of Columbia cast a blank ballot.

†One Democratic elector in Minnesota cast a vote for Edwards for president and Kerry for vice president.

Source: From Stephen Wayne, *The Road to the White House, 2008: The Politics of Presidential Elections.* Copyright © 2008. Reprinted with permission of Wadsworth, an imprint of Cengage Learning: www.cengage.com.

Inequalities also fuel attitudes toward government. One would think that people who perceive that government benefits those with money and power would be more critical and less trusting of it. And they have been, although recent surveys conducted since the election of 2008 indicate greater hopefulness among less-well-represented groups for what government can and may provide. Much of this optimism undoubtedly has to do with the election of the first African American president and the model he represents for those who have faced social, economic, and political barriers in their lives. Some of the optimism among those at the lower end of the socioeconomic scale may also be a product of partisanship—of Democratic Party gains in partisan identification and control of government.

Contemporary Views on Government

People are more upbeat about government and the beneficial effects it can provide than they were during the Bush administration. African Americans, in particular, are more supportive of government. During George W. Bush's first term, a majority of this racial group believed that government controlled too much; in 2009, a majority of African Americans rejected this view.[25]

A survey of attitudes toward government, conducted in May 2009 by the Pew Research Center for the People and the Press, also found that people under 30 years of age are more positively disposed today toward government than are their parents and grandparents.[26] The differential in age-group perceptions was larger than it has been in several decades.

Other groups that comprise the Democrats' electoral coalition—women, Hispanics, and Asians—are also more likely to be supportive of the president and the Democratic Congress. They are more likely to believe that Obama's promise to change policy and politics will be successful and benefit the society as a whole. These beliefs are reflected in the data in Table 3.5.

Although Democrats and the groups that make up their electoral coalition are more optimistic about the Obama-led government, their optimism has not thus far changed their beliefs about what the government should do, particularly for people with the greatest economic and social needs. Public support for a government safety net has actually declined since 2007. In that year a Pew survey reported that 69 percent agreed with the statement that it was a responsibility of government to "take care of those who cannot take care of themselves"; two years later, only 63 percent agreed. The 2009 survey also reported comparable declines across other items related to assistance to the needy.[27]

TABLE 3.5 Perceptions of Government

Question: Do you believe that government is run for the benefit of all?

	Agree					
	1987	1992	1997	2003	2007	2009
Total	57	44	48	52	45	49
White	58	44	47	54	46	45
Democrats	*55*	*40*	*55*	*43*	*38*	*58*
Republicans	*67*	*53*	*46*	*70*	*62*	*41*
African Americans	49	37	53	37	33	50
Democrats	*50*	*38*	*—*	*35*	*36*	*53*
Hispanic	—	—	—	62	55	66

Source: Pew Research Center for the People and the Press, "Independents Take Center Stage in Obama Era," May 21, 2009, 33, http://people-press.org/reports/pdf-bw/517.pdf.

Similar findings on health care suggest the persistence of a gap between a theoretical goal, "government needs to do more to make health care affordable and accessible," which 59 percent supported, and the belief that "the government would become too involved in health care," a belief in which the public was nearly evenly divided (46 percent agreed and 50 percent disagreed). The split was largely along partisan and ideological lines, with 68 percent of Republicans, 44 percent of independents, and 29 percent of Democrats agreeing with the statement.[28]

Age differences were also evident in fear of too much government involvement in health care. Young people, African Americans, Hispanics, and women expressed less fear than did older people, whites, and men.[29] According to the Pew study, "Women, blacks and Hispanics are also significantly more likely than others to completely agree that government needs to do more to improve the accessibility and affordability of medical care. Nearly two-thirds of women (65%) say this, compared with just 54% of men. More than three-quarters of African-Americans (77%) and 69% of Hispanics hold this view, compared with just 54% of whites."[30]

The differences reflected in the survey present an interesting dialectic. Those who have been less well represented in government favor a larger role for government while those who have been more effectively represented favor a more limited role. Since the 1930s, people with the greatest needs have tended to be more sympathetic to the Democratic Party and its policy goals. So naturally they would be more optimistic when the Democrats controlled government.

The Consequences of Representational Bias

Inequality in terms of election results and demographic representation makes an impact on public policy outcomes, particularly in a governmental system that impedes rather than facilitates change, a system in which it is easier to prevent policy change than achieve it. Remember that the status quo is no friend to the disadvantaged. Existing policy tends to reinforce conditions in which those with economic, social, and political power continue to reap more benefits than do others.

The relatively smaller percentages of women and minorities in government compared with their proportion in the general population make it less likely that the unrepresented or underrepresented will be heard, that their issues become salient, their opinions considered, and their policy goals achieved. Joe Soss and Lawrence R. Jacobs cite evidence that indicates ". . . that on issues where the policy preferences of rich and poor diverge, governmental policy is substantially more responsive to the preferences of more-affluent individuals and groups."[31]

Representational inequality lessens support for policy change. Sometimes it also raises questions about the legitimacy of government actions; it may even encourage the circumvention of those actions. Unequal representation also leads to cynical views by those who are less well represented, views about government, the officials who run it, and the politicians who compete for public office.

Although the evidence presented here suggests that a major attitudinal shift toward a larger role for government has not occurred in the United States, the terrorist attacks of September 11, 2001; natural disasters such as hurricanes, droughts, earthquakes, and other environmental disasters; health emergencies including plagues, pandemics, and food and drug-related medical problems; the availability and costs of energy; and law and order issues have all led people to turn to government for help when they have nowhere else to turn.

In short, representation is the critical link in the problem-resolution process. Representation holds the relationship between people and their elected representatives together. When representation is skewed, the policy outcomes, if any, are likely to be skewed as well.

Term Limits

The Twenty-second Amendment, ratified in 1951, limits a president to a maximum of two elected terms in office, or to only one if the president serves more than half his predecessor's term. Lyndon Johnson, who became president after John F. Kennedy's assassination in November 1963, would have been eligible for two elected terms; Gerald Ford, who succeeded Richard Nixon in August 1974, was eligible for only one.

The movement for term limits, which peaked in the 1990s, was spurred by dissatisfaction with the performance of government and the behavior of public officials. The public's perception continues to be that elected officials are unduly influenced by special interests, that they become increasingly self-interested and self-promoting, and that they use the perquisites of their office to gain an unfair reelection advantage—thus, the argument goes, the only effective way to ensure turnover in office is to limit the terms of office to a specified number of years or elections.[32]

Those who support this argument contend that legislatures were initially designed to be popular assemblies in which concerned citizens represented their brethren when formulating and overseeing public policy. The idea of an assembly composed of political professionals with job security gained through significant incumbency advantages is anathema to this original design and its intent. Rotation in office keeps elected officials more in touch with the needs and interests of the electorate. It also creates more nonincumbency elections in which competition is stimulated and more voters turn out. It is argued as well that term limits prevent special-interest groups from becoming too cozy with those in power and thus less likely to use their resources to "buy, rent, or influence" elected officials.[33]

The anti–term limits crowd contends that limits are unnecessary, undesirable, and undemocratic.[34] They are unnecessary because there is sufficient turnover in most legislatures, undesirable because they result in the election of less-knowledgeable and less-experienced public officials who initially lack the skills to be effective in office and thus become more dependent on staff, and undemocratic because they prevent the electorate from reelecting a particular representative who may have served well in office. Moreover, limits remove the incentive for an incumbent to be responsive in his or her last term and may contribute to the phenomenon of declining influence in that term.[35]

The Twenty-second Amendment is a good example of the negative impact term limits can have and the power vacuum it can create. The amendment that prohibits presidents from running for a third term weakens them as their second term progresses. The term lame duck is frequently used to describe their predicament. As power flows away from them, they usually seek refuge in ceremony, travel, and speeches; concentrate on foreign policy; and make much more use of their unilateral instruments of executive authority.

Supporters of term limits believe that the loss-of-power argument is overblown and that presidents are reelected to continue their policies already in place, not to create a lot of new domestic programs. The greater danger, they contend, is that the cult of personality can upset the balance of power and effectively undercut the democratic electoral process as Republicans claim that it did when Franklin Delano Roosevelt was reelected in 1940 and 1944 after having served two full terms in office.

Some states also sought to impose restrictions on how long their members of Congress could serve. Not only did they believe that turnover would bring new ideas to government, but they also wanted to provide more electoral opportunities for their term-limited state legislators. The Supreme Court, however, ruled that state-imposed limits on members of Congress were unconstitutional because they added an additional qualification for eligibility to serve in Congress, thereby conflicting with Article I of the Constitution, which specifies only age, citizenry, and residence requirements for members of Congress. The Court's decision effectively derailed the term-limits movement.

Age, Residency, and Citizenship Requirements

In addition to term limits, there are several other constitutional qualifications that limit public choice. At the national level, these include minimum-age and residency requirements for candidates for both Congress and the presidency and a native-born requirement for the presidency. Are such qualifications still necessary and desirable? Does it make sense to have a minimum-age requirement but not a maximum-age requirement? Ronald Reagan, the oldest president, suffered memory loss in his second term. Strom Thurmond, the oldest member of Congress, was reelected at the age of ninety-two and stood fourth in line for the presidency as president pro tempore of the Senate when the GOP controlled that body. About one-third of the electorate thought that Senator Robert Dole's age of seventy-four was a factor that could affect their voting decision when considering the 1996 Republican presidential candidate;

McCain's age of 72 was also cited by 39 percent as a factor in voting in the 2008 general election. [36]

The president has to be a native-born American. Being born in the United States might have been important in 1787, when the nation was young and people's patriotic ties to it were weaker than they are today, but is it relevant? Several prominent citizens have been precluded from the presidency by this requirement. They held high positions in government, some were in the official line of succession, and would have been considered qualified in every other respect, but they were born in other countries. Included among these individuals were secretaries of state Henry Kissinger (born in Germany) and Madeleine Albright (born in Czechoslovakia) and California governor Arnold Schwarzenegger (born in Austria).

Similarly, what is the purpose of a residency requirement, particularly in an age of international commerce in which business executives employed by multinational corporations often have to spend considerable time living abroad? Although the Constitution mandates residence in a state before a person can represent that state, it is still possible to achieve residency by moving there and declaring residence some time before the election. Former attorney general Robert Kennedy and then first lady Hillary Rodham Clinton both moved to New York to be candidates for the U.S. Senate. Both were elected, although Kennedy hadn't lived in the state long enough to vote.

SUMMARY: REPRESENTATIONAL DILEMMAS IN A NUTSHELL

American democracy rests on the concept of representative government. In such a government, all citizens have the right to be equally and fairly represented. But theory and practice diverge. Structural biases affect the representative character of the U.S. political system.

Plurality voting in single-member districts overrepresents majorities at the expense of minorities, but it also contributes to stability and accountability in government by maximizing the number of seats that the majority party holds and its ability to exercise power. A proportional voting system in multi-member districts increases minority representation, but frequently at the price of a coalition government.

Women are underrepresented but not as a consequence of structural bias. Their failure to achieve representation equal to their proportion of the population is largely a residue of the restrictions placed on women's suffrage before 1920, voting prejudices, differing gender career patterns, and the advantages that incumbents, who are still overwhelmingly male, have in getting reelected.

Winner-take-all voting in the Electoral College inflates the clout of the large states and the cohesive groups within them. More important, it encourages candidates to concentrate their campaigns in populous areas deemed by historical voting patterns and current public opinion polling to be most competitive and neglect most of the rest of the country. As a consequence, presidential elections are national, but presidential campaigns are not.

If states with more than half the electoral votes required their electors to vote for the national popular vote winner, an undemocratic result could not occur in the Electoral College. Under the current arrangement, however, it can and has. It also could occur if states were to apportion their electors on the basis of statewide and legislative district voting or on the proportion of the vote that candidates received in the state, although the results of the Electoral College vote would probably be closer than it has been in the winner-take-all system.

The underrepresentation of certain groups has been a source of discontent to them. It has affected attitudes toward government and public policy. Those who are economically disadvantaged and thus underrepresented in the electorate and in government tend to want a larger and more active government because they have nowhere else to turn.

Electoral and representational outcomes also are affected by restrictions placed on eligibility. Age and residency requirements shrink the pool of eligible candidates. Limits on tenure contribute to turnover of elected officials, which can adversely affect the operation of government.

To address representational bias and the policy problems that flow from it, the majority has to be more cognizant of the need for minority representation and willing to adjust the electoral system or its voting behavior to achieve it. A tall order, to be sure, and one that is not readily embraced by those who benefit from the current system.

Now It's Your Turn

Discussion Questions

1. Is it possible to have a democratic electoral system in which the majority decides and the minority is fairly represented?
2. If women constitute a majority of the voting-age population, why are fewer women than men elected to positions in government?
3. What difference might it make if there were a more equitable gender balance among elected officials?
4. Is it important for a representative democracy to have demographic, issue, and ideological groups represented in proportion to their percentages in the population? If so, how can this representation be achieved? Should a quota system be established?
5. Why do people who are worse off and less well represented want government to do more, whereas those who are better off, well represented, and more likely to benefit from public policy today want government to do less?

6. What consequences do you think a direct election of the president would have on the electorate, the electoral process, the operation of government, and the public policy it makes?

7. Are age, residency, and place-of-birth requirements consistent with a democratic electoral process in which the people are supposed to be able to choose their elected leaders? Should there be a maximum age requirement for voting, for service in government, neither, or both?

Topics for Debate

Challenge or defend the following statements:

1. Descriptive representation is irrelevant and may be harmful to substantive representation and effective government.

2. The system of plurality voting in single-member districts is inconsistent with the Supreme Court's interpretation of the Fourteenth Amendment's equal protection clause.

3. The underrepresentation of women in elected positions does not adversely affect public policy.

4. The direct election of the president is neither necessary nor desirable.

5. Term limits are a good idea and should be imposed for all elected officials, regardless of position.

6. Age qualifications for office are unnecessary, undesirable, and undemocratic and should be eliminated.

7. Tests of mental competency should be required for voting and for service in government.

8. Persons incarcerated for crimes should at least be permitted to vote for law enforcement officials and judges.

Exercise

A congressional committee is holding a hearing on how to improve representation in the national government. As an expert on representational issues, you've been invited to testify. Your assignment is to prepare and present your testimony. In your testimony, note the following:

1. how well the society is currently represented in the federal government and the public policy it makes,

2. the principal groups that suffer representational bias,

3. the source of their representational problems and what it would take to fix them,

4. the pros and cons of changing the system to remove these representational problems (including any unintended consequences that you think might occur), and

5. your recommendation to the committee on what (if anything) it should propose to Congress as a legislative solution to the problem.

INTERNET RESOURCES

- FairVote: www.fairvote.org
  Contains a wealth of information on various voting systems, especially proportional representation.
- National Popular Vote: www.nationalpopularvote.com
  Puts forward a proposal and arguments for the direct election of the president accomplished by an interstate compact and not by a constitutional amendment.
- The Pew Research Center for the People and the Press: www.people-press.org
  Conducts surveys on public knowledge, attitudes, and opinions toward candidates, government, and the media.
- U.S. Term Limits: www.termlimits.org
  Promotes term limits; provides information on states that have legislated or had initiatives on term limits.
- Voter Information Services: www.vis.org
  Provides a database on congressional voting that can be downloaded for analysis.

SELECTED READINGS

Bartels, Larry. *Unequal Democracy: The Political Economy of the New Gilded Age.* Princeton: Princeton University Press, 2008.

Best, Judith. *The Choice of the People? Debating the Electoral College.* Lanham, Md.: Rowman and Littlefield, 1996.

Brunell, Thomas L. *Redistricting and Representation: Why Competitive Elections Are Bad for America.* New York: Routledge, 2008.

Edwards, George C., III. *Why the Electoral College Is Bad for America.* New Haven: Yale University Press, 2004.

Gallagher, Michael, and Paul Mitchell, eds. *The Politics of Electoral Systems.* Oxford: Oxford University Press, 2005.

Gilens, Martin. "Inequality and Democratic Responsiveness." *Public Opinion Quarterly* 69 (December 2005): 778–796.

Guinier, Lani. *The Tyranny of the Majority.* New York: Free Press, 1994.

Hardaway, Robert M. *The Electoral College and the Constitution: The Case for Preserving Federalism.* Westport, Conn.: Praeger, 1993.

Lublin, David. *The Paradox of Representation.* Princeton: Princeton University Press, 1997.

Malbin, Michael J., and Gerald Benjamin, eds. *Limiting Legislative Terms.* Washington, D.C.: CQ Press, 1992.

Massicotte, Louis, Andrei Blais, and Antonine Yoshinaka. *Establishing the Rules of the Game: Election Laws in Democracies.* New York: University of Toronto Press, 2004.

Nye, Joseph S., Jr., Philip D. Zelikow, and David King. *Why People Don't Trust Government.* Cambridge: Harvard University Press, 1997.

Pitkin, Hanna F. *The Concept of Representation.* Berkeley: University of California Press, 1967.

Rehfeld, Andrew. "On Quotas and Qualifications for Office." In *Political Representation and Democratic Self Rule,* edited by Ian Shapiro, Susan Stokes, and Elisabeth Wood. New York: Cambridge University Press, 2009.

———. "Representation Rethought: On Trustees, Delegates, and Gyroscopes in the Study of Political Representation and Democracy." *American Political Science Review* 33 (May 2009): 214–230.

Swain, Carol M. *Black Faces, Black Interests: The Representation of African Americans in Congress.* Cambridge: Harvard University Press, 1993.

Urbinati, Nadia. *Representative Democracy: Principles and Genealogy.* Chicago: University of Chicago Press, 2008.

Vermeule, Adrian. *Mechanisms of Democracy: Institutional Design Writ Small.* New York: Oxford University Press, 2007.

Warren, Mark E. *Democracy and Trust.* Cambridge: Cambridge University Press, 1999.

Will, George. *Restoration: Congress, Term Limits, and the Recovery of Deliberative Democracy.* New York: Free Press, 1992.

NOTES

1. Although Clinton did appoint a more diverse administration than his predecessors, he did not achieve his objective of appointing an administration as diverse as America.
2. For a deeper discussion of the representational issue, see Andrew Rehfeld, "Representation Rethought: On Trustees, Delegates, and Gyroscopes in the Study of Political Representation and Democracy," *American Political Science Review* 33 (May 2009): 214-230.
3. Edmund Burke, "Speech to the Electors," *Burke's Politics,* quoted in Hanna F. Pitkin, *The Concept of Representation* (Berkeley: University of California Press, 1967), 171.
4. In a national survey conducted for the Center on Policy Attitudes, people were asked whether "elected officials would make better decisions if they thought more deeply about what they think is right." Almost 80 percent of the respondents said yes. They were also asked, "When your Representative in Congress votes on an issue, which should be more important: the way voters in your district feel about that issue, or the Representative's own principles and judgment about what is best for the country?" A majority of 68.5 percent answered "the way voters feel." Steven Kull, "Expecting More Say: The American Public on Its Role in Government," Center on Policy Attitudes, May 10, 1999, 35; Frank Newport, "Americans Want Leaders to

Pay Attention to Public Opinion, But Still Skeptical of Standard Sample Sizes Used by Pollsters," Gallup Poll, October 12, 2005, www.gallup.com/poll/19138/Americans-Want-Leaders-Pay-Attention-Public-Opinion.aspx.

5. "Polling and Democracy," *Public Perspective* (July/August 2001): 24. They also believe that public officials place too much attention on polls. Gallup Poll, "Public Opinion Polls," April 15, 1999.

6. "Polling and Democracy," 23.

7. U.S. Census Bureau, *Statistical Abstract of the United States: 2009* (Washington, D.C.: Government Printing Office, 2009), Table 6: Resident Population by Sex, Race, and Hispanic-Origin: 2000–2007, www.census.gov/compendia/statab/tables/09s0006.pdf.

8. *Reynolds v. Sims,* 377 U.S. 533 (1964).

9. *Wesberry v. Sanders,* 376 U.S. 1 (1964).

10. For an excellent discussion of this quandary, see David Lublin, *The Paradox of Representation* (Princeton: Princeton University Press, 1997).

11. *Shaw v. Reno,* 509 U.S. 630 (1993); *Miller v. Johnson,* 115 S.Ct. 2475 (1995); *Bush v. Vera,* 116 S.Ct. 1941 (1996); and *Meadows v. Moon,* 117 S.Ct. 2501 (1997).

12. Lani Guinier, a law professor and unsuccessful nominee for assistant attorney general for civil rights in the Clinton administration, argues in her book *The Tyranny of the Majority* (New York: Free Press, 1994) that only with cumulative voting in multimember districts can the minority hope to achieve fair and equal representation. Guinier's proposal is to give citizens as many votes as there are candidates and allow them to distribute their votes any way they choose. They could, for example, give all the votes to one of the candidates, perhaps a person who shares their demographic characteristics or attitudinal views, or they could divide them among several of the candidates. Guinier contends that such a system would accord with the one person–one vote principle but would not involve the state in racial districting. Without such a system, she contends, the prejudices of the majority will dominate. This proposal, which conservatives found alarming, forced Guinier to withdraw her nomination when she failed to obtain sufficient support in the Senate.

13. A 2006 Gallup poll and a 2007 Fox News poll indicated that a majority believed their fellow countrymen were not yet ready to vote for a homosexual candidate for president; the Gallup poll also indicated that atheists, Mormons, and people of Asian and Hispanic ancestry would have great difficulty getting elected. See Jeffrey M. Jones, "Six in 10 Americans Think U.S. Ready for a Female President," Gallup Poll, October 3, 2006, www.gallup.com/poll/24832/Six-Americans-Think-US-Ready-Female-President.aspx; Fox News/Opinion Dynamics Poll, February 27–28, 2007, as reported in the Polling Report, www.pollingreport.com.

14. National Civic Review, "Full Representation: Proportional Systems Promote Inclusion, Deliberation, and Better Policy," Spring 1998, on Web site of FairVote.org, www.fairvote.org/?page=511.

15. If no candidate received a majority, the House of Representatives would choose from among the top five candidates. The Twelfth Amendment later reduced this number to three when it provided for separate ballots for the president and vice president. In the event of a House election, voting would be by state, with each state delegation possessing one vote.

16. *Every Vote Equal: A State-based Plan for Electing the President* (Los Angeles: National Popular Vote Press, 2006), 85.

17. Even incumbent presidents keep their eye on the most competitive states when deciding where to travel and hold public events. Fifty-six percent of George W. Bush's non–White House events in his first year in office were held in states he won or lost by 10 percent of the

vote or less in 2000; similarly, Barack Obama has concentrated his domestic travel in his first six months in the states that were most competitive in 2008. Brendan J. Doherty, "The Politics of the Permanent Campaign: Presidential and the Electoral College," *Presidential Studies Quarterly* 37, no. 4 (2007): 749–773; Brendan J. Doherty, "Barack Obama's First Six Months of International and Domestic Travel in Historical Context," White House Transition Project, www.whitehousetransitionproject.org/resources/briefing/sixmonth.

18. Center for Voting and Democracy, "2008's Shrinking Battleground and Its Start Impact on Campaign Activity," December 4, 2008, www.fairvote.org/tracker/?page=27&pressmode=sho wspecific&showarticle=230.

19. In 1876 a dispute over twenty electoral votes and the resolution of it by a congressionally established commission resulted in the election of Republican Rutherford B. Hayes, who had fewer popular votes than his opponent, Samuel J. Tilden. In 1888 Republican Benjamin Harrison received a majority of the electoral votes; his opponent, President Grover Cleveland, received a majority of the popular votes. In 2000 Republican George W. Bush won a majority of the electoral vote; Democrat Al Gore had a plurality of the popular vote.

20. Darren K. Carlson, "Public Flunks Electoral College System," Gallup Poll, November 2, 2004, www.gallup.com/poll/13918/public-flunks-electoral-college-system.aspx.

21. Ibid.

22. *Every Vote Equal,* 243–274.

23. Two elections would be costly, might result in the candidate who came in second in the first round winning in the second, and would be time-consuming, thereby shortening the transition.

24. In Alabama and Mississippi, fourteen unpledged electors voted for Democratic senator Harry Byrd of Virginia.

25. Pew Research Center for the People and the Press, "Independents Take Center Stage in Obama Era: Trends in Political Values and Core Attitudes," May 21, 2009, http://people-press .org/report/517/political-values-and-core-attitudes.

26. Ibid., "Section 2: Views of Government and the Social Safety Net," http://people-press.org/ report/?pageid=1517.

27. Pew data, however, indicate public sentiment about the safety net today is much higher than it was in the mid-1990s after the Republicans had taken over Congress and were attempting to end large government welfare programs.

28. Pew Research Center for the People and the Press, "Section 2: Views of Government and the Social Safety Net," http://people-press.org/report/?pageid=1517.

29. Ibid.

30. Ibid.

31. Joe Soss and Lawrence R. Jacobs, "The Place of Inequality: Non-participation in the American Polity," *Political Science Quarterly* 124 (Spring 2009): 99; see also Martin Gilens, "Inequality and Democratic Responsiveness," *Public Opinion Quarterly* 69 (December 2005): 778–796; Larry Bartels, *Unequal Democracy: The Political Economy of the New Gilded Age* (Princeton: Princeton University Press, 2008).

32. For arguments in favor of term limits, see Mark Petracca, "Rotation in Office: The History of an Idea," in *Limiting Legislative Terms,* ed. Michael J. Malbin and Gerald Benjamin (Washington, D.C.: CQ Press, 1992), 19–52; and George Will, *Restoration: Congress, Term Limits, and the Recovery of Deliberative Democracy* (New York: Free Press, 1992).

33. The scandal in which a prominent Washington lobbyist, Jack Abramoff, provided benefits to members of Congress in exchange for their help in satisfying the public policy interests of his clients is a case in point.

34. Malbin and Benjamin, eds., *Limiting Legislative Terms*, 198–221.
35. John R. Hibbing, *Congressional Careers: Contours of Life in the U.S. House of Representatives* (Chapel Hill: University of North Carolina Press, 1991), 180; and John M. Carey, *Term Limits and Legislative Representation* (Cambridge: Cambridge University Press, 1996), 193–194.
36. Edison Media Research and Mitofsky International, "National Exit Poll," available on most major news networks' Web sites.

chapter 4

Has Money Corrupted Our Electoral Process?

Did you know that . . .
- Richard Nixon spent six times as much in his last race for the presidency in 1972 as he spent for his first in 1960?
- Barack Obama's campaign spent almost twice as much as did McCain and the Republican National Committee combined in the 2008 presidential election?
- the more money congressional incumbents spend in the general election the more likely they are in trouble?
- national party candidates for electoral office in 2008 raised and spent more than $2 billion?
- the candidates who had the most money in their presidential accounts at the beginning of 2008 failed to win their party's nominations that year?
- there may be no causal relationship between campaign spending and electoral success?
- the party that controls Congress tends to receive a larger proportion of its funds from political action committees (PACs) than does the party in the minority?
- only about 11 percent of taxpayers today check off the box that allows $3 of their taxes to go to a Federal Election Campaign Fund?
- Industry associations, labor unions, and corporations spend much more money lobbying elected officials at the national level than they do trying to influence their election?
- people believe that members of Congress are more beholden to special-interest groups than to their own electoral constituents?
- the Federal Election Commission seems permanently immobilized by its partisan composition of three Democrats and three Republicans?

Is this any way to run a democratic election?

MONEY AND DEMOCRATIC ELECTIONS

What does money have to do with democracy? The answer is "a lot" if it:

- gives wealthy people and groups an unfair advantage in influencing the election;
- affects who votes and how they vote;
- conditions who runs for office and who does not;
- affects information the electorate receives about the candidates and their issue positions;
- affects public perceptions of how the electoral system is working, whether it is fair or unfair, and whether it contributes to effective government or not;
- affects how elections are administered: the period of time in which citizens may vote, the places at which they can do so, the length of time it takes them to complete the voting process, the form and clarity of the ballots, the timeliness and accuracy of the vote tabulation, and the number of election officials available to help voters deal with problems, oversee the process, and plan for the next election.

Money can and does affect the democratic character of elections in the United States. If a basic tenet of an electoral democracy is the right of every adult citizen to have an equal opportunity to influence an election outcome, then the unequal distribution of resources within society threatens that right. Does the average citizen have the same opportunity to affect an election campaign as multibillionaires Bill Gates and George Soros do, or to run for office as multimillionaires George W. Bush and John Kerry did in 2004? Do two equally qualified candidates have the same chance to win if one is wealthy and willing to use a personal fortune to advance personal political ambitions while the other begins with much more modest means? Is everyone equally protected by the laws if some people are able to gain more access to policymakers by virtue of their campaign contributions and expenditures than those who cannot or do not contribute?

The difficulties in providing equal opportunities for all citizens stem in large part from the value Americans place on personal freedom and private property. The Constitution protects the right of people to use their own resources as they see fit, provided they do so legally. Moreover, the Supreme Court has equated campaign spending with freedom of speech. In 1976, in the case of *Buckley v. Valeo* (424 U.S. 1), the Court held that the independent expenditures by individuals and groups are protected by the First Amendment, as is the advocacy of issues by party and nonparty groups.

Not only does the Constitution protect the rights of people and groups to express their feelings and "petition the government for grievances," but the electoral and governing systems are designed to allow them to do so, to enable those who feel most strongly about a candidate or issue to try to convince others of the merits of their deeply felt beliefs and opinions and the arguments that support them.

Freedom to spend and speak are not the only two freedoms that produce inequality in the electoral process. Freedom of the press is another. Should the giant companies of the communication industry be able to condition the scope, content, and spin of the information the electorate receives? Should the mass media profit from their performance of a public service—covering election campaigns?

This chapter explores the impact of money on elections. It begins with a description of the rising costs of political campaigns, the problems associated with these costs, and the ways Congress and other governments have attempted to deal with these problems. It then assesses the intended and unintended consequences of recent election laws on the conduct of campaigns and the democratic character of the electoral system. Subsequent sections of the chapter deal with the relationship between money and electoral success, public perceptions of the money issue, and proposals for campaign finance reform.

CAMPAIGN FINANCE LEGISLATION AND ITS CONSEQUENCES

The costs of elections have skyrocketed in the last forty-eight years. In 1960 Richard Nixon spent about $10 million in his race for the presidency. Eight years later, he spent $25 million. Running for reelection against a weak opponent in 1972, he spent more than $61 million. Since then, campaign expenditures have risen dramatically. The Center for Responsive Politics, a public interest group that tracks campaign spending, estimated that $2.2 billion was spent on federal elections during the 1995–1996 election cycle, $3 billion during 1999–2000, $4 billion during 2003–2004, and more than $5 billion during 2007–2008. A little less than half of the expenditures were used on the 2008 race for the presidency, twice as much as in 2004 and three times as much as in 2000.[1]

A variety of factors has contributed to this rapid increase in spending. The nomination process has become more competitive and has lasted longer. The 2008 nomination campaign began in 2006 for many of the aspirants. Today, successful candidates have to run in two elections that occur over a two-year period. The techniques of modern campaigning—television advertising, survey research, direct-mail and e-mail fund-raising, database compilations, grassroots organizing, and communicating on the Internet—have added to the rising costs.

The Federal Election Campaign Act

Fearing that the election process had become too expensive, that candidates had to spend too much time raising money, that they had become too dependent on large donors, and that money was being given secretly and perhaps illegally to candidates and parties, Congress went into action. Legislation was enacted in the 1970s to reduce the costs of elections, decrease dependence on wealthy donors, reduce the amount of time candidates spend fund-raising, increase the number of viable candidates, make the races more competitive, and make contributions and expenditures subject to full public review. The Democratic Congress had an additional objective in passing this legislation—to reduce the Republican Party's financial advantage in elections.

The new laws were primarily directed at the presidential election, but some restrictions also were placed on congressional elections. The amount of money that individuals and groups could give to candidates for federal office as well as to the political parties was strictly limited. In addition, a restriction was placed on how much money candidates could contribute to their own campaigns. The law also allowed corporations and labor unions, previously banned from contributing money, to encourage their employees, members, and stockholders to form political action committees (PACs) and contribute up to $5,000 per candidate per election.[2] Federal subsidies and grants for major-party presidential candidates and funds for the major parties were provided, and spending limits for candidates in the presidential campaign who accepted these funds were established. The Federal Election Commission (FEC), composed of six members, initially to be appointed by both the president and Congress, was set up to monitor and police election activities.

The Federal Election Campaign Act (FECA) was the first comprehensive law to regulate campaign finance activity and the first to provide partial public funding for the presidential nomination and election. Previous legislation had prohibited direct business and labor contributions but had done little to regulate the source and amount of campaign contributions and expenditures.

Prior to the 1970s the only public funding was at the state level, and it paid for the conduct of the election. In providing public subsidies, the United States followed the practices of several European countries that also subsidized candidates or their parties' elections. (Table 4.1 summarizes the grants and subsidies of other democratic governments.)

The FECA, scheduled to go into effect after the 1972 elections, was immediately challenged as unconstitutional. Critics charged that the limits placed on contributions and spending violated the constitutionally guaranteed right to freedom of speech, that the funding provisions unfairly discriminated against third-party and independent candidates, and that appointment of some of the commissioners by Congress violated the separation of powers.

In 1976, the Supreme Court declared two parts of the law unconstitutional. Although the Court upheld the right of Congress to regulate campaign contributions for candidates who seek federal office, it held that independent spending by individuals and groups was protected by the First Amendment to the Constitution and thus could not be regulated. It also voided Congress's selection of four of the six election commissioners as an intrusion on the president's executive authority.

TABLE 4.1 **Public Subsidies for Elections**

Country	Direct subsidy	Free media access	Tax relief for parties	Tax relief for donors
Argentina	Yes	Yes	Yes	Yes
Australia	Yes	No	No	Yes
Austria	Yes	No	No	No
Belgium	Yes	Yes	No	No
Brazil	Yes	Yes	Yes	No
Canada	Yes	Yes	No	Yes
Czech Republic	Yes	Yes	Yes	Yes
France	Yes	Yes	No	Yes
Germany	Yes	Yes	Yes	Yes
India	No	Yes	No	No
Israel	Yes	Yes	Yes	Yes
Italy	Yes	Yes	Yes	Yes
Japan	Yes	Yes	Yes	Yes
Mexico	Yes	Yes	Yes	Yes
New Zealand	No	Yes	No	No
Peru	No	Yes	No	No
Russia	Yes	Yes	No	No
South Africa	Yes	Yes	No	No
United Kingdom	Yes	Yes	No	No
United States	No	No	No	No

Source: Institute for Democracy and Electoral Assistance, Political Finance Database, www.idea .int/parties/finance/db.

The Court's decision forced Congress back to the drawing board in the midst of another presidential election cycle. A new law was enacted at the start of the 1976 presidential nomination campaign. It retained the contribution and spending limits and public funding of the presidential campaign. But the funding was to be voluntary. Candidates did not have to accept government funds; if they did, they were limited in how much they could contribute or lend to their own campaign and how much their campaigns could spend. The FEC was reconstituted with all six members, specified as three Republicans and three Democrats, to be nominated by the president and appointed with the advice and consent of the Senate.

With limited money available, the candidates decided to spend the bulk of their resources in 1976 on television advertising to reach the widest possible audience. As a consequence, much of the political paraphernalia that normally accompanies presidential campaigns—buttons, bumper stickers, yard signs, campaign literature, and the like—was missing or in short supply. Voter turn-out continued to decline. Congress was concerned that the funding limitations, the emphasis on television advertising and on media-oriented events, and the drop in turnout were all related.

The 1979 Amendment and the Soft-Money Loophole

An amendment to the law was enacted in 1979 that enabled the parties to raise and spend unlimited amounts of money for their voluntary efforts to promote voting through educational campaigns, get-out-the-vote drives, and other party-building efforts. The only prohibition on the expenditure of this money was that it could not be spent advocating a specific candidate's election.

Known as the soft-money amendment, it created a gigantic loophole in the law, permitting, even encouraging, the solicitation of large contributions. Unlike the hard money that was strictly regulated and reported, soft money was not regulated and initially even unreported.[3]

In the first two presidential elections after the soft-money amendment was passed, the Republicans enjoyed a financial advantage. Helped by negative reaction to the Jimmy Carter presidency, Ronald Reagan's appeal among wealthy conservative donors and business interests, and, subsequently, Reagan's own general popularity, the GOP raised three times as much soft money as the Democrats.

The race for soft money increased exponentially in the 1990s. It did so as a consequence of a clever plan conceived by President Clinton's political advisers. Clinton needed to improve his public standing and image in the after-math of the Republicans' victory in the 1994 midterm elections, the failure of his health care initiative, and scandals that beset his White House and administra-tion. To do so, the president's political strategists recommended an advertising campaign in which the president's moderate policy positions were contrasted with the more conservative Republican stands.

Launched in the summer of 1995, the campaign was very expensive. In the first two months, almost $2 million was spent on it. Fearful that the continued expenditure of large sums of money could deplete Clinton's reelection treasury and leave him with insufficient funds to respond to an attack by the Republicans and their nominee, the president's advisers decided to raise and spend soft money for the advertising campaign rather than depend on the money that had been or would be contributed to his official reelection committee.

The Clinton fund-raising effort, in which the president, vice president, senior White House officials, and the first lady participated, raised the ante on soft-money contributions. It also embroiled the president and his staff in questionable fund-raising tactics, especially their use of public facilities for the purposes of private solicitation.

The Republicans protested the actions of Clinton and the Democrats, but to no avail. Unable to stop the Democrats from using their position in government to raise money, the Republicans then conducted their own soft-money campaign. After the election, the Republican-controlled Senate investigated Democratic fund-raising activities. No new campaign finance legislation was enacted, however.

Sen. John McCain kept the soft-money issue alive during his 2000 quest for the Republican presidential nomination. Other principal candidates in that election, notably Democrats Al Gore and Bill Bradley, also said that they favored campaign finance reform to close the soft-money loophole. After the election and several high-profile accounting frauds, business failures, and illegalities by corporate executives, Congress, swept up by public indignation over the fraudulent actions of the business and accounting firms, enacted the Bipartisan Campaign Reform Act (BCRA) in 2002.

The 2002 Bipartisan Campaign Reform Act

A principal purpose of the new law was to ban the national political parties from raising soft money. Another was to prevent them and nonparty groups from using advocacy advertising as a not-so-subtle vehicle for promoting particular candidates. A third objective was to increase the amount that individuals were permitted to give to candidates and their parties.

The BCRA prohibited the national parties from soliciting unregulated contributions. To compensate for their potential loss of revenue, the law raised the individual contribution limits from $1,000 to $2,000 and indexed the higher amount to inflation. Party and nonparty groups were not allowed to mention candidates by name in their advocacy ads thirty days or less before a primary and sixty days or less before the general election. Finally, the BCRA allowed candidates for Congress facing self-financed opponents to raise additional funds to level the playing field—the so-called millionaires' amendment.

As with FECA, the BCRA was immediately challenged by those who opposed the law and believed that it violated their First Amendment rights of freedom of speech. In December 2003, in the case of *McConnell v. FEC* (540 U.S. 93), the Supreme Court upheld the major provisions of the law, allowing the legislation to shape the financial aspects of the 2004 and subsequent election campaigns.

Opponents of the law had feared that the political parties would be unable to make up the loss of soft money. The Democrats, most of whom had supported the legislation, were particularly nervous since their party had relied on these funds to offset the Republicans' traditional fund-raising advantage. Moreover, being in the minority, the Democrats could not use the White House or Congress as they had in previous elections to bolster their fund-raising efforts.

To deal with this potential shortfall, Terry McAuliffe, then chair of the Democratic National Committee, created a task force of party operatives and supporters and charged them with designing a strategy to deal with the expected shortfall of funds. The task force recommended that nonparty, nonprofit groups, which had functioned under two provisions of the Internal Revenue Code, 527 and 501(c), be created and used as vehicles for raising and spending soft money. The spending, however, could not be coordinated with the party or candidates; it had to be done independently.

Beginning in 2003, these nonparty groups began to raise money for Democratic candidates. They were aided in their efforts by millions of dollars in seed money donated by financier George Soros and insurance magnate Peter Lewis. Outraged by the ruse, the Republicans appealed to the FEC, but unsuccessfully. The commissioners, by a 4-2 vote, decided not to intervene during the 2004 election campaign. As a consequence, the Republicans belatedly set up their own 527 and 501(c) organizations to raise and spend soft money. In the end, more than $417 million was collected by these groups and $420 million spent, according to Political Moneyline, a public interest group that tracks campaign money.[4]

The parties also took advantage of changes in the law to raise more money than they had in previous election cycles. The increase in the amount that individuals could contribute to candidates for national office, the computerization of their fund-raising databases, and the deep partisan divisions in the country that the policies of the Bush administration provoked fueled this effort.

Thus, the BCRA had a mixed impact on the parties. It encouraged them to improve and broaden their fund-raising base. It also increased the number of small donors, those who contributed $200 or less. In 2000, 25 percent of the total contributions came from small donors; in 2004 that percentage had increased to 34; by 2008, it had increased 40.4 percent.[5] The provision that limited advocacy advertising in the final thirty days before primaries and sixty days before the general election motivated the parties and groups to spend more money on grassroots efforts with the desired result—a higher voter turnout in 2004 and 2008.

However, soft money—lots of it—continued to find its way into the federal election campaign, especially by virtue of the fund-raising activities and expenditures of party-oriented nonparty groups.[6] Table 4.2 lists the revenues and expenditures of these groups in the period 2003–2008.

Nonparty groups, created to supplement their party's efforts, actually reduced the control the candidates and their parties had over their own campaigns. The prohibition against coordinating party and nonparty activities resulted in the conduct of separate, presumably uncoordinated campaigns. Moreover, the BCRA also allowed the parties to engage in independent spending, which they were able to coordinate with candidate campaigns. (For actual party revenue and expenditures, see Table 4.3.)

TABLE 4.2 **Revenue and Expenditures of 527s, 2003–2008 (in millions)**		
Year	Revenues	Expenditures
2003–2004	$599.2	$611.7
2005–2006	385.0	429.5
2007–2008	506.1	490.3

Source: Center for Responsive Politics, "527s: Receipts and Expenditures," www.opensecrets .org/527s/index.php.

The BCRA had another effect, partly anticipated and partly not. By doubling the amount that candidates could receive from individual donors and adjusting that amount to the rate of inflation, the law stimulated fund-raising and quickly increased the amount of money available to federal candidates. They had more, so they could spend more. The BCRA did not, however, raise the spending limits for presidential candidates who accepted federal funds except for an annual inflationary adjustment. Thus, a large spending gap developed between federally funded and privately funded candidates for their parties' presidential nominations.

Those who accepted federal matching grants were handicapped in three ways: They were limited in what they could spend in individual states, limits that were most harmful in the important early contests that attract so much media attention and tend to weed the fields of candidates quickly. Second, federally funded candidates had overall spending limits that could be fatal during an extended nomination process. In 2000, Senator McCain, fighting George W. Bush for the Republican Party nomination, had come to within $1 million dollars of his overall cap by the first Tuesday in March, whereas Bush had more delegates, more money, and no limits. The third problem was the lack of sufficient funds during the three- to five-month period after the nominee was effectively determined but before the nominating convention was held. How does a candidate who has reached the limit continue to stay in the news, campaign, and respond to criticisms of the opposing party's presidential candidate? These handicaps prompted Howard Dean and John Kerry not to accept matching grants in 2004 so they would not be at such a disadvantage against an unchallenged incumbent, George W. Bush. Both Bush and Kerry accepted the federal grant in the general election and, with the help of their parties and nonparty groups, had about the same amount of resources in the general election.

With no incumbent president or vice president running in 2008, the nomination contest started earlier than in previous years. The early start complicated the problem for federally funded candidates in two ways. It extended the period during which their expenditures counted against the state and

TABLE 4.3 Major Party Revenues and Expenditures, 1996–2008 (in millions)

		1996		2000		2004		2008	
		Revenue	Expenditure	Revenue	Expenditure	Revenue	Expenditure	Revenue	Expenditure
Democrats	Hard	$221.6	214.3	275.2	265.8	688.8	665.6	763.3	746.5
	Soft	$123.9	121.8	245.2	244.9	—	—	—	—
	Total	$345.5	335.1	520.4	510.7	683.8	665.6	763.3	746.5
Republicans	Hard	$416.5	408.5	465.8	427.0	782.4	752.6	792.9	766.1
	Soft	$138.2	149.7	249.9	252.8	—	—	—	—
	Total	$554.7	558.2	715.7	679.8	782.4	752.6	792.9	766.1

Source: Federal Election Commission, "Party Financial Activity Summarized for the 2008 Election Cycle," May 28, 2009, revised August 5, 2009, http://ffec.gov/press/press2009/05282009Party/20090528Party.shtml.

overall limits, but it also extended the period for raising funds. Under the circumstances, there was more incentive to fund campaigns solely with private funds and not accept federal matching grants. These incentives carried over into the general election.

Barack Obama's success during the nominations (he raised $326 million through the end of June 2008) prompted him to reject federal funds for the general election. McCain was forced to take them, $84.1 million, because he did not think he could raise nearly the amount that Obama could. Besides, McCain believed in public financing and had drafted much of the 2002 legislation—also called the McCain-Feingold Act. In the general election Obama's privately funded campaign enjoyed an almost five to one spending advantage over McCain's campaign and about a two to one advantage if Republican Party expenditures for McCain are included.

The lesson is clear for future nominations and elections. Unless the spending limits imposed on government-funded candidates are modified or lifted entirely, public financing of presidential elections is practically dead! It will be used only by lesser-known or fringe candidates who have no other option. The personal irony for McCain is also obvious. An opponent of soft money and architect of the legal structure that banned it, McCain's BCRA undermined his own presidential campaign and, with it, the public funding provision of presidential elections.

CONTINUING CAMPAIGN FINANCE ISSUES

Are elections too expensive? Former House majority leader, Tom DeLay, did not think so. In claiming that the campaign finance issue was overblown, DeLay stated, "Americans spend twice as much per year on yogurt than they spend on political campaigns."[7] Does it require millions or billions of dollars to educate the public about the candidates and issues?

Elections are much more expensive today, but public participation remains uneven. Most people do not contribute any money to candidates or their parties. Most do not get personally involved in the campaign and, with the exception of the presidential election held once every four years, most people do not even vote. Clearly, a lot of money that is being spent on get-out-the-vote activities has not been producing its desired effect, although if less effort was made and less money spent even fewer people might vote.

Nor is there much evidence that the public is any better informed and more attentive to election issues today than it was a decade or two ago when campaign expenditures were less. In fact, people may actually be less knowledgeable about the issues than they were when newspapers were the prime source of information and there was greater depth in policy discussions. The costs of elections do not seem to be paying off in terms of producing a more educated electorate, although spending less money might contribute to an even less-informed one.

Is Money Important?

Clearly, candidates and their managers believe that it is. Having a large war chest can often dissuade a credible challenger from running. In their quests for reelection, Presidents Clinton and George W. Bush raised millions of dollars to discourage a quality challenger in their own party from running against them for the nomination, a practice that is likely to continue for subsequent incumbents desiring renomination. Clinton and Bush also wanted the money so that they could respond quickly to attacks made against them.

Campaigns are more costly today because of the revolution in communications technology and the need to hire professional experts in the use of this technology. Polling, media advertising, grassroots organization, computer programming, database acquisition, networking, Web site design, and the equipment that these technologies use, and even election law reporting and accounting, require special skills and knowledge. In the past, political parties provided their nominees with campaign services and the personnel to run them. Today, most of these operations are outsourced to campaign professionals.

Having money up front also gives candidates greater flexibility in deciding when and where to campaign. It helps them get press coverage because the news media view money as an early indication of electability. Coverage follows the dollar, and that coverage, in turn, can generate more dollars. In addition to the psychological and public relations advantages that a large war chest, assembled early, can provide, up-front money also increases a candidate's strategic options. In contrast, accepting federal funds limits those options because of the state and national spending limits.

Although money buys recognition, hires political professionals, and satisfies other needs, such as fund-raising, staff support, and grassroots organizing, it may not buy much more than that. It certainly does not guarantee electoral success, as Ross Perot and Steve Forbes found out in 1992, 2000, and 2004. Surprisingly, the candidates who had the largest revenues in the year before the two most recent presidential nominations, Howard Dean in 2004 and Mitt Romney and Hillary Rodham Clinton in 2008, did not win their party's nomination. And when Barack Obama passed Hillary Clinton in fund-raising and exceeded her expenditures by margins of two or three to one, he too did not gain popular-vote victories in the big Democratic primary states of Texas, Indiana, and Pennsylvania. Had he spent less, however, he might have done worse.

In the general election, there seems to be a stronger relationship between the expenditure of money and electoral success. Between 1860 and 1972 the winning presidential candidates outspent the losers twenty-one out of twenty-nine times. Republican candidates spent more than their Democratic opponents in twenty-five out of twenty-nine elections during this period. The four times they did not, the Democrats won.

The relationship between money and electoral success holds even when independent expenditures, partisan communications, and soft money are considered. In the 1980s, considerably more was raised and spent on behalf of Republican nominees than on their Democratic opponents. In the 1990s, the Democrats narrowed the gap but still did not eliminate the GOP's fund-raising advantage. George W. Bush was the financial as well as electoral victor in 2000, but in 2004 the spending by and for the major-party candidates was about equal. In 2008, the money advantage shifted strongly to the Democrats. Did Obama win because he raised and spent the most, or did he raise and spend the most because more people perceived he would win or wanted him to do so?

Money alone did not decide the outcome of the 2008 presidential nominations or election although it may have contributed to the size of Obama's victory in both the nominations and general election. Had the general election been closer, however, Obama's financial advantage might have played a more pivotal role.

In congressional elections, the relationship between money and electoral outcomes presents a similar picture. In 2004, the candidates with the most money won 97.7 percent of the races for the House of Representatives and 88.6 percent of the Senate contests; in 2006, the percentages were 93.8 and 75.8, respectively.[8]

Challengers need more money to defeat incumbents but frequently find raising it more difficult. When incumbents spend a lot of money, it is usually a sign that they are in trouble, not that they are assured of victory; open seats in competitive districts tend to attract the most donors and dollars. When the candidates lack recognition, money seems to be important, particularly at the beginning of the campaign. Not only can it be used to air more advertising and contact more voters, but it can also create the impression of a momentum swing.[9]

The bottom line is that money can buy recognition, but it usually cannot buy victory. Even so, candidates take few chances; they and their aides tend to devote a great deal of effort to filling their war chests and keeping them full. Even if they will not need all the money during the current campaign, it represents a cushion for the next one and, if it is large enough, a hurdle that may discourage a quality challenger.

Who Contributes to Campaigns and What Do Donors Get for Their Money?

In addition to the inequality that unequal resources create for the candidates, there is another problem many consider equally troubling and harmful to a democratic electoral process. That is the problem of a political payoff. Do the contributors, directly or indirectly, receive a personal or policy benefit for their contributions?

Contributors are unequally distributed among the society. Only a small percentage of the population regularly gives to the candidates and the parties. The Center for Responsive Politics estimated that only about 1 percent of the adult population in the United States contributed money in the 2008 national elections; of those who contributed, 61 percent gave donations in amounts of $200 or less (37 percent women and 74 percent men) while 13 percent made contributions of $2,300.[10] As with voting, public opinion surveys conducted before and after elections indicate that more people say that they contribute than actually did so.

The FEC requires candidates for national office to file reports on all their contributions and expenditures. The commission and various public interest groups analyze these data and make them available to the public. Table 4.4 lists the top twenty-five organizations that gave the most money in 2008, the amounts they gave, the percentage of funds that went to Democrats and Republicans, and the total contributed by individuals within these organizations or by PACs affiliated with them.

The concentration of contributors among wealthy individuals and campaign expenditures among corporations, trade associations, and labor unions raises important issues for an electoral democracy. To what extent can and do the people and groups influence who runs and wins, and to whom are the winning candidates likely to be most responsive once in office?

From the public's perspective the answers are clear: the big contributors, and particularly the individuals—called "bundlers"—who raise the contributions for the candidates, and the industries, unions, associations, and other nonparty groups that contribute to the candidates as well as spend even larger amounts during elections promoting their beliefs and interests and the candidates who are sympathetic to them. Mistrust of politicians and their motives and public officials and their responsiveness remains high. Right or wrong, the perceptions are that money buys political influence, that members of Congress are more likely to respond to campaign donors outside of their districts than to nondonors within their districts, and that members support policies primarily because these policies are desired by their donors and not because elected officials believe them to be in the best interests of the country.[11] The public has also been troubled by the accusations of foreign money being spent in U.S. elections to influence the outcome and the implications that those expenditures may have for national security.[12]

Whether or not these public perceptions accord with reality, the fact that most people believe them is significant, and both presidential candidates, Barack Obama and John McCain, responded to them during the 2008 campaign. Obama railed against government by special interests, refused to take money from PACs, said he would not appoint lobbyists to top positions in his administration, and established new and stringent ethical requirements for public officials. McCain criticized legislation that earmarked special projects and the appropriations that funded them for groups in members' constituencies. Both candidates said that they would oppose special-interest politics and government policies that furthered it. The widespread belief that government is conducted of, by, and for the special interests rather than the public interest undermines the democratic character of the political system.[13]

TABLE 4.4 **Individual Contributions Coming from Large Organizations in the 2007–2008 Election Cycle, 25 Top Overall Donors**

Rank	Contributor	Total contributions	To Democrats	To Republicans	Contributions tilt
1	ActBlue	$24,482,402	100%	0%	Solidly Dem
2	Goldman Sachs	$7,140,170	74%	23%	Strongly Dem
3	JPMorgan Chase & Co	$6,026,091	54%	36%	On the fence
4	AT&T Inc	$5,685,012	39%	39%	On the fence
5	Citigroup Inc	$5,562,707	61%	33%	Leans Dem
6	National Assn of Realtors	$4,947,940	49%	35%	On the fence
7	Intl Brotherhood of Electrical Workers	$4,912,946	69%	1%	Strongly Dem
8	Morgan Stanley	$4,375,164	53%	43%	On the fence
9	General Electric	$4,303,528	59%	26%	Leans Dem
10	Microsoft Corp	$4,030,134	64%	23%	Leans Dem
11	Comcast Corp	$3,893,961	53%	28%	On the fence
12	American Bankers Assn	$3,840,311	33%	44%	On the fence
13	Bank of America	$3,782,710	46%	36%	On the fence
14	North Carolina Republican Executive Cmte	$3,595,000	0%	0%	On the fence
15	American Assn for Justice	$3,535,090	74%	3%	Strongly Dem
16	American Federation of Teachers	$3,529,361	66%	0%	Leans Dem
17	International Assn of Fire Fighters	$3,483,250	62%	18%	Leans Dem
18	University of California	$3,448,172	93%	7%	Solidly Dem
19	Time Warner	$3,413,096	83%	15%	Strongly Dem
20	Merrill Lynch	$3,392,241	44%	54%	On the fence
21	Honeywell International	$3,387,528	42%	41%	On the fence
22	PricewaterhouseCoopers	$3,340,192	40%	44%	On the fence
23	National Auto Dealers Assn	$3,296,500	29%	57%	Leans Repub
24	UBS AG	$3,281,494	56%	43%	Leans Dem
25	Lockheed Martin	$3,269,137	40%	42%	On the fence

Source: Center for Responsive Politics, based on data released by the Federal Election Commission on May 12, 2009, http://www.opensecrets.org/bigpicture/topcontribs.php?cycle=2008.

The issue is also one of equity. If the groups that contribute and spend the most money were representative of the population as a whole, the situation would be better than if they represented a particular economic stratum within society. But, alas, they do not, as Table 4.4 suggests. Business interests spend the most; the expenditures of consumer groups pale in comparison. Organized labor spends less, directs most of it to the Democrats, and represents the interests of blue-collar union workers. Who represents the interests of nonunionized blue-collar workers or white-collar employees? And when is the last time you heard that a group representing the poor had elected or influenced a public official through campaign contributions or expenditures?

As the people see it, politicians are also winners in the money game. Although the public thinks of both parties and their candidates as involved in excessive and even questionable fund-raising activities, Republican and Democratic partisans differ over the most egregious campaign finance problems. Republicans direct their outrage at the incipient influence of foreign money and labor unions, whereas the Democrats see special-interest money, flowing in large part from business and conservative groups to Republicans, as the issue that most needs rectifying.[14] According to national surveys, the public wants the financial system to be reformed and the abuses ended, but people doubt that politicians in Washington will do so.

Why Has Congress Been So Slow to Deal with These Problems?

The unintended consequences of campaign finance legislation have made members of Congress reluctant to act quickly. Some members are reluctant to legislate at all because they are philosophically opposed to government regulation in general and campaign finance regulation in particular. They see spending as free speech protected by the First Amendment. Some also object to using taxpayer money to fund national elections, partially or wholly.

Besides which, members of Congress are probably the most inappropriate group to fix a problem from which they have personally benefited by virtue of their election and, for most of them, reelection. They are hardly disinterested policymakers. As incumbents, they can raise more money. This built-in advantage naturally makes them hesitant to change the system and level the playing field. Whichever party has been able to raise the most money tends to oppose legislation that would reduce its competitive edge.

There also has not been much recent public pressure on Congress to act. Although people say that they desire campaign finance reform, most do not regard it as a major policy priority. It was not even mentioned on the Gallup poll's most important problems facing the United States during the 2004–2008 period.[15]

What Else Could Congress Do to Fix Campaign Finance? Although a consensus has not emerged on how to reform the system, certain practices have been subjected to considerable criticism: the solicitation of soft money by nonparty groups and state and local parties; PAC contributions, especially to

members of Congress; the money from foreign and other questionable sources that flows into American political campaigns; the spending restrictions placed on candidates who accept government funding; and the independent expenditures of individuals, parties, and nonparty groups.

Should All Soft-Money Contributions Be Banned? When Congress enacted the BCRA in 2002, it prohibited the national parties from soliciting and spending soft money. This prohibition has encouraged the national parties and their supporters to form sympathetic nonparty groups to raise soft money and mount stealth campaigns. Should new legislation be enacted to ban soft money for these groups as well?

Congress could probably do so if the issue threatened the national parties or equity in their fund-raising capacities. But, so far, it has not. In fact, the revenues and expenditures for these groups have decreased from their 2004 highs. In 2008, approximately $500 million was raised and spent by groups classified as 527s; in off-year elections, the figure has been about half that amount.[16] Congress cannot limit these group expenditures, however, because such limits violate the First Amendment.

Nor does Congress have the authority to extend its soft-money ban to party affiliates at the state and local levels. Only the states can do so, and some have enacted restrictive laws that have also raised constitutional issues.[17]

Should PAC Contributions Be Eliminated or Reduced? Another possible reform would be to eliminate or reduce PAC contributions to candidates. The law currently restricts the amount donated to $5,000 per candidate, per election. But it sets no overall limit on how much PACs can contribute and spend on their own. One proposal would be to reduce the amount that they could give directly to candidates. Alternatively, Congress, which created PACs in the legislation that established the campaign finance system, could prohibit them from making individual contributions at all, set an overall cap on the total amount of their contributions in any election cycle, specify a maximum percentage of funds candidates could receive from PACs, or, in the most extreme case, eliminate PACs altogether.

Reducing or eliminating PAC contributions would certainly appeal to the general public, who perceive these nonparty groups as a large part of the problem. In reality, however, PAC contributions are relatively insignificant for presidential candidates. They are more important for congressional candidates, but even for members of Congress $5,000 from any one group is also a relatively small amount in most campaign chests. Campaign spending by PACs is another story, but again, restricting these expenditures would put Congress on a collision course with the Supreme Court's view that independent campaign spending is protected by the First Amendment.

Besides, if PACs were eliminated, it is doubtful that their interests would vanish as well. Rather, they would find other ways to affect the political process.

PACs are required to report their contributions and expenditures to the FEC. Whether and to what extent other entities that might replace them would also be required to report is unclear.[18]

Should Contributions and Expenditures from Foreign and Illegal Sources Be Prohibited? Another source of public concern is foreign contributions and those emanating from individuals with prison records or axes to grind. Under the existing law, contributions are restricted to U.S. citizens and noncitizens who are permanent residents. American subsidiaries of foreign-owned companies also may create PACs or make contributions, provided they do so with money earned in the United States. A foreign company cannot give its American subsidiary money to spend in U.S. elections.

Congress could prohibit any individual contribution from a person who is not a U.S. citizen. It also could prevent foreign-owned companies from making contributions. It probably could not, however, prevent American employees of these companies from forming PACs and making contributions. Nor would Congress want to do so because this could potentially discriminate against American workers.[19]

In today's interdependent, international economic environment, Congress must be very careful about how it treats foreign companies for fear of hurting American interests abroad. Although the problem is perceived as foreign influence, as often as not the beneficiaries are American companies that do business abroad.

There is little need for legislation that might restrict donations from criminals or others of questionable character. These contributions cost more in the form of bad publicity and potential loss of public support than they are worth, and they tend to be returned by candidates and parties just as quickly as they become a public source of embarrassment.

Should the Amount of Public Funds Available to Presidential Candidates Be Increased? The flip side of constricting contributions is expanding government grants. One of the original aims of the FECA was to enlarge the field of potential candidates and level it, giving lesser-known and less-well-funded candidates opportunities that they had lacked in the past. Providing matching funds during the presidential nominating period was designed to provide such an opportunity, allowing candidates to demonstrate their qualifications and establish their electability. And it accomplished that until increases in private contributions were permitted in the 2002 legislation and spending limits imposed on candidates who accepted government funds changed the revenue-expenditure equation to the disadvantage of federally funded candidates.

A task force commissioned by the Campaign Finance Institute, a nonprofit public interest organization devoted to campaign finance disclosure and reform, has proposed increasing the amount of money candidates who are seeking their party's presidential nomination would receive by upping the size of the match on the first $100 contributed. The task force also recommended that candidates receive public funding the year before the election.

Providing the grant earlier would give candidates funds when they need it most—at the beginning of the process. Increasing the size of the initial match would increase the motivation for candidates to seek small contributions rather than focus their efforts on those who give the larger amounts. Enlarging the amount of funds from the Treasury would also be necessary if more candidates received larger federal grants. To provide for these additional public funds, the task force has proposed a $2 increase in the income tax checkoff, from $3 to $5 per taxpayer.[20]

The grant for the federal election could be increased and would need to be, given the higher costs of election campaigns, the increased expenditures by candidates and their parties, and the greater opportunities and incentives for raising private funds instead of taking government money. Candidate expenditures have risen at a rate greater than inflation during the more than thirty-year period since the initial campaign finance legislation went into effect. Yet the amount that the major-party candidates receive is still tied to the $10 million figure established in 1974, adjusted by the rate of inflation. Providing candidates with more money or allowing them to supplement federal funds with private contributions in the general election would make federally funded candidates more competitive with privately financed opponents and also less dependent on their parties and nonparty groups, which now regularly supplement presidential campaigns.

It is unlikely, however, that Congress and the general public would support an increase in tax checkoffs that would be necessary to enlarge the pool of election funds. Only about 11 percent of taxpayers are currently checking the box to put $3 of their taxes into the fund for presidential candidates. Given all the other expensive policy issues that must be addressed, rising concern about the magnitude of annual budget deficits and the national debt, the relatively tepid support for government-financed elections in the United States, and the increasing willingness of the public to permit funding with private contributions, it is extremely unlikely that Congress will enact legislation to increase public funding of election campaigns.[21]

The revenue side is only half of the campaign finance equation; spending is the other. Can campaign expenditures be equalized without denying candidates, their parties, and the groups that support them freedom of speech? Some reformers say that they can if spending limits were eased or eliminated or if independent expenditures were subject to some controls.

Should the Federal Campaign Spending Limits Be Modified? For the first time since the enactment of FECA, passage of the BCRA tied individual contribution limits to inflation. However, the law did not do the same to the state and overall spending limits or to the matching funds. As a consequence, federal funds have become much less attractive. The spending discrepancies between publicly and privately funded candidates are enormous. In 2008, the principal candidates for their party's nomination spent considerably more than the $42.05 million plus legal and accounting funds (a total of about $50 million) that the law allowed. Clinton and McCain each spent more than $200 million and Obama more than $300 million.

Increasing the expenditure limits substantially would make federal funds a more viable option for candidates faced with the dilemma of not being able to raise or spend as much as their primary and general election opponents. It could help extend the contested phase of the nomination and make that phase more equal. Easing or eliminating the contribution and spending limits after the nominee was effectively determined also would equalize the preconvention campaign in the period after the primaries and before the national nominating conventions.

Raising the spending limits, however, would also force the candidates back into the fund-raising game for extended periods of time. More fund-raising by the candidates would create greater competition for funds within the party and among allied groups and even congressional candidates. Cohesion between the party and nonparty groups and the nominee might be loosened as a result. It might put pressure on Congress to increase once again the amounts that individuals and groups can contribute. Nevertheless, raising spending limits and allowing federal funds to be supplemented by private money seem to be the only viable ways of preventing the effective demise of the public funding system in presidential elections.

Can Independent Spending by Individuals and Groups Be Reduced or Eliminated? Limiting spending in a campaign would obviously cut down on the costs of elections and make candidates less dependent on outside sources of revenue. But the limits would have to be voluntary because the Supreme Court has stated that involuntary restrictions on campaign spending violate freedom of speech. Several countries, such as the United Kingdom and Canada, impose spending limits on candidates for national office although they do not limit party spending.

One proposal that has received considerable attention would set voluntary ceilings for House and Senate elections, such as $600,000 for House races (about one dollar per person in the district) and $950,000 to $5.5 million for the Senate, depending on the population of the state. Candidates who abide by these limits would receive free or reduced-cost time on television and cheaper mailing rates.

Voluntary limits with inducements for compliance would equalize spending and keep costs from getting out of hand. Incumbents who can raise more money might seem disadvantaged by this arrangement, but most would not be. Challengers usually need more money to balance the incumbent's advantages of recognition, constituency service, and record of accomplishments.

But voluntary spending limits also could give greater advantage to wealthy candidates who do not have to abide by them.

Providing free or low-cost communications also might be a problem for traditional for-profit communication companies, notably those in television, radio, and print media. Most oppose providing free time or space for the purpose of enhancing public debate and facilitating partisan communications. Countries such as Germany, Mexico, and the United Kingdom do require their television broadcasters to provide free time to political parties but not to individual candidates; the United States could do the same as a condition for renewal of television licenses. But what about minority parties and independent candidates? What about stations that do not use the airwaves but operate via cable or satellite? Lowering mail rates is another option, but one that would require an additional government subsidy.

With the development of the Internet; the expansion of social networking sites; and other advances in faxing, teleconferencing, cell phone technology, texting, twittering, and a variety of other electronic interactive mechanisms, the problem of improving campaign communications and providing voters with more information about the candidates and election issues may prove to be much less difficult than getting voters to take advantage of these opportunities and learn from them. (See Chapter 8 for an extended discussion of campaign communications and their impact.)

SUMMARY: CAMPAIGN FINANCE DILEMMAS IN A NUTSHELL

American elections are getting more and more expensive. For some candidates it seems almost as if the sky is the limit when it comes to campaign spending. Each election has become more costly than the previous one.

The need for money has become an obsession for candidates and has encouraged them to spend increasing amounts of time, energy, and money raising it. Their drive to fill their own campaign coffers, often well in advance of the election, has created (at least in the public's mind) a political system in which the wealthy exercise the most influence and thereby undermine the equity principle in a democracy.

For the past thirty-five years, Congress and the president have had to contend with a range of campaign finance issues stemming from the need to fund higher and higher campaign expenditures, many of which resulted from the professionalization of campaign operations, weakening of party control, and introduction of new communication technologies. Initially, the solution was thought to lie in requirements that limited individual and group contributions to candidates for federal office, established spending limits for presidential candidates who accepted government funds, and mandated filing detailed reports on revenues and expenditures to the FEC.

The legislation enacted in the 1970s achieved some of these objectives. It broadened the base of campaign contributions, initially decreased the perceived influence of the wealthy, lessened the amount of time and energy that presidential candidates had to spend on fund-raising, and leveled the playing field and thereby gave more candidates an opportunity to demonstrate their qualifications for office and electability. Very important, it also brought campaign finance into the open, to full public view.

But some of these achievements have been short-lived. The Supreme Court's judgment that campaign spending is free speech and protected by the First Amendment has undercut the goal of cutting campaign expenses. Although limits could legally be placed on contributions to federal candidates, overall expenditure limits on individuals and groups cannot be imposed. For a time, turnout declined; Congress's response to what it deemed to be an unfortunate development for a democratic electoral system was to permit unlimited contributions to parties to boost their get-out-the-vote and other grassroots activities. Known as the soft-money loophole, it was exploited in 1996 and 2000, first by Clinton and later his Republican opponents, each of whom wanted to maximize his election opportunities. In 2002, the loophole was closed for the national parties and, contrary to fears, has not impeded their fund-raising abilities.

The law increased private contribution limits, making it possible for presidential and congressional candidates to raise more and more money. The revolutions in computing and Internet communications further increased the private funding potential. Although government grants were also increased by the rate of inflation, the gap between private and public funding opportunities has widened. The real culprit here is the spending limits imposed on candidates who accept government funds. These limits have become such a disadvantage that unless the law is changed candidates will take public funds in the future only if they have no other viable option. Reviving the public funding system will require legislation that not only raises spending caps but permits publicly funded candidates to supplement their campaign treasuries with private contributions.

Restrictions were also placed on issue advocacy advertising by nonparty groups in the closing thirty days of the campaign before a primary and sixty days before a general election by the BCRA. These restrictions have limited stealth advertising for the presidential candidates by advocacy groups, but they have also raised constitutional issues. Nonetheless, they have encouraged parties and their nonparty-group allies to place greater emphasis on grassroots organizing. Spurred by advances in communication technologies, this emphasis helped increase turnout in the presidential elections of 2004 and 2008.

Although the problems of high costs, large contributions, and increasingly unlimited expenditures remain, there seems little that Congress can do without violating the Supreme Court's opinion that independent spending is a form of free speech. It is this dose of liberty that makes equality so hard to achieve in the American electoral process.

Can campaign spending be reduced or equalized without impinging on constitutionally protected freedoms? Can candidates be assured that they will have sufficient money to get their messages across without increasing the burden on taxpayers, forcing the news media to provide free time, or maintaining a situation in which those who have access to money are advantaged? And, finally, can incumbents who have profited from the current system be induced to change it in a manner that reduces their advantage?

In addition to the free speech–equal influence quandary, fixing the problem of federal funding is difficult because of the ideological opposition to any federal subsidies by some elected officials, primarily Republicans, and the lack of public support for public funding of elections.

Now It's Your Turn

Discussion Questions

1. Is money really as corrupting an influence on politics and government as people believe?
2. Do the wealthy exercise disproportionate influence on the conduct of elections and, through that influence, on the operation of government?
3. Are American elections too expensive? What would be a reasonable criterion by which to evaluate whether the costs of elections are excessive?
4. Can money in elections ever be regulated as long as the Supreme Court considers expenditures as freedom of speech?
5. Does money buy electoral success? Did it in the 2008 presidential and congressional elections?

Topics for Debate

Challenge or defend the following statements:

1. All laws regulating campaign finance, except for the reporting requirements, should be abolished.
2. All federal elections should be publicly funded.
3. Congress should increase the matching funds and decrease the spending limits on candidates seeking their party's presidential nomination.
4. The required political composition of the FEC should be abolished and replaced by independent, nonpartisan commissioners who are appointed.
5. The Bipartisan Campaign Reform Act is fatally flawed and should be repealed.
6. The Constitution should be amended to exclude campaign spending from the free speech protection of the First Amendment.

Exercise

This exercise has two parts. The first is to design a nonpartisan public relations campaign on the need for campaign finance reform in the United States. In formulating your campaign, indicate why the system must be reformed and what those reforms should be. Make sure that you try to anticipate the objections that different groups may raise.

For the second part of the exercise, assume that your campaign has worked and that you have generated enough of a public outcry to move Congress into action. At this point, assume the role of a Democratic or Republican member of a committee (your choice depending on your own political persuasion) charged with investigating the issue and proposing a legislative solution.

1. Outline the major points of a bill that addresses the problems you have cited in your public relations campaign. (Remember you are now a partisan, so your bill should not adversely affect the interests of your party. If it is to be enacted into law, however, it must not adversely affect the interests of the other party.) In your statement anticipate the criticisms that members of the other party on the committee are likely to make and respond to them.

2. With your class as the full committee, have a vote at the end to see whether your proposals should be sent forward to the floor of Congress. Would the current administration support such a bill?

INTERNET RESOURCES

- Campaign Finance Information Center: www.campaignfinance.org
  Contains archives of campaign finance stories from around the country, databases, lists of experts, links, and other reporting tools.
- Campaign Finance Institute: www.campaignfinanceinstitute.org
  Associated with the George Washington University, the institute collects and analyzes detailed finance information from recent federal elections and makes recommendations on how to improve the electoral system.
- Center for Responsive Politics: www.opensecrets.org
  Focuses on money and elections; publishes alerts, news releases, and major studies on campaign finance issues.
- Common Cause: www.commoncause.org
  Considers itself a citizens' lobbying group; for years, it has been at the forefront of campaign finance reform.
- Public Citizen: www.publiccitizen.org
  Provides information about problematic relationships among money, elections to office, and governance.
- Political Money Line: www.politicalmoneyline.org
  Provides up-to-date financial data on candidates, campaigns, and public officials.

- Federal Election Commission: www.fec.gov
Official source for data on campaign revenues and expenditures for federal elections; puts candidate finance reports on its Web sites as well as analyzes data from these reports and makes them available to the public.

SELECTED READINGS

Corrado, Anthony, and David B. Magleby, eds. *Financing the 2008 Election: Assessing Reform.* Washington, D.C.: Brookings Institution Press, 2010.

Magleby, David B., Anthony Corrado, and Kelly D. Patterson, eds. *Financing the 2004 Election.* Washington, D.C.: Brookings Institution Press, 2006.

Malbin, Michael, ed. *The Election after Reform: Money, Politics, and the Bipartisan Campaign Reform Act.* Lanham, Md.: Rowman and Littlefield, 2006.

————. "Rethinking the Campaign Finance Agenda." *The Forum* 6 (2008): Article 3.

————. "Small Donors, Large Donors, and the Internet: The Case for Public Funding after Obama." Campaign Finance Institute, April 22, 2009. www.campaignfinanceinstitute.org/pr/prRelease.aspx?ReleaseID=228.

Mann, Thomas E. "The U.S. Campaign Finance System under Strain: Problems and Prospects." In *Setting National Priorities: 1999,* edited by Robert D. Reischauer and Henry J. Aaron. Washington, D.C.: Brookings Institution Press, 1999.

Princeton Survey Research Associates. "Money and Politics: A National Survey of the Public's Views on How Money Impacts on the Political System." Commissioned by the Center for Responsive Politics, Washington, D.C., March 1977.

Sorauf, Frank J. *Money in American Elections.* Glenview, Ill.: Scott Foresman, 1988.

NOTES

1. Center for Responsive Politics, "U.S. Election Will Cost $5.3 Billion, Center for Responsive Politics Predicts," October 22, 2008, www.opensecrets.org/news/2008/10/us-election-will-cost-53-billi.html.
2. In an effort to control spiraling media expenses, the law limited the amount that could be spent on advertising. That provision was later eliminated.
3. Congress subsequently imposed a reporting requirement similar to the one that existed for all other contributions.
4. Political Moneyline, "Money in Politics Databases," www.politicalmoneyline.com.

5. Michael J. Malbin, "A Public Funding System in Jeopardy: Lessons from the Presidential Nomination Contest of 2004," in *The Election after Reform: Money, Politics and the Bipartisan Campaign Reform Act,* ed. Michael J. Malbin (Lanham, Md.: Rowman and Littlefield, 2006), 226–232. Percentage for 2008 calculated by author from data available from the Federal Election Commission, "Presidential Campaign Finance: Contributions to All Candidates," www.fec.gov/DisclosureSearch/mapApp.do.

6. Campaign Finance Institute, "501(c) Groups Emerge as Big Players Alongside 527s: Outside Soft Money Groups Approaching $400 Million in Targeted Spending in 2008 Election," October 31, 2008, http://campaignfinanceinstitute.org/pr/prRelease.aspx?ReleaseID=214.

7. Tom DeLay, "Statement on Shays-Meehan Bill," August 3, 1998.

8. Calculated by author from data from the Center for Responsive Politics for the 2003–2004 and 2005–2006 election cycles; see "The Big Picture: Winning vs. Spending," www.opensecrets.org/bigpicture/bigspenders.php?cycle=2006 (accessed July 10, 2009).

9. Gary C. Jacobson, *The Politics of Congressional Elections* (Boston: Little, Brown, 1983), 42.

10. Center for Responsive Politics, "2008 Overview: Donor Demographics," www.opensecrets.org/overview/DonorDemographics.php.

11. According to the 1992 "Money and Politics" survey conducted by Princeton Survey Research Associates for the Center for Responsive Politics, the following percentages of respondents say that the use of money to buy political influence occurs "often":
    - Leads elected officials to support policies they don't think are best for the country: 45%
    - Leads elected officials to spend too much time fund-raising: 63%
    - Leads elected officials to vote against constituent interests: 44%
    - Keeps important legislation from being passed: 48%
    - Gets someone appointed to office who would not otherwise be considered: 50%
    - Gives one group more influence by keeping another from having its fair say: 55%

12. A poll of 1,347 adults conducted April 2–5, 1997, by the *New York Times*/CBS News asked "Whose attempts to buy influence bother you the most?" Responses were:

Wealthy people	21%
Foreign governments	45%
American special-interest groups	25%
Don't know	8%

    See "Financing Campaigns: Skepticism, and a Need for Change," *New York Times,* April 8, 1997, sec. A.

13. Less than one-third of the American people in 2007 believed "they could trust the government to do what was right just about always or most of the time"; see Gallup Poll, "Topics A-Z: Trust in Government," http://www.gallup.com/poll/5392/Trust-Government.aspx; see also "Money and Politics," 1992.

14. "Money and Politics," 1992.

15. Gallup Poll, "Topics A-Z: Most Important Problem," http://www.gallup.com/poll/1675/Most-Important-Problem.aspx.

16. Center for Responsive Politics, "527s Advocacy Group Spending," http://www.opensecrets.org/527s/index.php.

17. In 2006 in the case of *Randall v. Sorrell,* 548 U.S. 230, the Supreme Court invalidated the state of Vermont 's strict election contribution and expenditure limits as unconstitutional.

18. A related concern is the practice of bundling. Pioneered by EMILY's List, a PAC that supports women candidates, the bundling procedure solicits individual contributions for candidates, collects them, and sends them to the candidates. In this way, the PAC's activities can

result in much more money for a candidate than the $5,000 maximum a PAC can contribute. Could Congress prohibit this practice? Probably not.

19. Congress would probably not want to prevent what has become a widespread practice in the United States: having foreign corporations and even governments hire American firms to represent their interests in the United States.

20. Another objective of the task force's recommendations was to reduce the need for and the amount of generic advertising that the national parties have to air during the period that follows the contested phase of the nomination process and before their national nominating conventions. The task force's proposals, however, would not impede fund-raising and independent spending by party and nonparty groups.

21. Stephen R. Weissman and Ruth A. Hassan, "Public Opinion Polls Concerning Public Financing of Federal Elections, 1972–2000: A Critical Analysis and Proposed Future Directions," Campaign Finance Institute, 2005.

chapter 5

News Media
Watchdog or Pit Bull?

Did you know that . . .

- there are more free and accessible sources of campaign information than ever before, yet the level of public knowledge has not significantly increased?
- although Americans say they believe in freedom of the press, almost 40 percent also believe that the media have too much freedom?
- the more education people have, the less they trust the news media?
- a majority of the population wants to prevent the broadcast and cable networks from projecting a winner in presidential elections while people are still voting?
- the voting-age group least informed about campaigns is the youngest: those between eighteen and twenty-nine?
- television is the primary source of election news in almost every advanced democratic nation?
- television news covers campaigns and elections as if they were sporting events?
- when the public has been asked to evaluate news media's coverage of recent national campaigns, the average grade given is a C?
- the spin put on campaign coverage today is more negative than positive?
- television anchors and correspondents received six times more airtime than the candidates on the evening news shows of the major networks during recent presidential campaigns?
- people rate the honesty and ethical standards of funeral directors and accountants higher than those of journalists while members of Congress and lobbyists are evaluated even lower?
- almost two out of three people believe the press is biased in reporting the news?
- 1996 was the first presidential election in which all the major candidates for president and Congress had Web sites?

- Barack Obama had twice as much favorable press as did John McCain during the 2008 presidential campaign?
- according to the nonpartisan Center for Media and Public Affairs, Fox News coverage of the 2008 presidential campaign was the most "fair and balanced"?

Is this any way to run a democratic election?

A free and fair press is essential to a democratic electoral process. In theory, the news media expand the information available and reach more people than would a campaign conducted by word of mouth, printed literature distributed by parties, or an event-driven campaign. Journalists provide a more objective presentation and analysis of that information than could be expected from self-interested candidates and parties. Reporters make it easier for the electorate to compare candidates running for office, to place the campaign in some historical and contemporary perspective, and to gain information they deem relevant to make an enlightened judgment. For all these reasons, press coverage of election campaigns is important, more so as the electorate has expanded and the number of news sources has dramatically increased.

In the course of covering elections, however, the news media become part of the story. They affect the campaign by the news they present and the manner in which they present it. They help focus the electoral agenda for the campaign, emphasize the qualifications of the candidates, and report on the positions they take on the issues as well as other statements they make. The news media analyze how the candidates are doing, how the public is reacting, and how the election may turn out. After the election is over, they explain who voted for whom and why. In addition, they indicate the impact the election is likely to have on public policy making and governance in the years ahead. The news media then become the watchdogs of that government. Both during the election and after it, these informational reporting and evaluative functions give the press enormous power.

To the extent that the information presented is accurate, comprehensive, relevant, and impartial, the electorate is well served. To the extent that the information is incomplete, inaccurate, incomprehensible, truncated, skewed, biased, or in any other way unfair, the electorate is shortchanged, and the democratic electoral process suffers. In short, the scope, content, and spin of the news can enhance or warp the public's vision, energize or turn off voters, facilitate or impede its electoral decisions, and provide realistic or unrealistic policy expectations of the newly elected government. All of this can and does affect attitudes toward politicians and government.

Has the United States been well served by the way the news media cover campaigns, assess candidates, monitor public opinion, and then explain election outcomes and the public policy that follows from them? To answer these questions, the chapter begins by examining the evolution of the press in American elections, with an emphasis on the changes in communications technology that have affected coverage in the last several decades. The second part of the chapter looks at the ways contemporary campaigns are communicated to voters and the impact of that communication on the electorate and the electoral process. The final section presents proposals for improving the scope and content of campaign communications, with the goal being a more informed and involved public.

THE EVOLUTION OF ELECTION NEWS

Newspapers were published in America long before the country gained its independence. They were never neutral observers. In fact, the first paper, *Publick Occurrences, Both Foreign and Domestick,* was banned after only one issue by the British for its "offensive content." Since that time, newspapers have taken part in the debates on the country's most critical political, economic, and social issues.

The early newspapers, sold by subscription and delivered by mail, were more like today's op-ed pages than papers that reported events. They were intended for the educated and businesses classes who were interested in public affairs. Most papers had a discernible political perspective that shaped the news they reported. These perspectives, written in the form of essays, debated contemporary issues such as independence and the ratification of the Constitution. It was in such papers that Madison, Hamilton, and Jay published their famous essays, known today as *The Federalist Papers,* in support of ratification.

The audience for and content of newspapers began to change during the 1830s, as the political parties began to expand their popular base. Technological improvements, a growth in literacy, and the movement toward greater public involvement in political affairs all contributed to the rise of the "penny press"—newspapers that sold for a penny and were profitable by virtue of their advertising and mass circulation. To sell more papers, news stories had to be entertaining and exciting. Electoral campaigns fit this mold better than most other news about politics, government, and public policy. As a consequence, campaigns have received extensive coverage through the years.

Technology has played its part. The invention of the telegraph helped make it possible for an emerging Washington press corps to communicate information about national political issues to the entire country. Other advances followed. The first radio station began operating in 1920, and radio remained the principal electronic news medium from the 1920s to the 1950s. The 1924 presidential election was the first to be reported on radio; the conventions, major speeches, and election returns were broadcast to a national listening audience. During the 1928 election, both major presidential candidates, Republican Herbert Hoover and Democrat Alfred E. Smith, spent campaign funds on radio advertising.

Television and the Broadcast News Networks

Television became a major source for news reporting in the 1950s. The number of television sets and the hours that people watched quickly grew. TV soon became the primary source of fast-breaking news and the primary communication vehicle for people to acquire their knowledge about the candidates and issues. In contrast, newspaper readership declined, particularly among the younger generations, and has continued to do so.

The primary source for televised news used to be the half-hour news broadcast on the three major networks, ABC, CBS, and NBC, during the early evening. The effect of television was felt as early as 1952, when Republican vice presidential candidate Richard Nixon denied allegations that he had obtained and used campaign gifts for himself and his family. The speech in which Nixon also vowed not to give up a dog named Checkers that had been given to the Nixon family by political supporters generated favorable public reaction and testified to the power of television if used effectively by candidates. Forty years later, Bill Clinton turned to television first to deny and then acknowledge accusations of extramarital affairs that threatened to derail his presidency. He later used that medium to repackage himself as a mainstream moderate, contrasting his public policy positions on health, education, and the environment with the more extreme views of the Republican Congress.

The marketing of candidates on television, through paid political advertising and newsworthy speeches and events, revolutionized the electoral process, particularly the strategy and tactics of campaigning. It has enabled candidates to craft their own images and to challenge those of their opponents. Another example of the power of television came during the four debates held in 1960 between the two major presidential candidates, Senator John F. Kennedy and Vice President Richard M. Nixon. In their first debate, the vice president's pallid appearance, darting eyes, and unrehearsed responses damaged his image; overall, the debates probably contributed to Kennedy's narrow election victory.

The growing importance of television affected the print media as well. Because television reported events at or close to the time they happened, newspapers and magazines had to supplement their coverage and commentary in order to provide an additional dimension to maintain a product that people would want to buy. One way they did so was to "find" news by investigating activities that on the surface might not have appeared newsworthy.

Cable news challenged the dominance of the broadcast networks beginning in the 1980s. Its 24-7 news cycle, begun by the Cable News Network (CNN) and later supplemented by MSNBC and Fox News, changed the way in which Americans got their news. The ability of cable to report developing stories as they happened rather than at scheduled times ultimately changed viewing habits. The broadening of programming options on cable as well as the competition among cable providers that lowered the monthly rates increased cable's share of the viewing audience from about 20 percent of American households in 1980 to 56 percent in 1990, 68 percent in 2000, and 72.4 percent in 2006.[1]

The broadcast networks responded by changing the content and reducing the length of their news stories. Their news got softer, "more sensational, more personality-centered, less time-bound, more practical, and more incident-based."[2] Broadcast media paid less attention to policy matters, political leadership, and major events and their consequences. In style, network news was redesigned to be captivating, current, and concise to compete more effectively with the hundreds of channels that cable and satellite companies offered and with the shorter attention spans and remote control devices never far from the hands of their viewers. The evening news shows became the functional equivalent of news and entertainment magazines rather than the leading providers of national news and analysis.

The major networks also cut back on their news staffs. During the 1990s, sizes of foreign bureaus were reduced or eliminated and less attention devoted to foreign policy matters until the terrorist attacks of September 11, 2001, and the subsequent U.S. military actions in Afghanistan and Iraq forced the major networks to increase their coverage of international events. However, most did not increase their staffs. Instead they hired independent journalists and bought the film clips that went with their stories. Here, too, technology played a role by reducing the costs and increasing the speed by which words and pictures could be transmitted around the world.

Local television stations increased their news coverage as well and gained a larger share of the market. One study of eleven regional markets during the 2004 presidential election found that almost two out of three local news shows contained at least one election story, half of which concerned the presidential race.[3]

The Impact of Cable News

The cable news networks now have the largest share of the news audience (46 percent). Of the three major cable news networks, CNN is watched by the most viewers (25 percent), followed closely by Fox (21 percent) and MSNBC (10 percent).[4] Only 24 percent of the population continues to cite the broadcast network news outlets (ABC, CBS, and NBC) as its principal source of election news, while another 13 percent mention local news as its most important source.[5]

Cable audiences are more partisan than the audience for the broadcast networks. Conservatives and Republicans prefer Fox News; liberal and Democrats turn to MSNBC and CNN.[6] These news networks, in turn, orient their spin to reflect the preferences of their viewing audience. They are part of the new niche journalism community.

The Internet and Beyond

The Internet has become the fastest-growing source for campaign and election news. Although television, both cable and broadcast, is still the medium to which most people turn, the Internet has quickly developed as both a supplementary and primary source (see Table 5.1). About 11 percent of the

TABLE 5.1   **Changing Sources of Campaign News, 1992–2008 (percentages)**

Question: How did you get most of your election news?

November	1992	1996	2000	2004	2008
Television	82	72	70	76	68
Newspapers	57	60	39	46	33
Radio	12	19	15	22	16
Magazines	9	11	4	6	3
Internet	n/a	3	11	21	36

Note: Numbers add to more than 100 percent because voters could list up to two primary sources.

Source: Pew Research Center for the People and the Press, "High Marks for the Campaign, A High Bar for Obama," November 13, 2008, www.people-press.org/report/471/high-bar-for-obama.

population reported the Internet to be its primary source of election news in 2000; four years later that percentage had risen to 21; in 2008, 36 percent indicated that the Internet was its primary source of campaign news.[7]

The Internet remains more popular for younger Americans than older ones (Table 5.2). According to Pew researchers:

> Nearly three times as many people ages 18 to 29 mention the Internet than mention newspapers as a main source of election news (49 percent vs. 17 percent). Nearly the opposite is true among those over age 50: some 22 percent rely on the Internet for election news while 39 percent look to newspapers. Compared with 2004, use of the Internet for election news has increased across all age groups.[8]

It is noteworthy that among eighteen- to twenty-nine-year-olds, television has also has lost ground to the Internet.[9] The demographic profile of Internet users has also changed. Users better reflect the general population today than they did one or two decades ago.

The reason that so many have turned to the Internet for news is that it has become user friendly, quick, and cheap; with almost all new sources maintaining free-access Web sites, the amount of information is enormous. Thus far, however, there is little evidence that the availability of this information has led to a more informed public. In fact, Pew reports that the most informed people use the Internet more than those who are less informed about electoral politics. If this trend continues, then the availability of more sites and

TABLE 5.2   **Demography of the Internet, 2008**

Characteristics	All adults	Internet users
Gender		
Male	49	50
Female	51	50
Age		
18–29	19	24
30–49	37	42
50–64	26	25
65+	17	8
Race/ethnicity		
White (non-Hispanic)	70	71
Black (non-Hispanic)	11	9
Hispanic	11	12
Education		
Less than high school	13	8
High school grad	36	32
Some college	23	27
College grad	27	34
Household income		
Less than $30,000	26	19
$30,000–$49,999	17	19
$50,000–$74,999	14	17
$75,000 or more	24	32
Geography		
Urban	30	29
Suburban	53	55
Rural	18	15

Source: Pew Research Center for the People and the Press, "The Internet's Role in Campaign 2008," Pew Internet and American Life Project, April 15, 2009, www.pewinternet.org/Reports/2009/6—The-Internets-Role-in-Campaign-2008.aspx?r=1.

more information on them may be expanding the knowledge gap between people who follow politics closely and those who do not.

In addition to widening the knowledge gap, other problems arise from the revolution in communications technology. Not only has the diversity of programs and Web sites increased, but so has the speed at which information travels. Rumors move so fast these days that the establishment press has had to relax its two-source verification rule, often giving unsubstantiated allegations as much attention as verifiable items. Coverage of a rumor or allegation lends credibility to it, clouding the line between fact and fiction.

To make matters worse from the candidates' perspectives, a credibility gap has also emerged: the news media no longer give politicians and public officials the benefit of doubt. The press regularly imputes political motives of the candidates when they make statements and take policy positions. In turn, candidates see the press as hostile and overly negative. In fact, they often point to that negativism when justifying their own attempts to put a favorable spin on the news.

THE ADEQUACY OF CONTEMPORARY CAMPAIGN COVERAGE

To what extent do the news media present information about elections fairly and accurately? To what extent do they skew the news toward the desires of their audience, presenting what they believe people want to know, not necessarily what they need to know to fulfill the informational needs of a democratic electoral process?

Journalistic Bias: Ideological or Professional?

In deciding what to report, the news media impose their bias. Some believe that it's an ideological bias. Conservatives and Republicans, in particular, see the national press as liberal, Democratic, and likely to favor candidates who share this political orientation. To support their contentions, these conservative critics often point to studies about the media that show the overwhelming number of national news reporters and correspondents to be Democratic, liberal, and from large metropolitan areas and to content analyses that show more favorable treatment of Democratic presidential candidates than Republican candidates.[10]

Others, however, point to the influence of the conservative corporate executives who oversee the communication empires of newspapers, radio stations, and television networks; to the corporate interests that advertise on these media and contribute to their profits; and to the editorials that reflect the conservative views of the owners, the publishers, and corporate advertisers.[11] They also note that news spin rarely coincides with electoral outcomes, suggesting that if the news media have biases, they are directed toward the underdog rather than the expected winner.

Most people see some political bias in the news. A majority believes that stories are often inaccurate (see Table 5.3).[12] Perceptions of bias vary with partisanship, with Republicans being more critical of the news media than independents who are more critical than Democrats.[13]

Whereas politicians and partisans perceive an ideological bias, academic observers believe that there is a more pronounced professional bias, one reflected in the definition of what is newsworthy. All events, activities, and

TABLE 5.3   Perceptions of Political Bias, 1989–2008

Responses	Aug. 1989	Jan. 2000	Jan. 2004	Jan. 2008
A great deal	25	32	30	31
A fair amount	51	37	35	31
Not too much	19	20	24	25
Not at all	3	6	9	9
Don't know / refused to answer	5	2	2	4

Source: Pew Research Center for the People and the Press, "Internet's Broader Role in Campaign 2008," January 11, 2008, http://people-press.org/report/384/internets-broader-role-in-camapign-2008.

statements during elections are not equally newsworthy. The criterion of audience interest is the principal one the press uses to determine the newsworthiness of an item or event. From the perspective of the press, if an item is new, surprising, exciting, different, dramatic, action oriented, or involving conflict, then it is more newsworthy than one that does not exhibit any of these characteristics. The first utterance is more newsworthy than the second one, the unexpected development more newsworthy than the predicted outcome, the misstatement more newsworthy than the standard speech, the contest more newsworthy than the substance of the issues, and controversy is usually deemed more newsworthy than consensus.

The media's orientation also extends to the format in which news is reported. It must be direct and, above all, simple. Positions are presented and contrasted as black or white; gray areas get less attention. The story usually has a single focus. There is a punch line or bottom line toward which the report is directed.

A Sound-Bite Mentality

The concepts of what is news and how news is reported create incentives for candidates to come up with new angles, new policies, and new events to galvanize public attention. It also encourages them to play it safe, not think out loud, and not take chances. Words, expressions, and ideas are pretested in focus groups to gauge the likely effect before candidates express them in public. To combat a press eager to highlight the critical and the unexpected, candidates stage their events, recruit their audiences, and try to engineer an enthusiastic response from them. They speak in sound bites designed to capture public attention and do so in an environment tailored to reinforce them. The size of the bite serves an additional need of the news media, particularly radio and television. It facilitates the compartmentalization of news, compressing it into proportions that the press believes the public can digest.

To the extent that the public gains its information about the campaign from these short, simple statements, the amount of knowledge and especially the depth of that knowledge suffer. Newspapers, particularly national ones such as the *New York Times, Christian Science Monitor,* and *Wall Street Journal* and comprehensive regional dailies such as the *Chicago Tribune, Los Angeles Times,* and *Washington Post,* provide more extensive coverage. But only a small portion of the electorate regularly reads these papers, much less focuses on election news in them, although people may access newspaper Web sites for individual stories. Nonetheless, the bulk of the electorate receives a snapshot, a partial and truncated piece of the campaign. Is it any wonder that people are poorly informed, that they retain so little of the news they see on television?

Interpretive Reporting

There's another problem with contemporary campaign coverage in the mass media: it is highly mediated. People today see and hear more from the correspondents reporting the news than from the candidates making it. S. Robert Lichter and his associates reported that the average campaign story on network evening news had correspondents and anchors on the air six times longer than the candidates.[14] In fact, the candidates are seen and heard only briefly (Table 5.4). The average length of a quotation from a candidate on the evening news since the 1988 presidential election has been less than ten seconds! Compare this with 42.3 seconds in 1968. Today, to communicate their messages themselves, candidates seek alternative channels such as talk radio, entertainment television, and the Internet.[15]

A major part of the media's interpretation of campaign news is the story line into which most campaign events are fitted. According to Thomas Patterson, a dominant story emerges and events within the campaign are explained in terms of it. In 1992 the story was the vulnerability of President George H. W. Bush, first revealed by Pat Buchanan's surprising showing against him in the early caucuses and primaries, then by the "conservative takeover" of the Republican National Convention, and, finally, by the president's weak showing in the general election. The character issues that Bush raised about his opponents, and his own plans for future policies, weren't nearly as newsworthy in that election. Patterson describes this particular story line as the "likely-loser scenario."[16] That story line also plagued Robert Dole in 1996 and John McCain in 2008. In its analysis of media coverage for the 2008 presidential election, the Project for Excellence in Journalism concluded:

> The story of the media coverage of the general election phase of this race, at least so far, is the snowball effect on John McCain. In the press, this race became substantially defined around the troubles that began for McCain in mid-September and the difficulties he had in trying to change the trajectory of the race in the weeks that followed. With a press corps heavily focused on horse race, and a candidate whose strategy was apparently thrown off by events, he has been unable to change that narrative.[17]

TABLE 5.4 **Election News Coverage, 1988–2008**

	1988	1992	1996	2000	2004	2008
Amount of coverage						
Number of stories	589	728	483	462	504	683
Minutes per day	1,116	1,400	788	805	1,007	1,606
Average number of stories per day	10.5	11.5	7.7	7.3	9	9.4
Average sound bite (seconds)	9.8	8.4	8.2	7.8	7.8	—
Focus of coverage (percentage of stories)						
Horse race	58%	58%	48%	71%	48%	55%
Policy issues	39%	32%	37%	40%	49%	31%
Tone of coverage (percentage with good press)						
Democratic nominee	31%	52%	50%	40%	59%	68%
Republican nominee	38%	29%	33%	37%	37%	33%

Note: Based on evaluations by nonpartisan sources in election stories on ABC, CBS, and NBC evening newscasts and the first half hour of Fox Network's *World News.*

Sources: Center for Media and Public Affairs, "Campaign 2004 Final: How TV News Covered the General Election," *Media Monitor* (November/December 2004): 5; "Election Watch: Campaign 2008 Final: How TV News Covered the General Election Campaign," *Media Monitor* 23 (Winter 2009), www.cmpa.com/pdf/media_monitor_jan_2009.pdf. Used by permission of the Center for Media and Public Affairs.

For Clinton, the story line, especially in 1996, was just the opposite. It was that of the "front-runner" who had a large lead and skillfully maneuvered to keep it. In this particular story, the press attributed Clinton's lead and inevitable success to a beneficial economic environment, superior resources, the perquisites of the presidency, and an extremely well-organized and well-run campaign.[18] The news media's depiction of Ronald Reagan's 1984 presidential campaign had been presented in a similar manner, providing yet another illustration of the media's use of the front-runner script.[19] Similarly, during 2008, Obama was depicted as a historic candidate during a historic period. His command of the issues, unifying and upbeat message, and the country's dire economic conditions were the major ingredients of the story that explains his successful presidential campaign.

Many people believe that members of the news media often let their personal preferences influence the way they report the news. Interpretive reporting contributes to the perception of media bias. It has made voters more wary and less trusting of television correspondents. According to a Gallup poll conducted in 2009, only 23 percent of respondents expressed a great deal or quite a lot of confidence in television news, and only 25 percent felt the same about newspapers compared with 34 and 33 percent, respectively, a decade earlier.[20]

Contributing to the news media's problems have been their revelations of their own errors, such as the acknowledgment by CBS News, prior to the 2004 election, that the documents its evening news presented as evidence of George W. Bush's questionable service in the Alabama National Guard were not authentic.

The speed at which information flies on the Internet and the increased competition to report a story first and to anticipate events before they happen have pressured the news media to relax their two-source rule,[21] go live to cover an event as it is happening, and report rumors as if they were true. The need to preempt media rivals has also led the press to rely increasingly on unnamed and unidentified sources for information. As a consequence, accuracy in reporting has suffered.

Pack Journalism

Despite the desire for breaking news and finding it through investigative reporting, the press corps operates more as a pack than as individuals looking for distinctive stories. They do so because they lack the personnel and resources (and perhaps the drive) to find new information on their own. As a consequence they follow the leader—newspapers, news networks, and wire services that have more resources, reliability, and reporters, such as the *New York Times, Wall Street Journal, Washington Post,* CNN, Fox News, and the Associated Press. This coverage tends to magnify and extend stories that are already in the news and to minimize others that do not make the mainstream media.

A study by the Project for Excellence in Journalism describes the echo effect:

> . . . the press first offers a stenographic account of candidate rhetoric and behavior, while also on the watch for misstatements and gaffes. Then, in a secondary reaction, it measures the political impact of what it has reported. This is magnified in particular during presidential races by the prevalence of polling and especially daily tracking. While this echo effect exists in all press coverage, it is far more intense in presidential elections, with the explosion of daily tracking polls, state polls, poll aggregation sites and the 24-hour cable debate over their implications. Even coverage of the candidate's policy positions and rhetoric, our reading of these stories suggest, was tied to horse race and took on its cast.[22]

The ability of the pack to influence public consumption of information by its coverage forces candidates to anticipate and respond to news media coverage. Political campaigns orchestrate and compartmentalize their newsworthy activities and statements into morsels that they hope the press will devour and then regurgitate. They do so by researching and then leaking negative information about their opponent, faxing or texting information to select reporters, staging media events, and crafting speeches with the sound bites they want included in the article. They also use advertising as a ploy to get the media's attention as well as to reinforce or challenge perceptions that may have been created by news stories. Political advertising is not subject to the same standards for truthfulness and accuracy as is commercial advertising (see Chapter 8).

All of this information from the press and candidates swirls about during the election campaign and can confuse as well as inform voters. It's almost as if three interrelated campaigns were going on at once. In one, the candidates are appealing directly to the electorate for votes. In another, they're attempting to win the media campaign by controlling the agenda, spinning their news, leaking unfavorable stories about their opponents, and reacting quickly to controversies highlighted in the news media about themselves and their supporters. The third campaign is the one the media report to the electorate. It consists of entertaining news that commands the attention of their consumers rather than news intended primarily to educate the polity in the exercise of its civic responsibilities. Table 5.4 summarizes these aspects of election news coverage in the six most recent presidential elections.

The Election Game

The story about the election is almost always reported as if it were a sporting event. The candidates are the players, and their moves (words, activities, and images) are usually described as strategic and tactical devices to achieve their principal goal of winning the election. Even their policy positions are evaluated within this game motif and are often described as calculated attempts to appeal to certain political constituencies.

The metaphor used most frequently is that of the horse race. A race—especially if it is close and if the result isn't readily predictable—generates excitement. Excitement holds interest, which sells newspapers and magazines and increases the size of radio and television audiences. Surprise, drama, and human-interest stories do the same. When these elements are present, elections get more coverage than when they are not.

In addition to conveying excitement and stimulating public interest, there is another reason why the media use the game format. It lends an aura of objectivity to reporting. It encourages the press to present quantitative data on the public's reaction to the campaign. Public opinion surveys, reported as news, are usually the dominant news item during the primaries and caucuses and share the spotlight with other campaign-related events during the general election.

Emphasizing the horse race is not a new phenomenon, but it often occurs at the expense of the policy debate. Table 5.4 indicates the amount of time given on the evening news to horse race, policy, and other campaign issues in the last six presidential elections. With the war in Iraq as the principal focus of the 2004 presidential campaign, policy issues received barely more attention than did the horse race; in 2008, although the economy was the principal issue of the campaign and Obama had a sizable lead in the polls beginning in mid-September, there were still more election stories about the race, the strategy and tactics of the candidates, and the competitive nature of the debates than about the range of policy issues that the candidates discussed and their Web sites detailed.

A study conducted by the Project for Excellence in Journalism on the 2008 presidential campaign reached similar conclusions about the focus of media attention:

> Horse race coverage predominated. Such accounts, which principally involved tactics, strategy, and polling, accounted for 53% of all the coverage. Closely related political matters, such as examination of advertising, fund-raising and political endorsements, which weren't quite so focused on who was ahead or behind, made up another 10%. Policy, the second largest category of coverage, accounted for 20%. Coverage of the personal life of candidates filled 5% and examination of public records of the candidates made up 5%.[23]

What's the consequence of this type of coverage on the electorate? Simply put, it results in people's remembering less about the policy issues and about the candidates' programs for dealing with them. Although the candidates' positions get attention in the news media, the costs and consequences of their proposed solutions don't get nearly as much focus. A few national newspapers and magazines do provide this type of coverage, and occasionally the major broadcast networks have a special program on a particularly vexing economic or social issue, but for most people it is the horse race, the candidates themselves, and their strategies and tactics that are highlighted.

The Bad-News Campaign

Campaign news coverage also tends to be highly critical. Of course, criticism per se isn't harmful to a democratic electoral process; in fact, it's a necessary part of that process. But an overemphasis on the negative, particularly on negative personal and character issues, can disillusion voters, decrease turnout, and render the election a contest among lesser evils.[24]

Why all the negativism? Are the candidates less qualified now than they were in the past? Most scholarly observers don't think so. They offer three principal reasons for the contemporary press's negativism: underlying skepticism about the motives and interests of politicians and elected officials; increasing emphasis on character issues combined with scrutiny of private behavior; and increased competition with tabloid journalism in the news and entertainment marketplace.

The Vietnam War and the Watergate scandal ushered in an era of investigative journalism in which the media adopted an attitude of distrust and disbelief in their coverage of politics and government. Public officials and candidates for office were no longer taken at their word, no longer given the benefit of doubt. The press assumed that the statements and actions of those in power or vying for office were self-interested and not necessarily in the public interest, and that it was the job of the media to reveal hidden motives, strategies, and goals. In other words, it was their responsibility to present the other side.

Campaign coverage became more candidate centered as investigative journalism began to focus more on the people seeking office than on their partisan connection. Pretty soon the line between public and private was obliterated, with the press trumpeting the importance of character as its rationale for reporting what used to be considered private (and therefore not reportable) behavior.

With the tabloid press eager to highlight the personal foibles and relationships of prominent people, even if only rumored, the mainstream press found itself pressured to follow suit. They often use a report in the tabloid media, a news conference, or an unsubstantiated investigative report as the pretext for presenting this type of information as news. Thus the allegations of Gennifer Flowers that she was Bill Clinton's lover for eleven years became front-page news during the 1992 Democratic nomination, as did facsimiles of memos questioning George W. Bush's service in the Alabama National Guard and ads in 2004 disputing John Kerry's heroism in the Vietnam War.

Opposition research by campaigns regularly stimulates and supplements this type of media coverage. As previously mentioned, leaks have become a common and accepted way to alert the press to negative facts and rumors about one's opponents. Because the negative often is surprising and unexpected, this type of news feeds into the media's addiction to information that grabs their audience.

From the candidates' perspective, the bad news is magnified by the fact that they don't get the opportunity to respond in kind, to explain their side of the story in anywhere near the detail as the charges made against them. Moreover, if the charges prove to be inaccurate, any corrections made by the press don't get nearly the amount of coverage as the story that prompted them.

As a result, candidates are left with little alternative but to defend themselves against even the most reckless charges, thereby giving even more attention to the charges. Not only must candidates respond quickly to allegations against them so as not to allow an unfavorable image to become part of the public's perception, but they have an incentive to get dirt on their opponents as well. To make matters worse, candidates also have an incentive to reinforce negative personal news reported by the press by running negative personal advertising.

A number of unfortunate consequences for a democratic electoral process follows from this type of campaign behavior and media coverage. The electorate gets a jaundiced view of the campaign. It becomes more of a personal contest between two or more gladiators than an issue-oriented policy debate or a campaign between two parties with opposing philosophies and goals. The news is presented by television anchors, correspondents, and star newspaper reporters and not by the candidates themselves. It emphasizes the bad over the good.

How did coverage of the 2008 election fare? Was it more thorough, more objective, and more informative than previous elections? According to the Project for Excellence in Journalism, it was not. The coverage in the 2008 election was similar to that of past campaigns.[25] The principal presidential candidates received about the same amount of coverage during the general election, but the stories of the campaign were more favorable to Obama than to McCain.

Why did Obama receive better coverage? A study by the nonpartisan Project for Excellence in Journalism concluded that it was due to the news media's horse-race emphasis and the fact that Obama was in the lead for most of the general election campaign:

> . . . winning in politics begat winning coverage, thanks in part to the relentless tendency of the press to frame its coverage of national elections as running narratives about the relative position of the candidates in the polls and internal tactical maneuvering to alter those positions. Obama's coverage was negative in tone when he was dropping in the polls, and became positive when he began to rise, and it was just so for McCain as well. Nor are these numbers different than what we have seen before. Obama's numbers are similar to what we saw for John Kerry four years ago as he began rising in the polls, and McCain's numbers are almost identical to what we saw eight years ago for Democrat Al Gore.[26]

Obama's more favorable coverage may also be a product of his newness, the first African American to be nominated by a major party, his skillful campaign that utilized new methods of communication, and his hopeful message of policy and political change. Newness and change are more newsworthy than traditional candidates running traditional campaigns and making traditional promises. In short, the press might have also viewed Obama as a more interesting candidate and likely to be a more interesting president.

The Project for Excellence in Journalism saw two trends in the 2008 presidential election news coverage:

> The first is the focus on tactics and strategy. The candidate who was perceived to be winning this year got better coverage. We have seen that pattern before. In 2000, our research saw George Bush receiving more positive coverage than Gore. In 2004, our studies of a narrower time frame saw Kerry enjoying better coverage, as polls perceived his closing the gap on Bush.

The second phenomenon is an almost instantaneous reinforcing and echoing effect of the press. Presidential elections are now so heavily polled, with various daily tracks and compilations of state-by-state polls, that every campaign event is almost instantly measured for its political impact and that in turn is immediately analyzed by the political press. Each event has in a sense three echoes. The event is covered. The effect is measured. And the reaction to that measurement by the campaigns is then examined and covered.[27]

PUBLIC CYNICISM ABOUT THE MEDIA

Not only does the news media's coverage of campaigns focus on the contest and the contestants rather than on the consequences of their policies, not only does it lessen respect for the candidates, not only does it impute their motives, but it also contributes to cynicism about the press itself.

In theory, there is broad support for a free press. Although many people may not understand the protections that the First Amendment provides media in the United States today, they do believe that newspapers, radio, television, and news magazines are necessary for a democratic society. However, the numbers are not overwhelming. In a survey published in June 2007 by the Pew Research Center for the People and the Press, 44 percent agreed with the statement that the press protects democracy, but 36 percent did not.[28] A survey conducted by the Annenberg Public Policy Center found that most people also believe that a government may restrict the right of the press to report a story, a position to which most journalists do not subscribe.[29]

Despite the support for a free press, the desire to keep up with events, and the dependence on the media for election news, criticism of how the media do their job has been growing. Surveys conducted by the Gallup organization indicate that a substantially smaller proportion of the population has a great deal or a fair amount of confidence in the press today (43 percent) than in 1972 (68 percent) and 2000 (51 percent).[30] Put simply, people today find the press less believable, less accurate, and more biased than they did in the past.

The public's ambivalence toward the news media; the people's desire for gossip, scandal, and conflict; and their criticism of the press for providing and emphasizing this type of information create a situation in which the marketplace dictates the outcome. The mass media give their audience what they believe their audience wants. In this sense they are responding to their consumers' demands.

The interests of the public and the orientation of a profit-oriented media toward satisfying these often conflicting needs pose a real dilemma for a democratic society.

The Dumbing of the Electorate: Does It Matter?

The time frame for the first question about the level of information that the general public possesses is relatively short if answered with survey data. National polls of public knowledge, attitudes, and opinions were not conducted with any regularity until after World War II. Moreover, to make comparisons, responses to similar survey questions have to be analyzed. Finally, the vast majority of public affairs polls ask attitude and opinion questions rather than informational ones. In fact, information is frequently provided in the question or statement so that people can respond intelligently.

In the few polls that do ask informational questions, the evidence of campaign learning is modest at best. In July 2008, a Pew survey found that a majority of people said that they had little knowledge of the candidates' foreign policy positions but that they knew a bit more about their domestic policy positions.[31] Although Americans said that they followed the 2008 presidential campaign more closely than they followed previous campaigns, the Annenberg Public Policy Center reported on September 26, 2008, that many people were still not able to identify the major candidates' stands on a variety of issues from health care to free trade to the closing of the U.S. military detention facility at Guantánamo Bay in Cuba.[32] In a later survey released on October 29, 2008, the Center reported, "From September to October, we detected a few increases in learning on topics such as mandatory health insurance for children and elimination of the Bush tax cuts for people above a certain income level, but those increases were small."[33] Basic knowledge of the political system was also weak.[34]

In short, campaign news coverage, political advertising, and coverage of such events as conventions and debates contribute to the learning process,[35] but how much people really learn is unclear. The critical question is whether they know enough to make an enlightened judgment on election day. Most people believe that they do, as indicated in Table 5.5.

TABLE 5.5	**Voters' Perceptions of Information Adequacy, 1988–2008 (percentages)**					
Perception	1988	1992	1996	2000	2004	2008
Learned enough to make an informed choice	59	77	75	83	86	85
Did not learn enough from the campaign	39	20	23	15	13	14
Don't know/refused	2	3	2	2	2	1

Sources: Pew Research Center for the People and the Press, "Voters Like Campaign 2004, but Too Much 'Mud-Slinging'," November 11, 2004; Pew Research Center for the People and the Press, "High Marks for the Campaign, a High Bar for Obama: Republicans Want More Conservative Direction for GOP," November 13, 2008, http://people-press.org/report/471/high-bar-for-obama.

Information and Democracy: Three Views

How much public knowledge and activity are necessary to maintain the health and vitality of a democratic society? There are several schools of thought.

Those who subscribe to the **elitist model** of democracy believe that as long as the leadership is informed, involved, and responsible to the people through the electoral process, the political system can function properly. This minimalist theory of public involvement maintains that democratic criteria are satisfied if the citizenry has the opportunity to participate in elections and enough basic information to do so. Citizens need to be able to differentiate among the candidates and their principal policy positions, factor in their own perceptions of reality, and make voting decisions. But not everyone has to be informed and participate in civic affairs for the system to work.

The **pluralist model** sees the system as democratic if it permits people to pursue their interests within the political arena. Elections are one of the political processes in which they can do so, but not the only one. Public demonstrations, letter-writing campaigns, e-mails, texting, and personal contacts are other means by which those outside of government can influence those in it. Again, the burden of being informed and involved rests primarily on the group leadership, on those in and out of power; the requirement for the populace is that its interests can be discerned, expressed, and pursued.

In both the elitist and the pluralistic models, the process by which people express their views is the main criterion for claiming that the system is democratic. The **popular,** or **plebiscitary, model** demands more. It requires a higher level of public involvement in politics and government. Within the electoral arena, this translates into more public debate, more interaction between the candidates and the electorate, and more people voting.

Those who adopt this perspective see the decline in public trust and confidence in politics and government as dangerous because it can lead to a concentration of power in the hands of a few. It also can reduce support for governmental decisions and for the people who make them and weaken the legitimacy of the rules and processes of the political system. One sign of alienation would be the growth of organized, armed vigilantes or militias, those who see it as their mission to take the law into their own hands. Another would be an increase in civil disobedience. A third might be the failure of a significant portion of the population to participate in elections and to vote.

It is difficult to answer the question of how informed and involved a citizenry must be to maintain a democratic political system. But there is little doubt that the more information, involvement, and active support the general population gives to the candidates who run for office, the more attention they will pay to the party platforms on which those candidates run, to their qualifications for office, and their performance in it.

Of course, people don't get all their information about campaigns from the news media. Candidate advertisements are another source of information, as are personal contacts and experience, particularly when those experiences reinforce or refute the claims candidates make. News coverage, however, is still a very important component of the process of gathering sufficient information to make an informed voting decision—hence the issue addressed in the last part of this chapter: how to better educate the public about the campaign through the mass media.

WHAT CAN BE DONE?

Criticizing contemporary press coverage of elections is much easier than making constructive suggestions for changing that coverage. The electorate may be getting what it wants but not necessarily what it needs. It is all well and good to berate the news media for not presenting a detailed discussion of the issues, but what good would it do to present such a discussion if the public was not interested in it, did not follow it, or was turned off by it? Besides, there is plenty of detailed and easily accessible information about the candidates and their campaigns, the parties and their platforms, and the voters and their interests and desires. And that information is readily available in national newspapers and magazines; on public radio and television; and on the Web sites of candidates, parties, nonparty groups, and the news media.

We can wring our hands and bemoan the fact that most people don't regularly consult these sources. We can say that they should, but we certainly aren't ready to reinstitute literacy tests as a condition for voting. We can blame this state of affairs on the failure of civic education in the schools, a claim that probably has some merit, but shaking our heads sadly about underinformed, uninvolved, generally apathetic citizens won't change the situation, although it might enable some people to rationalize it more satisfactorily.

We can blame the problem on the news media, as Thomas Patterson does. Patterson believes that those who determine media markets have made a wrong-headed assumption that people interested in news want an endless diet of soft, tabloid-oriented pabulum to consume. Not so, he says. In a study of the news preferences of television audiences, he found hard news to be more appealing to more people than soft news. Moreover, he also discovered that consumers of hard news were less tolerant of soft news than consumers of soft news were of hard news.[36] Patterson concludes that in their effort to compete with the increasing variety and number of news-entertainment shows, the national news networks have done themselves and our democracy a disservice by increasing their emphasis on soft news, gossip, and celebrities.[37] So the question becomes what can be done to change contemporary media coverage of elections.

Redefine Election News

One suggestion is to induce those who control the scope and methods of election news coverage to change their definition of news, their standards for reporting it, and their game-oriented emphasis. A task force on campaign reform has urged such an approach. The task force suggests that the press "use the campaign controversies as spring boards for reporting on the real substance of politics and political careers, rather than treating them as self-contained episodes."[38] Similarly, instead of entertaining horse-race stories that report polls of who is ahead and by how much, the task force recommends more analysis of why different groups seem to be supporting different candidates; more in-depth reporting, be it on character or substantive policy concerns; and more emphasis on the big issues that transcend day-to-day events. The report also makes the observation that election news could be more repetitive, that news does not always have to be new, and that the test for including information should be the level of public knowledge on a subject, not the level of the press's knowledge about it.[39] Too often the catalyst for a story is the desire to scoop other journalists for something new and different rather than the salience of the issue to the voters and the country.

Thomas Patterson reaches much the same conclusion when he argues that the hard-news component must be strengthened if people are to have the information they need to make an informed judgment when voting. "What is good for democracy is also good for the press," he writes.[40]

These are excellent suggestions, but they require the news media to change their journalistic orientation. Such changes tend to come slowly, if at all, and they are usually dictated by the economics of the marketplace, not by politics. Citizens could vote for these reforms with their television remotes and radio dials by tuning in to news programs that provide more in-depth, policy-oriented coverage, such as public radio and television, two media outlets whose audiences have increased during the past two decades.[41] The bottom line is that without a massive, negative reaction to contemporary election coverage or a massive public relations campaign like those for eating healthy foods, refraining from smoking, or not drinking and driving, people are unlikely to change their reading, listening, and viewing habits quickly or easily.

Shorten the Campaign

A different type of suggestion, proposed by Thomas Patterson several years ago in his book *Out of Order,* was to shorten election campaigns, particularly the long and arduous nomination contests that now consume more time than the general election.[42] A more compact campaign, he believes, would of necessity focus the news media on the more important issues, cut down their interpretations and negativity, and force the political parties to play a greater role in communicating with the voters.[43] But it also would provide less time for an inattentive public to learn about the candidates and issues.

Moreover, national legislation would probably be required to impose the time period in which campaigning could occur, thereby increasing even more the regulatory role of the federal government in elections and possibly conflicting with the free speech protections of the First Amendment and the authority of the states to conduct elections for federal officials. Unless campaign finance laws were changed, candidates would still have to raise considerable sums of money and do so before the official campaign began. How would they obtain money without campaigning? If candidates were forbidden to raise early money, and if the current laws remained in place, incumbents and wealthy candidates would be even more advantaged than they are today. Besides, what guarantee would there be that the news media would become any less interpretive and negative?

Communicate More Directly With Voters

Another recommendation, made in some campaign finance proposals as well as by several bipartisan groups and commissions, is to conduct more of the campaign spontaneously and directly though the mass media. That could be done by extending the number of debates among the candidates, as well as by providing them with free broadcast time. Most European democracies feature debates among the principal candidates or party leaders, and some require on-air time to be provided to the parties. But most of these countries also operate government-controlled networks on which to provide such time; the United States does not.

If these suggestions were implemented in the United States, they might reduce but not eliminate the press's role as mediator between the candidates and the electorate. Depending on the amount of free time to which candidates were entitled, these changes would give those running for office greater opportunity to address the issues in their own words. Candidates and parties also would exercise more control over the agenda of the campaign.

Debates are useful for several reasons. They enable the public to see, compare, and evaluate candidates in the same setting, at the same time, and on the basis of the same criteria: their knowledge of the problems, their priorities and issue positions, and their communicative skills. Debates attract relatively large audiences, larger than most other political events. They allow candidates to speak in their own words uninterrupted for a specified time to which the participants have agreed. Coincidentally, certain debate formats reduce the press's role as intermediary.[44]

Not all candidates benefit equally from debates. Front-runners, particularly incumbents, see little advantage in debating their challengers; when they do, they are usually able to dictate the timing and format of the debate to their perceived advantage. Most candidates play it safe, anticipating their opponents' arguments and rehearsing lines in advance. Spontaneity is minimized. As the campaign progresses, candidates begin to sound like their ads.

Nor do the parties gain much from debates held during the nomination phase. Candidates usually try to distinguish themselves from one another rather than indicate what good partisans they are and with what party policy positions they concur. Moreover, nomination debates are rarely carried on the major broadcast networks, although they may be aired on local affiliates in the region or state in which the primary is to occur. The cable networks may cover some of them, and C-SPAN usually does, but the audience is quite small. The greater the number of debates—there were 47 during the 2007–2008 nomination cycle, 21 among the Republicans and 26 among the Democrats—the smaller the television audience tends to be.

Moreover, during the early stages of the nomination quest, there are usually many candidates, particularly if an incumbent is not seeking renomination. A debate involving more than three or four people is not usually a debate but simply an opportunity for the participants to distinguish themselves, declare their positions, and try to project a presidential image. In-depth discussions are precluded by multiple candidates and limited time. Not much learning occurs unless a candidate states a position that is unpopular with that candidate's partisan supporters, such as Rudolph Giuliani's position on same-sex unions or Ron Paul's opposition to the war in Iraq, makes a mistake, or says or acts in an inappropriate way.

At the presidential level in the general election, the audience is larger (see Table 5.6). But the availability of many other entertainment shows, including competition with the baseball playoffs and World Series, reduces the size of the viewing audience and the duration of time people watch.[45] Thus, even if the debates were more easily available on television, it is likely that once their aura wore off, the principal audience would probably be composed of strong partisans who root for their candidate and inadvertent viewers who watch for a few minutes and then move on to other channels.

Until 2004, there was a decline in the proportion of the viewing audience that watched the presidential election debates since they started being held regularly in 1976. Political polarization and the war in Iraq renewed interest in the debates in 2004, and that interest continued into 2008. Table 5.6 shows the estimated debate audience in terms of numbers of voters.

There are other problems with having debates as the principal vehicle through which the candidates communicate with voters. Debates reward performance skills. They benefit telegenic candidates who are well prepared, well coached, and comfortable with television, essentially those who can give quick and catchy responses to the questions of moderators or the comments of their opponents. Those who take longer to make a point, who agonize over the complexities of issues, who don't communicate easily or quickly in short sound bites may be disadvantaged. Are debate skills important for elected officials? Should they be a major factor potentially affecting the election outcome?[46]

A shorter campaign combined with a required debate format could reduce the news media's role although, if the past is any indication, the press would still analyze the debates, solicit and report public reactions, and declare winners and losers. Would voters benefit from this arrangement? Would they gain and retain more objective information about the candidates, their positions, and their intellectual, communicative, and political skills? Would they be better able to make considered judgments in the voting booth?

TABLE 5.6　**Presidential Debates: Audience Size, 1976–2008**

Year	Candidates	Networks	Dates	Total viewers (millions)
1976	Carter-Ford	ABC, CBS, NBC	10/22	62.7
			10/6	63.9
			9/23	69.7
1980	Carter-Reagan	ABC, CBS, NBC	10/28	80.6
1984	Mondale-Reagan	ABC, CBS, NBC	10/21	67.3
			10/7	65.1
1988	Dukakis-Bush	ABC, CBS, NBC	10/13	67.3
			9/25	65.1
1992	Clinton-Bush-Perot	ABC, CBS, NBC, CNN	10/19	66.9
			10/15	69.9
			10/11	62.4
1996	Clinton-Dole	ABC, CBS, FOX, NBC, CNN	10/16	36.3
			10/6	46.1
2000	Gore-Bush	ABC, CBS, FOX, NBC, CNN, FOX NEWS, MSNBC	10/17	37.7
			10/11	37.5
			10/3	46.6
2004	Bush-Kerry	ABC, CBS, FOX, NBC, CNN, FOX NEWS, MSNBC	10/13	51.1
			10/8	46.7
			9/30	62.4
2008[a]	Obama-McCain	ABC, CBS, FOX, NBC, CNN, FOX NEWS, MSNBC	10/15	56.6
			10/7	63.2
			9/26	52.4

[a]More people usually watch the debates between the presidential candidates than watch the vice presidential debates. Not so in 2008 when the Biden-Palin debate drew an audience of 69.9 million.

Source: Commission on Presidential Debates, "Debates History," www.debates.org/pages/history .html.

However these questions are answered, the candidates and their handlers would not be satisfied with a debate format alone. They want time to communicate their message without interruption and criticism, and they wish to do it in a setting that enhances their image and message.[47] And the Constitution protects their right to do so, much as it protects the reporters' right to cover the election as they see fit.

Occasionally some candidates have been given a little free time by a major cable or broadcast network. The limited time and partisan nature of the presentation normally attracts a small audience composed primarily of loyal supporters. These appearances have produced little discernible impact on public knowledge and voter decision making.[48]

Nonetheless, various free-time proposals have been advanced—from keeping the current voluntary system to requiring the networks to provide a certain amount of time to meet their public interest obligations. Naturally, the major corporations that control the communications industry oppose a free-time requirement imposed on them by government, particularly one that obligates them to provide airtime during prime time. They fear that they would lose money. They point to the large number of candidates for national office who would want to avail themselves of free time on television. Could minor party candidates be excluded? Who would decide? And how could the free time be monitored?

Although most candidates would probably use free time were it made available to them, it is unlikely that when doing so they would forgo other forms of communication, such as political advertising, or even deviate very much from the message of their ads. So would more free time really be more of the same political "propaganda," little more than advertising in another form?

SUMMARY: NEWS MEDIA DILEMMAS IN A NUTSHELL

The press is a critical link between the candidates and the electorate. Since the 1830s, the mass media—first newspapers, then radio and television, and now the Internet—have brought campaigns to the voters. Over the years the news media have evolved from a local to a national press, from individual ownership to newspaper chains, from print to radio to television, from broadcast to cable and satellite to the Internet, and from once-a-day reporting to constant and instantaneous news. Not only have the media become diverse, but they have also become omnipresent. If these changes had contributed to a more attentive, informed, and involved electorate, then the democracy would have been well served, but, alas, they have not.

The scope, content, and format of the election news that is reported is not as informative as it needs to be. A journalistic orientation toward making the election news as captivating as possible (in light of greater competition) has resulted in media coverage that lacks substance. The emphasis is on newness, controversy, and drama rather than on partisan and policy debates. The coverage has become more compartmentalized, more interpretive, and, with the advent of investigative reporting, more negative. The candidates are presented as players in an unfolding drama. The campaign story is told with sports metaphors and analogies, is strewn with juicy personality tidbits, and features the contending forces, each trying to manipulate the electorate to its advantage.

Coverage affects the campaign. It forces the candidates to orchestrate their activities for television with irresistible sound bites in their speeches, engaging pictures and personalities at their events, and well-known talking heads to spin their messages. It also forces them to have war rooms to respond quickly and decisively to any attack or allegation against them.

The public is informed primarily by this coverage. From the media's perspective, it is what their audience desires, although Thomas Patterson's research indicates that the news media may be wrong about this marketing judgment. From the perspective of democratic theory, it isn't enough of what an informed electorate needs in order to make meaningful decisions when it votes. The public, too, is critical of news coverage yet continues to consume it and claim that it has sufficient knowledge to render intelligent judgments when voting. But what good would it do to present more of the substantive policy debate if people were turned off by it and tuned it out? How can the electorate be energized and people made more positive about the electoral process without government regulating the form and content of news coverage?

Suggestions have been made to shorten the campaign and facilitate more direct communication between the candidates and voters with more debates and free airtime. Whether these could or should be imposed on profit-making media and, if so, whether they would provide more of the substantive debate that is presently lacking is unclear.

Now It's Your Turn

Discussion Questions

1. What is the connection between public interest in politics and news about politics?
2. How does journalistic bias affect the scope and content of information that people learn about elections?
3. Is sufficient information available for the electorate to make informed judgments when it votes? If not, who's at fault: the news media, the candidates, or their parties? If so, what's the problem? Does it lie with the news media or the electorate, and how can it be fixed?
4. Should government exercise more control over the scope and content of campaign coverage?
5. What inducements might encourage the news media to provide more substantive policy information about contemporary election issues and more in-depth studies of the qualifications of those who seek elective office?
6. Can campaigns for federal office be made less dependent on media coverage? Should they be?
7. Do you think that the press exercises too much influence on people's judgments and election outcomes?

Topics for Debate

Challenge or defend the following statements:

1. A free press cannot be a fair and objective press.
2. If voters lack the information they need to make an informed voting decision today, it's their own fault.
3. A democratic electoral process requires the electorate to be opinionated but not necessarily informed.
4. Government should require the principal broadcast and cable news networks to give all candidates for federal office free and adequate airtime.
5. The private behavior of candidates is relevant to their public performance in office and should continue to be reported as election news.
6. The news media have a liberal ideological bias that has been evident during the most recent presidential elections.
7. The news media have an obligation to report substantive policy debate in depth, whether or not the people are interested in that debate.

Exercises

1. A major television network asks for your advice on how to improve its campaign coverage of the next election. The network would like you to prepare a memo with three goals in mind: meeting the network's public responsibility to inform voters, satisfying the interests of the viewing audience, and gaining audience ratings that are higher than its competitors' ratings. Draft the memo. In your analysis, indicate the following:
   a. the aspects of the campaign that you would cover and the proportion of coverage you would give to each,
   b. the attention to be given to third-party and independent candidates versus major-party candidates, to national versus local coverage, and to primaries versus the general election,
   c. the ways in which the media should cover the campaign to maximize their ratings and perform their public service.
   In addition, the network would like to know whether it should:
   - relax its two-source verification rule in the interest of competition;
   - air rumors and allegations about personal behavior if they appear credible;
   - include in the candidates' personality profiles information about their physical and mental health; and
   - give attention to candidate misstatements, inconsistencies, and off-color remarks.

2. Critique the news coverage of a current election campaign on one of the twenty-four-hour news networks, on public television, and on one of the broadcast networks on the basis of its adequacy, fairness, and information quality. In your critique, indicate the following:

a. what you consider to be the most important issues of the campaign and the scope and emphasis given to each,
b. whether the reporting was objective and the analysis fair and helpful,
c. whether the candidates and parties were treated equally, and
d. which medium provided the best coverage from the perspective of a democratic electoral process.

On the basis of the individual coverage provided, do you think voters would have enough accurate information to make informed voting decisions?

INTERNET RESOURCES

- Annenberg Public Policy Center: www.annenbergpublicpolicycenter.org
  Conducts studies on the media, which it makes available on this Web site; part of the Annenberg School for Communication of the University of Pennsylvania.
- Center for Media and Public Affairs: www.cmpa.com
  Evaluates the amount and spin of the major broadcast networks' coverage of the news; associated with George Mason University.
- Commission on Presidential Debates: www.debates.org
  Dedicated to the sponsorship, production, and archiving of presidential debates; nonpartisan and nonprofit organization.
- Freedom Forum: www.freedomforum.org
  Provides information on media issues, particularly as they relate to the First Amendment; is sponsored by the Gannett Foundation and links to other Gannett groups, Newseum, and Press Watch, which also contain useful information on coverage of elections.
- Newspaperlinks.com: www.newspaperlinks.com
  Provides links to the online editions of local newspapers across the country through NewsVoyager site.
- Politics Online: www.politicsonline.com
  Good source for presidential campaigning on the Internet.
- Project for Excellence in Journalism: www.journalism.org
  Excellent source for an ongoing content analysis of media coverage of campaigns as well as an evaluation of that coverage
- Other media sources with campaign Web sites:
  ABC News Politics: http://abcnews.com
  Associated Press: www.ap.org/
  CBS News: www.cbsnews.com
  CNN: http://cnn.com
  C-SPAN: www.cspan.org
  Fox News: http://foxnews.com
  Los Angeles Times: http://latimes.com

NBC News: www.msnbc.com
New York Times: www.nytimes.com
USA Today: www.usatoday.com
Washington Post: http://washingtonpost.com

SELECTED READINGS

Ansolabehere, Stephen, and Shanto Iyengar. *Going Negative: How Political Advertisements Shrink and Polarize the Electorate.* New York: Free Press, 1995.

Baum, Matthew A., and Samuel Kernell. "Has Cable Ended the Golden Age of Presidential Television?" *American Political Science Review* 93 (1999): 99–111.

Cappella, Joseph N., and Kathleen Hall Jamieson. *Spiral of Cynicism: The Press and the Public Good.* New York: Oxford University Press, 1997.

Davis, Richard, and Diana Owen. *New Media and American Politics.* New York: Oxford University Press, 1998.

Denton, Robert E., Jr. *The 2004 Presidential Campaign: A Communication Perspective.* Lanham, Md.: Rowman and Littlefield, 2005.

Druckman, James N. "The Power of Television Images: The First Kennedy-Nixon Debate Revisited." *Journal of Politics* 65 (2003): 559–571.

Farnsworth, Stephen J., and S. Robert Lichter. *The Nightly News Nightmare: Network News Coverage of U.S. Presidential Elections, 1988–2004.* Lanham, Md.: Rowman and Littlefield, 2005.

Graber, Doris A. *Mass Media and American Politics,* 8th ed. Washington, D.C.: CQ Press, 2009.

Iyengar, Shanto, and Donald Kinder. *News That Matters: Television and American Opinion.* Chicago: University of Chicago Press, 1987.

Iyengar, Shanto, Helmut Norpoth, and Kyu S. Hahn. "Consumer Demand for Election News: The Horserace Sells." *Journal of Politics* 66 (2004): 157–175.

Jamieson, Kathleen Hall. *Everything You Think You Know about Politics and Why You're Wrong.* New York: Free Press, 2000.

Just, Marion, et al. *Crosstalk: Citizens, Candidates, and the Media in a Presidential Election.* Chicago: University of Chicago Press, 1996.

Kerbel, Matthew R. *If It Bleeds It Leads.* Boulder, Colo.: Westview, 2000.

———. "The Media: The Challenge and Promise of Internet Politics." In *The Elections of 2004,* edited by Michael Nelson, 88–107. Washington, D.C.: CQ Press, 2005.

Lawson-Borders, Gracie, and Rita Kirk. "Blogs in Campaign Communication." *American Behavioral Scientist* 49 (2005): 548–559.

Lichter, S. Robert, Stanley Rothman, and Linda Lichter. *The Media Elite*. Bethesda, Md.: Adler and Adler, 1986.

Mutz, Diana C. "How the Mass Media Divide Us." In *Red and Blue Nation? Characteristics and Causes of America's Polarized Politics*, edited by Pietro S. Nivla and David W. Brady. Washington D.C.: Brookings Institution Press, 2006.

Patterson, Thomas E. *Out of Order*. New York: Knopf, 1993.

Prior, Markus. "News vs Entertainment: How Increasing Media Choice Widens Gaps in Political Knowledge and Turnout." *American Journal of Political Science* 49 (July 2005): 577–592.

Sabato, Larry J. *Feeding Frenzy: Attack Journalism and American Politics*. Baltimore, Md.: Lanham Publishers, 2000.

NOTES

1. *Statistical Abstract of the United States*, "Utilization of Selected Media: 1980–2006," Table 1090, www.census.gov/compendia/statab/tables/09s1090.pdf.
2. Thomas E. Patterson, *Doing Well and Doing Good: How Soft News and Critical Journalism Are Shrinking the News Audience and Weakening Democracy—And What News Outlets Can Do About It* (Cambridge: Harvard University Press, 2000), 4.
3. Martin Kaplan, Ken Goldstein, and Matthew Hale, "Local New Coverage of the 2004 Campaigns: An Analysis of Nightly Broadcasts in 11 Markets," University of Southern California, Annenberg School for Communication, www.localnewsarchive.org.
4. Pew Research Center for the People and the Press, "Key News Audiences Now Blend Online and Traditional Sources," August 17, 2008, http://people-press.org/report/444/news-media.
5. Pew Research Center for the People and the Press, "Internet Now Major Source of Campaign News: Continuing Partisan Divide in Cable TV News Audience," October 31, 2008, http://people-press.org/report/467/internet-campaign-news.
6. Ibid. Among those who name the Fox News Channel as their main source for campaign news, 52 percent identified themselves as Republicans and only 17 percent as Democrats. By contrast, among those who rely on MSNBC for their campaign news, 50 percent said they were Democrats and only 11 percent said they were Republicans. Similarly, CNN's campaign news audience is largely Democratic: 45 percent Democrats and 13 percent Republicans.
7. Pew Research Center for the People and the Press, "The Internet's Role in Campaign 2008," Pew Internet and American Life Project, April 15, 2009, www.pewinternet.org/Reports/2009/6—The-Internets-Role-in-Campaign-2008.aspx?r=1.
8. Ibid.
9. Ibid.
10. The study most often cited on the political attitudes of journalists is S. Robert Lichter, Stanley Rothman, and Linda Lichter, *The Media Elite* (Bethesda, Md.: Adler and Adler, 1986).
11. Republican candidates have traditionally enjoyed the endorsement of more newspapers than have Democratic candidates. Doris A. Graber, *Mass Media and American Politics*, 5th ed. (Washington, D.C.: CQ Press, 1997), 250.
12. Pew Research Center for the People and the Press, "Views of Press Values and Performance: 1985–2007," August 9, 2007, http://people-press.org/reports/pdf/348.pdf.

13. Pew Research Center for the People and the Press, "Media Seen as Fair, but Tilting toward Gore," October 15, 2000, 1, http://people-press.org/reports/display.php3?ReportID=29.

14. "Take This Campaign—Please," *Media Monitor* (September/October 1996): 2; "Campaign 2000 Final," *Media Monitor* (November/December 2000): 2. Why do reporters and correspondents dominate election coverage? From the producers' perspective, interpretive news is more interesting, more focused, more likely to hold an audience, and more likely to present the big picture than are one-sided extended remarks by candidates. From the reporter's perspective, explaining the story makes it more understandable to more people and at the same time contributes to the correspondent's professional career, salary, lucrative speaking invitations, book contracts, and future opportunities for fame and fortune. From a candidate's perspective, reporters and producers are interpreting the news for their own benefit rather than reporting what the candidates actually say. In their view and that of their handlers, the news media present an incomplete, often inaccurate and warped perspective of the campaign.

15. The use of the talk-entertainment format has several advantages for candidates. They are treated more like celebrities than politicians. Hosts tend to be more cordial and less adversarial than news commentators and reporters. Moreover, the audience is different. Those who watch these shows tend to be less oriented toward partisan politics and thus may be more amenable to influence by the candidates who appear on them.

16. Thomas E. Patterson, *Out of Order* (New York: Knopf, 1993): 119–120.

17. Project for Excellence in Journalism, "Winning the Media Campaign, How the Press Reported the 2008 General Election," October 22, 2008, www.journalism.org/node/13307.

18. Senator Dole was portrayed as a weak candidate hopelessly trailing the popular incumbent president. Moreover, his low rating in the polls, compared with President Clinton's ratings, was used as a basis for evaluating and assessing the status of his campaign and how his strategy and tactics were not working. The news media repeatedly referred to Dole's struggling campaign and to his attempts to jump-start it.

19. Two other narratives are about a "bandwagon" that attracts supporters and allows candidates to build a lead and about "losing ground." In the first scenario, the image of strong and decisive leadership generates support; in the second, the image of weak and vacillating leadership contributes to erosion. Jimmy Carter's primary spurt in 1976 provides an illustration of the bandwagon; his decline in the 1980 general election exemplifies the losing-ground story. Patterson, *Out of Order*, 118–119.

20. Gallup Poll, "Topics A to Z: Confidence in Institutions," June 2009, www.gallup.com/poll/1597/Confidence-Institutions.aspx.

21. The two-source rule, which was used to such great effect by *Washington Post* reporters Bob Woodward and Carl Bernstein in their reporting of the Watergate burglary and the White House's involvement in it, requires two independent sources to confirm the accuracy of a description or statement before it will be published.

22. Project for Excellence in Journalism, "Winning the Media Campaign, How the Press Reported the 2008 General Election."

23. Ibid.

24. Negativism has been particularly evident at the presidential level and has been directed against incumbents. In 1980 Jimmy Carter was treated more harshly than Ronald Reagan, and in 1984 Reagan was treated more harshly than Walter Mondale. Vice President George H. W. Bush, running for president in 1988, fared poorly as well, but so did his Democratic opponent, Michael Dukakis. Much the same pattern emerged in 1992. S. Robert Lichter and his associates at the Center for Media and Public Affairs found that 69 percent of the

evaluations of Bush—his campaign, his positions, his performance, his general desirability—were negative, compared with 63 percent for Clinton and 54 percent for Perot. Bill Clinton did better in 1996, but Robert Dole did not. Only half of Clinton's coverage on the evening news was negative; two out of three comments about Dole were negative. George W. Bush got more negative coverage than John Kerry in 2004, as indicated in Table 5.4. "Campaign 2004 Final: How TV News Covered the General Election," *Media Monitor* (November/December 2004): 5.

25. "Winning the Media Campaign, How the Press Reported the 2008 General Election."

26. Ibid.

27. Ibid.

28. "Views of Press Values and Performance: 1985–2007."

29. Annenberg Public Policy Center, "Public and Press Differ about Partisan Bias, Accuracy and Press Freedom," May 24, 2005, www.annenbergpublicpolicycenter.org/NewsDetails.aspx?myId=209.

30. Gallup Poll, "Topics A to Z: Media Use and Evaluation," www.gallup.com/poll/1663/Media-Use-Evaluation.aspx.

31. Pew Research Center for the People and the Press, "Candidates' Policy Positions Still Not Widely Known," July 16, 2008, http://people-press.org/report/437/candidates-policy-positions-still-not-widely-known.

32. Annenberg Public Policy Center, "American Public Has Much to Learn about Presidential Candidates' Issue Positions, National Annenberg Election Survey Shows," September 26, 2008, www.annenbergpublicpolicycenter.org/Downloads/Releases/NAES%202008/Political%20Knowledge%20final.pdf.

33. Annenberg Public Policy Center, "American Public Still Has Much to Learn About Presidential Candidates' Issue Positions as Campaign End Draws Near," October 29, 2008, www.annenbergpublicpolicycenter.org/Downloads/Political%20Knowledge%20Round%20II.pdf.

34. "About two-thirds (66 percent) knew that the Supreme Court was the institution which has the final responsibility of determining whether or not a law is constitutional. A little over one-third (36 percent) of respondents knew that it takes two-thirds of the U.S. Senate and House to override a presidential veto." Ibid.

35. See, for example, Annenberg Public Policy Center, "Voters Learned Positions on Issues since Presidential Debates; Kerry Improves Slightly on Traits, Annenberg Data Show," National Annenberg Election Survey, October 23, 2004, www.annenbergpublicpolicycenter.org/Downloads/Political_Communication/naes/2004_03_%20Voters-and-the-issues_10-23_pr.pdf.

36. Patterson, *Doing Well and Doing Good,* 5–15.

37. Ibid., 7–9.

38. Task Force on Campaign Reform, "Campaign Reform: Insights and Evidence," Report of the Task Force on Campaign Reform, Woodrow Wilson School of Public and International Affairs, Princeton University, September 1998, 23.

39. Ibid., 21–26.

40. Patterson, *Doing Well and Doing Good,* 15.

41. Ibid., 8.

42. Patterson, *Out of Order,* 207–242.

43. Ibid., 210.

44. A less intrusive format for the press could include a single moderator to start the debate and regulate time allotted the candidates, or a single moderator to serve as a master of ceremonies who would preside over a town meeting at which the audience, not journalists, asked the questions.

45. In 2004, the third debate between Bush and Kerry drew an estimated 51.2 million viewers, compared with 15.2 million who watched the baseball playoffs.

46. There are also important procedural questions that could have a major impact on the electorate. When would debates occur? Who would set the dates? Who would be invited? Would candidates have to participate? What would the format be? Which institution would determine the rules, choose the moderators, and oversee the debate? Would instant commentary by news media representatives be permitted? Such commentary may color public perceptions, as it did of the second Ford-Carter debate in 1976. That debate concerned foreign policy. Initial public reaction was favorable to President Ford. However, Ford made a misstatement in the debate, leading some to conclude that he was unaware of the Soviet Union's domination of countries in Eastern Europe. The media pointed out Ford's error in their commentary. The president's failure to correct himself for three days, combined with the media's emphasis on his mistake, changed public perceptions about the debate, its winner, and Ford's competence in foreign affairs.

47. In the 2000 Democratic nomination process, Vice President Al Gore challenged his rival Bill Bradley to forgo ads and simply debate. Bradley refused, claiming that he needed to advertise because he was not as well known as Gore and did not have the vice presidential podium.

48. Christopher Adasiewicz, Douglas Rivlin, and Jeffrey Stronger, "Free Television for Presidential Candidates: The 1996 Experiment," Annenberg Public Policy Center, University of Pennsylvania, March 1997.

chapter 6

Are American Parties Still Representative?

Did you know that . . .

- the Democratic Party of the United States is the oldest political party in the world?
- in this age of telegenic candidates and carefully scripted candidate appeals, partisanship still remains the most important influence on voting behavior?
- more people claim to be independent today than vote consistently in an independent manner?
- the least and most educated voters tend to vote Democratic in presidential elections?
- no political party in the United States today commands the loyalty of a majority of the population?
- although changes in the nomination process were designed to give greater influence to rank-and-file partisans, the process continues to be controlled by party elites?
- a key factor that has led to a resurgence of party influence during electoral campaigns is money and lots of it?
- no third-party or independent candidate has ever won the presidency?
- only two independent or third-party candidates have been elected as independents to the House of Representatives since the end of World War II?
- people who usually are most supportive of third-party candidates are those between the ages of eighteen and twenty-nine?
- the more cohesive the parties, the more divisive the government is apt to be, particularly if one party controls the White House and the other controls one or both houses of Congress?
- the United States is one of the few democratic countries with a two-party system?

Is this any way to run a democratic election?

PARTIES AND AMERICAN DEMOCRACY

Political parties are considered an important part of a democratic electoral system. In fact, some scholars consider them absolutely essential.[1] They provide critical links among the electorate, the candidates, and the government. Parties help orient, organize, and energize voters. They tie candidates to one another and allow them to make both generic and specific appeals replete with partisan imagery. And they provide people with a basis for evaluating the performance of elected officials and holding them collectively responsible for their actions or inaction in office. Responsiveness and accountability are two critical components of a representative democracy.

In a heterogeneous society like that of the United States, interests are many, varied, and often conflicting. Political parties provide a structure for aggregating these interests, packaging them, and presenting them to voters. Parties articulate interests in their platforms, their campaign communications, and the campaigns of their candidates. Parties also provide a mechanism for governing and for bringing together elected officials on the basis of their shared values, interests, and policy goals.

In elections, as in government, parties are likely to be the most effective coalition builders. They can unite diverse elements of the electorate as well as overcome the institutional separation of powers to facilitate the operation of governance. But parties also can have the opposite effect. Divided partisan control of government reinforces the separation of powers and impedes consensus building across institutional bodies.

Each of these functions—interest aggregation, articulation, and electoral accountability—is critical to a viable democratic political system.[2] That is why parties are important.

What Parties Do in Elections

Within the populace, parties organize and orient voters. They create alliances among groups and allegiances among individuals. They inform people about the issues, get them involved in the campaign, and encourage them to vote.

Parties also structure electoral choices. They enable voters to transcend the many individual decisions they must make and allow them to superimpose a collective judgment that both guides and justifies their micro-level decisions. For the vast majority of voters, a major-party label conveys legitimacy, whereas a third- or minor-party label does not. Parties anchor policy preferences. Political parties have an organizational history and a policy record that the electorate uses to evaluate how successful they have been and anticipate how successful they are likely to be.

For the candidates, parties provide a collective presence and perspective, an organizational base, and the potential for enhancing their individual influence if elected. The collective entity is the party organization and its

BOX 6.1   Multiparty Politics: Pros and Cons

There are those who believe that two parties can never satisfactorily represent a country as large and diverse as the United States. Instead of having two major parties reflecting, even exaggerating, the views of their most active and ideological partisans, wouldn't representation be enhanced if a range of narrow-based parties existed and competed across the entire political spectrum?

Countries smaller and less diverse than the United States, such as France, Germany, and Spain, have such a system and have been able to maintain stable and effective governments for relatively long periods of time. Others, however, such as Italy and, to a lesser extent, Israel, have not been as successful in maintaining stability and continuity. Over the years, governments in both of these countries have had to depend on the support of minor parties to gain and sustain a parliamentary majority.

The types of party systems in major democratic countries are listed here.

Types of Party Systems

	STRICTLY BY NUMBER OF PARTIES			
	Predominant party systems	Two-party systems	Party systems with three to five parties	Party systems with more than five parties
Predominant party systems	Japan			
Two-party systems		Great Britain New Zealand United States		
Two-and-a-half party systems			Australia Austria Canada Germany Ireland	
Systems with more than two-and-a-half parties				
One large party			Norway Sweden	
Two large parties				Israel Italy Belgium
Even-party systems			France Denmark Israel Netherlands	Finland Iceland Luxemburg Switzerland

TAKING ACCOUNT OF RELATIVE SIZE OF PARTIES

(continued on next page)

perspective and the shared values, beliefs, and positions on the issues. As organizations, parties have the resources, money, media expertise, and grassroots mobilizing abilities to aid candidates in their campaigns and extend their influence in government.

Partisanship provides candidates with a core of faithful supporters; it also gives them the opportunity to reinforce some of the ideas, beliefs, and interests they have in common with fellow partisans. The benefits that parties give to candidates have led one astute observer, John H. Aldrich, to theorize that parties exist because office seekers and officeholders find them useful. They contribute to the outcomes that these ambitious politicians desire.[3]

Parties also provide a framework for evaluating election results, organizing the government, and subsequently assessing its performance. In doing so, they convert individual victories into a collective effort, help define priorities for newly elected officials, and provide a continuing incentive—renomination and reelection—for keeping public officials sensitive to the interests and opinions of those who elected them.

But how many parties are necessary to represent the views of a heterogeneous society such as the United States? There is no right answer. Although countries less diverse than the United States have multiparty systems (as indicated in Box 6.1), the United States has had a viable two-party system throughout most of its history.

The Two-Party Tradition in the United States

The persistence of Democratic and Republican parties is explained in part by their flexibility and their willingness to adjust and survive in light of the changes that have affected American society. The major parties have successfully weathered these changes because, until recently, they have been more

---

BOX 6.1   **Multiparty Politics: Pros and Cons** (continued)

In a multiparty system, the parties combine to form governing coalitions, and compromise occurs among them. In the United States, if there is a majority party, as there was between 1932 and the late 1960s, compromise occurs within it, among the various groups competing for influence. If the major parties share power, as they have for much of the time since 1968, then they must compromise within and between themselves.

Whether a two-party or a multiparty system is best may depend on the priorities placed on representation, accountability, and effective governance. But the question also may be academic, given the long and dominant two-party tradition in America, to which both major parties are committed, from which both derive benefit, and for which many of the laws governing the structure and operation of the system have been designed.

Source: Alan Ware, *Political Parties and the Party System.* Copyright © 1998, Oxford University Press. Reprinted by permission of Oxford University Press.

pragmatic than ideological, more inclusive than exclusive, and more decent-ralized than centralized.

They also have not attempted to impose their beliefs and issue positions on their supporters, their candidates for office, or even their elected officials as a condition of party affiliation or electoral acceptability, although obviously they try to persuade them to toe the party line.[4]

Moreover, the major parties have advantages in the political system, advantages that they built into it and jealously guard. They are well recognized and have standing. They have organizations in all the states, a leadership struc-ture, and core supporters and financial benefactors. Independent candidates and especially third parties generally lack these resources.

The major parties have systemic advantages as well. They are automati-cally on the ballot in all fifty states as long as they win a certain percentage of the vote. Third parties are much less likely to have won that percentage. Third-party and independent candidates usually have to collect a certain number of signatures of registered voters just to get on the state ballots. Besides, as noted in Chapter 3, the single-member district system in which the person with the most votes wins also benefits major-party candidates at the expense of minor-party candidates.

The presidential election system confers the same advantage on the major parties. The winner-take-all method of Electoral College voting used by forty-eight of the fifty states disadvantages third-party candidates whose support is widely distributed across the country, as Ross Perot's was in 1992 and 1996. If the election moves into the House, the major parties also benefit. The major parties and their candidates are automatically eligible to receive grants during the presidential election, whereas third parties and independent candidates are not.[5] Major parties and their candidates also receive much more extensive media coverage.

Despite public opinion, which periodically looks to third parties and inde-pendent candidates when the people are dissatisfied with the major parties, third parties have had difficulty gaining acceptance and maintaining public support. The argument that they cannot win in single-member districts or the Electoral College contributes to their difficulty in winning in those electoral arenas. In addition, the reforms that were initiated at the end of the nineteenth and begin-ning of the twentieth century—the secret ballot for voting and primary elections for choosing party nominees—provided those with views that differed from party leaders an opportunity to pursue those views within the major parties rather than outside of them. The threat of internal challenges forces party leaders to be more flexible and sensitive to a range of policy positions, with the consequence that parties have often incorporated the views of those outside the party hierarchy, thereby bringing outsiders into their electoral coalition rather than encouraging them to compete with the party from the outside.

The Democratic Party at the outset of the Great Depression provides a good example of a party shifting its position to incorporate the views of people who favored a more liberal, pro-government approach for solving the nation's

FIGURE 6.1   **Evaluations of the Major Parties, 1992–2009**

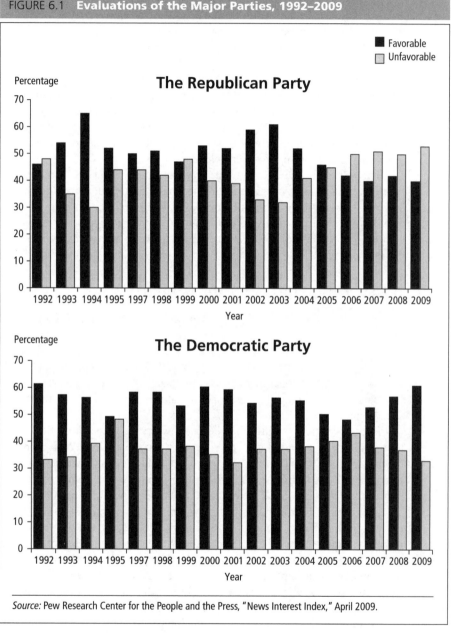

Source: Pew Research Center for the People and the Press, "News Interest Index," April 2009.

economic problems, an approach that neither of the major parties advocated prior to the 1930s. The Democrats' New Deal took the wind out of left-wing third parties during the Depression and after it.[6] Figure 6.1 indicates how Americans evaluate the major parties today.

If third parties and independent candidacies were the only ways minority viewpoints could be heard and minority groups represented, then the bias of the two-party system would be a serious failing in a democratic political process. But, as already noted, there are many other ways minorities can and do get representation and exercise influence on elections and government. In fact, many believe that demographic and ideological minorities are overrepresented within the major parties and exercise disproportionate influence on them, much to the dismay of moderate, mainstream, rank-and-file voters. And outside of the parties, interest groups have proliferated in the form of political action committees (PACs) and other groups within the electoral arena and lobbying groups within the governing arena.

The rest of this chapter examines each of the ways parties help electoral democracy. It looks at parties and the electorate, parties and electoral choice, and parties and electoral accountability. First, however, it presents a brief overview of the evolution of American political parties to provide a historical context for evaluating how well parties are serving the needs of electoral democracy today.

THE EVOLUTION OF U.S. POLITICAL PARTIES

Parties are not mentioned in the Constitution, nor did the framers anticipate them when they created the electoral system. They did anticipate that groups would be active within the political arena, however. Fearing domination by any one of these groups, they divided institutional spheres of authority and created separate but overlapping constituencies as a hedge against any one group, including a majority, disproportionately influencing the formulation of national policy.

Implicit in this constitutional design, however, was the assumption that a lot of public policy would not be needed at the national level. With an ocean for protection, a huge frontier, and seemingly unlimited natural resources, the nation composed largely of self-sufficient farmers was thought not to need or desire a very active national government. Although economic and social needs have changed and government has grown and become more involved in the everyday life of most Americans, its constitutional structure has essentially remained intact—hence the dilemma of how to bridge the institutional divide and facilitate the functioning of government. By providing common perspectives, policy goals, and political structures, parties can unify what the Constitution separates if one party controls the principal institutions of government. However, if institutional control is divided, partisanship can reinforce the constitutional division, thereby impeding government. Over the course of American history, parties have done both.

Birth and Infancy

The creation of parties at the end of the eighteenth and beginning of the nineteenth centuries presented the political system with both a challenge and an opportunity. The challenge was to prevent a major party from dominating the system in such a way as to deny the minority its rights and disregard its interests. The opportunity was to utilize common beliefs, goals, and interests as a consensus-building mechanism within and among the institutions of government.

Thomas Jefferson's Democratic-Republican Party, which emerged as the first broad-based political party in the United States, controlled national politics and government for more than twenty-five years, beginning at the end of the eighteenth century. It was the majority faction that the framers feared, but it also bridged the gap that was developing between an expanding and more diverse electorate and the national elites who had controlled the government since its founding. By the 1820s, the Federalist Party, which supported the policies of the Washington and Adams administrations, had faded from the scene, and the Democratic-Republicans were the only viable party remaining, although that party was becoming divided along regional lines. Two of these partisan divisions eventually evolved into broad-based parties: the Democrats, who backed Andrew Jackson, were one of them, and the Whigs, who opposed Jackson, were the other.

Adolescence: A Growth Spurt

Between 1828 and 1844, state party organizations loosely affiliated with the two major parties developed and subsequently changed the character of the two-party system by federalizing it.[7] The parties increasingly began to reflect America's federal structure. The national parties became little more than collectivities of state parties, and the state parties began to aggressively build a mass base.

Beginning in the 1840s, both parties used their presidential campaigns to mobilize voters. During nonelectoral periods, they employed their resources and exercised their political influence to provide supporters with tangible economic and social benefits to gain and maintain their electoral support. By energizing the electorate, the parties not only extended their political influence but also began to address the economic and social needs of the society at large.

In the 1850s, sectional rivalries, inflamed by the passions of slavery and westward expansion, splintered the parties and eventually led to the demise of the Whigs and the division of the Democrats into northern and southern factions. The Republican Party emerged out of this political chaos. Organized in 1854, the Republicans appealed to former Whigs and to northern Democrats, who supported the abolition of slavery; to white laborers and small farmers who objected to its expansion; and to industrial workers who feared that the influx of new immigrants would lower their wages or cost them their jobs.

The turmoil created by the Civil War and Reconstruction led to the emergence of new partisan coalitions. Big-business tycoons who had profited from the industrial revolution gained control of the Republican Party and dominated it for more than fifty years. The Democrats remained divided into a rural southern faction, controlled by a socially conservative white elite, and a more industrialized northern one that was influenced by banking and commercial interests.

The popular bases of both parties shrank in the second half of the nineteenth century,[8] voter turnout declined, and the partisan political environment became less competitive. Poorer farmers, blue-collar workers, and newly arrived immigrants increasingly found themselves alienated from both major parties.[9]

Adulthood: The Eras of Partisan Majorities

The Republican Era, 1896–1928. A recession in 1893 during the administration of Democrat Grover Cleveland, combined with the Populist movement in the West that further splintered the Democratic Party into "free silver" supporters and opponents, resulted in the emergence of a new Republican majority. Strong in the North, popular among Protestants and older immigrant groups, buoyed by the support of business and also increasingly by labor, and benefiting from the country's economic prosperity, the Grand Old Party (GOP), as it came to be called, dominated American politics for the next three decades. Although the Democrats were still a major party, ruling the South and even managing to gain control of both the White House and Congress from 1912 to 1918, the Republicans held onto their numerical advantage with voters until the Great Depression.[10]

The Democratic Era, 1932–1968. A major realignment of the parties occurred during the 1930s. The Democrats, riding on the coattails of Franklin Roosevelt and his New Deal policies, broadened their base by appealing to those at the lower end of the socioeconomic scale, whereas the Republicans held onto the allegiances of the business community and the more well-to-do members of society. The principal exception to this economically based division of the electorate was in the South, where, regardless of socioeconomic status, voters retained their Democratic loyalties.

The economic division between the parties became evident in their policy perspectives as well. The Democrats looked to government to take the lead in solving the nation's economic and social policies, whereas the Republicans viewed government involvement in the economy as a threat to the free enterprise, private ownership system. The Democrats supported Roosevelt's efforts to redistribute resources on the basis of individual need; the Republicans did not. The GOP continued to believe that a capitalistic system, free from government control, would provide the greatest benefit to the society as a whole.

The Democrats maintained the allegiances of a majority of voters until the end of the 1960s. As time passed, however, changes in the economic environment following World War II, growing prosperity nationwide, an expanding middle class, and gains for organized labor all weakened the economic foundation on which the Democrats had built their electoral and governing coalitions. New social and international issues—the civil rights movement; the Korean and Vietnam wars and the public's reaction to them; violent demonstrations on college and university campuses; deteriorating conditions in the cities, with associated increases in crime, drug trafficking, and racial unrest—divided the Democrats and helped unify the more socially conservative Republicans. By the 1970s, the Democrats had lost their status as the majority party; by the 1980s, they had lost their electoral plurality; by the 1990s, the parties were operating at rough parity with each other and continued to do so at the beginning of the twenty-first century. Discontent with the George W. Bush administration, the war in Iraq, the economic recession of 2008–2009, and a host of other domestic issues led to an erosion of the Republican support beginning in 2006 and the emergence of a Democratic plurality by the 2008 general elections.

Transitional Politics: The Volatile '60s and '70s. The dealignment of the American electorate began in the late 1960s. During this period, voters became more independent, more candidate centered, and more volatile in their voting behavior. Party leaders lost control of the nomination process to party activists (see Chapter 7); the party organizations no longer ran their candidates' campaigns. Television became the principal means of electioneering, and candidates hired campaign professionals to raise money, poll public attitudes and opinions, design media, and identify and mobilize supporters. Outside groups became more active as well during the campaign, performing many of the same tasks as the candidate organizations. These changes weakened the major parties and reduced their role as the major intermediary between candidates and voters.

Moreover, the growing parity between the Republicans and Democrats during this period, combined with more split-ticket voting, ushered in a era of divided government, with control of the White House and Congress shifting between the parties.

Decline in Partisanship. The weakening of partisan allegiances, beginning in the late 1960s and continuing into the mid-1980s, decreased turnout and increased split-ticket voting. It did so because partisanship acts as a lens through which political activity is viewed, a conceptual framework that helps people sort out the candidates and the issues, tell the "good guys" of one party from the "bad guys" of the other. For those who identify with a political party, partisan attitudes reduce the burdens of voting by providing an easy guide to follow when ballots are cast. Partisan attitudes also provide an incentive to become more involved, to get more information, and to vote along party lines.[11]

As partisan loyalties weakened, people looked to other factors when deciding how to vote. They focused on the candidates themselves and their positions on salient issues. Television encouraged this focus as candidates depended more and more on the mass media to create a favorable image and communicate it to voters along with their specific policy appeals. The more independent behavior of candidates also contributed to the personification of electoral politics; most candidates tapped themselves to run, organized their own campaigns, raised their own money, and took their own policy positions on salient issues. In fact, their independence was often a selling point in their campaigns, allowing them to argue that they were beholden to no one but their constituents. The news media also began to emphasize personal qualities, blurring the distinction between private and public behavior.

To counter the image making of their opponents, candidates and their handlers placed more and more emphasis on the negative—why people should not vote for their opponent—rather than simply trumpeting their own achievements and qualifications for office.[12] News coverage became more negative as well (see Chapter 5).[13]

To overcome their own negative portrayal in the news and by their opponents, candidates began to turn to professional image makers, public relations experts, and pollsters to design personal images and policy appeals that resonated with voters. Sometimes, in their desire to win, they made promises and created expectations that they could not possibly fulfill, particularly in a political system that shares responsibilities and checks and balances powers. The emphasis on individuals rather than on parties undermined accountability in government.

The Division of Government. The personalization of politics produced another effect; it increased the probability of divided government. By voting for the person and not the party, the electorate ended up with a mixed government composed of individuals who did not share as many common unifying priorities as did loyal partisans who had been recruited by party officials, funded by local and state party committees, and beholden to the organization of the party for guiding and financing their campaigns. Instead, elected officials increasingly thought of themselves as free agents, more oriented to their constituents who had elected them than to their party. Nor did many of them develop the close-knit personal relationships that facilitated compromise, so essential to policymaking in a large and diverse democratic society.

Under such circumstances, consensus building became harder to achieve, policy coalitions shifted from issue to issue, and legislative output decreased. Table 6.1 indicates the decline in the number of laws during this period. Individually and collectively, these factors contributed to public disillusionment, disengagement, and, when conditions merited it, discontent.

The Reemergence of Partisanship

The changes in electoral behavior were short-lived, however. Beginning in the 1980s, the parties began to regain strength. Partisan voting patterns reemerged, and the policy differences between the major parties became clearer.

The resurgence of the Republican and Democratic parties was helped by their national parties' improved fund-raising; their acquisition of the skills and

TABLE 6.1 **Legislation, 1987–2008**		
Congress	Public laws	Private laws
100th (1987–1988)	713	48
101st (1989–1990)	404	7
102nd (1991–1992)	589	14
103rd (1993–1994)	465	8
104th (1995–1996)	234	2
105th (1997–1998)	394	10
106th (1999–2000)	580	24
107th (2001–2002)	377	6
108th (2003–2004)	498	6
109th (2005–2006)	395	1
110th (2007–2008)	416	0

Source: Harold Stanley and Richard G. Niemi, *Vital Statistics on American Politics, 2009–2010* (Washington, D.C.: CQ Press, 2009), 198.

technologies of the new communications age; and their increasing involvement in the recruitment, training, and funding of candidates for national office.

The strengthening of the electorate's partisan attitudes is a bit more difficult to explain. Part of it may have been a reaction and readjustment to the turbulent 1960s and 1970s, to the policies that generated this turbulence, and to the government that exercised its power to effect social change.

The attractiveness of an alternative conservative philosophy, championed by Ronald Reagan, to those discouraged by the liberal policies of previous Democratic presidents and Congresses, contributed to a realignment of partisan attitudes along ideological lines. Liberals remained Democrats, but conservatives drifted to the Republican Party. As a consequence, the two parties became more internally cohesive and externally distinctive. Partisan allegiances were strengthened, while partisan cleavages within government became more pronounced. When more than one branch of government was controlled by the same party, partisanship unified what the constitutional system divided, thereby approaching a model of responsible party government (see Box 6.2.)

The Contemporary Parties

Today, the electoral coalitions that comprise the Democratic and Republican parties are distinct economically, socially, and culturally. The Democrats continue to attract the allegiances of those at the lower end of the socioeconomic

BOX 6.2 The Responsible Party Model

The doctrine of having more responsible parties was first proposed by Professor Woodrow Wilson in his book *Congressional Government*.[1] Wilson lamented the fact that American parties were not as cohesive as those in the British parliamentary system; he urged the adoption of practices designed to make American political parties more responsible, recommending that each party propose a national program, campaign for it, and carry it out if elected.

But no matter how good the idea sounded in theory, it would have been difficult to implement in practice. U.S. parties are more heterogeneous than their British counterparts in large part because the United States is a larger, more diverse country than the United Kingdom. Power is more dispersed within the American governmental system. In Britain, control of the House of Commons amounts to control of the government; in the United States, control of the House of Representatives, the people's house, is a far cry from control of the government. So is control of Congress, for that matter, if the president is of the opposite party. Besides, even when the same party has a majority in both houses, it may still be unable to dictate public policy outcomes. The committee and subcommittee systems in both houses, the unlimited-debate rule in the Senate, and the strong constituency orientation of most members of Congress make it difficult for the parties' legislative leaders to impose discipline on their members, much less assume collective responsibility for the policies and practices of government.[2]

Nonetheless, the idea of having more responsible parties has surfaced from time to time. It appealed to political scientists as their discipline developed after the Second World War. E. E. Schattschneider, a proponent of this view, headed a committee of the American Political Science Association that called for the Democrats and Republicans to offer clear-cut alternatives to voters, pursue those alternatives if elected, and be held accountable for their success or failure.

The period during which this idea gained currency, however, was not one in which the major parties strove to be different. After World War II both accepted the need for a strong national government; both were strongly anticommunist; and both were divided internally over social issues, particularly civil rights. When the Republican Party gained control of Congress in 1946–1947 and 1952–1953, it did not try to reverse New Deal policies as much as improve their administration and moderate their effects. In 1968, when independent candidate for president George Wallace said "There's not a dime's worth of difference" between the major parties, he was probably more right than wrong.

Contemporary parties are more consistent with the responsible party model than were the Democrats and Republicans in the mid-twentieth century. They are more divisive along ideological lines. They also have become more unified in government. Whether these changes make elections more democratic and government more effective remains a hotly debated issue. Critics still complain about the parties—that they are not representative of their own rank and file, much less the country; that they do not reflect the popular will in elections; and that they have not produced a more effective and efficient government.

1. Woodrow Wilson, *Congressional Government* (1885; reprint, New York: Meridian Books, 1960).
2. Morris P. Fiorina, "The Decline of Collective Responsibility in American Politics," *Daedalus* 109 (Summer 1980): 25–45.

scale: people with lower incomes, less formal education, and fewer professional job skills. These core Democratic supporters want and need more social services from government, including better public schools, more public housing, and a variety of health care and welfare services. They tend to favor government policies that redistribute resources and provide help to those less able to help themselves. The disproportionate concentration of certain minority groups, such as African Americans and Hispanics, among this economic sector of the population added a racial and ethnic dimension to the Democrats' base of support.

In contrast, the GOP attracted most of its supporters from the majority racial group in the population, from people in the upper-middle and higher income brackets who have had and benefited from more education and the job skills and personal contacts that education and skills provide. This Republican support group remained less enamored of a large government role within the economic sphere and programs that extended government social services. Republicans, however, continued to support and emphasize government efforts to protect the security of the citizenry and the nation.

Cultural factors such as religion, language, and community and family values also distinguish the major parties and their electoral bases from each other today. People who hold traditional religious beliefs and regularly attend religious services tend to be Republican; those who hold more secular views or do not attend religious services as regularly are more likely to consider themselves Democrats. The religious divide is evident on such issues as abortion, same-sex marriage, and government-sponsored stem-cell research, all of which Republicans are more likely to oppose than Democrats. Republicans are also more apt to back government policies and action to make English the nation's official language, to allow voluntary prayer in school, to increase the government's policing powers, and to make desecration of the American flag a criminal offense. Democrats place a higher value on the exercise of political freedoms, particularly as that exercise relates to First Amendment rights. They are more supportive of social and cultural diversity and the policies that promote or permit such diversity.

Partisan loyalties ebb and flow. Shifts in partisanship can be observed in election returns and national public opinion polls. The results of the election of 2008, a series of Gallup polls, a Pew national survey conducted during the spring of 2009, the preelection and postelection surveys by the American National Election Studies indicate that partisan parity of the parties may have ended with the Democrats emerging as the dominant of the two major parties (see Table 6.2).

The Republican base has eroded, shrinking about one quarter since the election of George W. Bush.[14] The party's electoral coalition has become whiter, more conservative, and more religious. Evangelical and fundamentalist Protestants constitute core constituencies while the support of mainline Protestants has declined. With its base more homogeneous, the GOP has maintained its strong ideological orientation, which its leaders articulate in their

TABLE 6.2 **Partisan Identification of the American Electorate, 1960–2008 (percentages)**

| | Democrats | | | Republicans | | |
Year	Strong	Weak	Leaners	Independents	Leaners	Weak	Strong
1960	20	25	6	10	7	14	16
1964	27	25	9	8	6	14	11
1968	20	25	10	11	9	15	10
1972	15	26	11	13	10	13	10
1976	15	25	12	15	10	14	9
1980	18	23	11	13	10	14	9
1984	17	20	11	11	12	15	12
1988	17	18	12	11	13	14	14
1992	18	18	14	12	12	14	11
1996	18	19	14	9	12	15	12
2000	19	15	15	12	13	12	12
2004	16	16	17	10	12	12	16
2008	19	15	17	11	11	13	13

Source: Harold Stanley and Richard Niemi, *Vital Statistics on American Politics, 2009–2010* (Washington D.C.: CQ Press, 2009), 105.

policy pronouncements. In contrast, the Democrats have become more heterogeneous, attracting more diverse racial and ethnic groups to its electoral coalition. As a result the party has become less ideological, although liberals still influence basic policy positions that the party adopts.

The makeup of each party's electoral coalition presents challenges for each of them. For the Republicans, the challenge is how to broaden their base of support while maintaining the ideological purity of their core; for the Democrats, it is how to unify such a diverse coalition around a set of acceptable public policy choices.

The Republicans' problem is accentuated by demographic trends in the United States, specifically the failure of the party to attract the fastest-growing ethnic group in America, Hispanics. In addition, the party has done most poorly in recent elections among people in the lowest age cohort eligible to vote, those who are between the ages of 18 and 29. This is a problem for the Republicans because voting preferences, once established, tend to harden over time. The entrance of new voters in the 1930s helped the Democrats build and sustain their partisan advantage for more than 30 years. The Republicans also have a gender problem, particularly with unmarried women who have consistently voted Democratic since the mid-1980s.

Attracting these and other disaffected groups will require the Republicans to become more pragmatic and less ideological. The question is, will core Republicans, who tend to be the activists within the party, the people who participate most regularly in the nomination process, be receptive to candidates whose views do not adhere with their own? Judging by the case of Senator Arlen Specter, who was forced to defect to the Democrats because he did not believe that he would be renominated by Pennsylvania Republicans, others who take moderate policy positions may meet resistance as well. Moreover, elected Republicans who survived the 2006 and 2008 Democratic victories tend to represent the most conservative districts and could jeopardize their own renomination by moving to the center of the political spectrum.

The Democrats face a similar type of dilemma: how to maintain their partisan advantage without alienating their traditional liberal base. Appealing to the young and the elderly, racial and ethnic minorities as well as the white majority, and to women and men will be a difficult task despite the "common ground approach" that President Obama has taken. If Democrats cannot produce legislation that successfully addresses the most salient issues, they too will be criticized. The Democrats must also contend with a populace that is far more conservative and moderate than it is liberal,[15] that remains suspicious of big government despite its reliance on that government in time of crisis,[16] and that has become less trusting of public officials and cynical of government performance.[17] Internal and external battles over health care, energy and the environment, immigration, and entitlement programs illustrate the party's dilemma.

PARTIES, ELECTORAL REPRESENTATION, AND DEMOCRATIC GOVERNANCE

Has the reemergence of partisan voting patterns, the strengthening of party organizations as campaign entities and governing coalitions, and the reappearance in 2002 and in 2008 of unified government strengthened or weakened the democratic character of the American electoral process? Have these changes helped or hurt democratic governance?

These developments have contributed to a more responsible party system and to more accountable government. They help rectify the criticism of American parties as being too much like each other; pursuing policies that are centrist, often ambiguous, and sometimes inconsistent; and sacrificing principle for pragmatism in order to welcome all comers into their "big tent."

Critics of the contemporary parties cite the rise of cynicism, decrease in trust, and downward spiral in election turnout through the 1990s as evidence that something is wrong and that the major parties should shoulder much of the responsibility for the current unhappy state of political affairs. They point to the lack of representation for moderate views and voters, the ideological rhetoric and rigidity that divide and inflame governmental policymaking, and the use of extreme political positions to create wedge issues.

Do Contemporary Political Parties Facilitate or Inhibit Democratic Elections?

The answer to this question depends on how satisfied people are with the candidates running and with the views they express. To the extent that the candidates are more extreme in their beliefs than the electorate as a whole, the choices they provide are less satisfactory. So why would parties nominate candidates like these? This question is answered in Chapter 7, where the discussion focuses on reforms in the nomination process that have shifted power to activists who feel more strongly about issues and exercise disproportionate influence in the selection of party nominees.

The reemergence of partisanship has increased turnout and that, of course, is good from a democratic perspective. Partisanship has encouraged the parties to concentrate on their base, devoting more time, effort, and money to developing grassroots operations. When doing so, however, they neglect independents and do not reach out to others who do not share their views because these individuals are less likely to vote, much less vote down the line for the party's candidates. Moreover, contemporary parties have less incentive to modify policies that are inconsistent with the beliefs of their ideological base. In addition, parties and their nominees also are encouraged to use negative stereotypes to demonize their opponents. Negative campaigning energizes and mobilizes the party's base.

Increasing turnout, creating distinct choices, providing information on the candidates and their proposals, advocating a governing agenda, and, if elected, converting that agenda into public policy are certainly consistent with a democratic electoral process. So are soliciting contributions, hiring campaign professionals, mobilizing volunteers, and engaging in get-out-the-vote activities, all functions that political parties perform during elections. What is more problematic are activities that exaggerate claims or provide false and negative information, shape legislative districts in such a way as to make them less competitive, and adhere to policy positions that do not reflect the more moderate views of mainstream America.

Do Contemporary Parties Facilitate or Inhibit Democratic Governance?

The transitional period in American politics created by the weakening of partisan attitudes, the rise of split-ticket voting, and the growing advantages of incumbents produced a Congress of individualists more intent on furthering their own constituency needs and personal goals than their party's. Partisan unity suffered as a consequence.

Congress also decentralized power to accommodate more members of both the majority and minority parties. A standing subcommittee system was established in the mid-1970s, and the seniority rule for picking committee chairs was substantially modified. Shared power, combined with many more veto points in the legislative process, made agenda setting and coalition building more difficult. Divided government created even more hurdles. Legislative output declined.

Although party leaders were able to forge legislative majorities on specific issues, they were not able to maintain those majorities across issue areas. President Reagan was successful in building bipartisan support for his economic program (with the help of conservative southern Democrats) and maintaining that support for his national security plan, but by the end of his term his party had lost control of the Senate and Reagan's support declined in the Democratic-controlled House. And the number of southern Democrats and moderate Republicans to whom presidents could appeal across party lines diminished. Ideology began to reinforce the partisan divide.

Beginning in the 1980s, increasing ideological consensus within the major parties resulted in greater party unity in Congress. When government is divided, unity, flamed by ideology, discourages compromise and can result in a political and institutional stalemate; when government is unified, however, it can result in the majority party achieving its legislative goals. Such conditions occurred in 2002 and were augmented by President Bush's focus on national security issues in the aftermath of the September 11, 2001, attacks. They recurred in the fall of 2008 and the spring of 2009 when President Obama used the economic crisis as a unifying and action-forcing mechanism in Congress to secure passage of key parts of his domestic legislative agenda.

With majority rule comes significant costs for those in the minority. They lose influence, particularly in the House of Representatives, in which the rules adopted by its members facilitate plurality voting decisions. In the Senate, rules that permit any senator to put a hold on a nomination and require the support of sixty senators for most authorization bills give the minority leverage to achieve compromises or prevent the Senate from acting, leverage that the minority does not have in the House of Representatives.

Another consequence of majority rule in unified government is that the minority has to shout to be heard. Rhetoric becomes shrill, heightened by the ideological character of contemporary partisan debate. Civility and comity in Congress have suffered as a result. The fact that many members of Congress do not move their families to Washington and do not socialize as much with one another has also adversely affected their working relationships, camaraderie, and legislative output. Bills tend to be amalgamations of individual preferences, special interests, and constituency needs; they are larger in size and more detailed and often parochial in content, with benefits accruing to entrenched groups.

The more ideological orientation of members of Congress, the more visible public arena in which decisions were made and votes cast—all covered by C-SPAN and the twenty-four-hour television news networks—as well as the decline of the civility and informality that facilitated compromise in the past have contributed to the warring-camps atmosphere prevalent in Congress during the last decade of the twentieth century and the first decade of the twenty-first.

Partisan bickering has been highlighted by national press coverage, with the consequence being that the public approval of Congress has been low. Before the 2006 midterm elections, only 24 percent of the population approved of the way Congress was handling its job; 68 percent disapproved. Although the approval level of Congress increased after the legislature enacted some of President Obama's policies, more people still express more disapproval of Congress's performance than approval.[18] Individual members still tend to get more positive assessments from their constituents than does Congress as a whole. The discrepancy between these two evaluations creates a significant and persistent ambiguity in public assessments of Congress.

Is Collective Accountability Possible?

Throughout this book the argument has been that elected officials must be held accountable for their decisions and actions. Since the 1970s it has become easier to hold individual government officials accountable because of the increasingly public arena in which policy decisions are made, the greater amount of information available to people about government, the increasingly investigative bent of the news media, and the continuous scrutiny of policymaking by interested outside groups. Personal accountability has also been enhanced during elections by the amount of research that parties and candidates conduct about their opponents.

But what about collective responsibility? Do contemporary parties contribute to that as well? The answer is that they may. Cohesive parties within a unified government provide an opportunity for the electorate to nationalize a congressional election and make a collective judgment on those in power. A negative judgment can result in a new congressional majority.

Every decade or so, the conditions for such a judgment occur. In the elections of 1946 and 1952, the Democrats were repudiated by the voters. Republicans gained power only to lose it two years later in each instance. In the 1974 election, following President Nixon's resignation, the opposite occurred. The Democrats substantially increased their congressional representation at a time when their proportion in the electorate was declining. Democrats lost control of the Senate in the Reagan landslide of 1980 but won it back six years later. In 1994, an electorate upset with the internal dissent and scandalous behavior of some Democrats voted that party out of power in the political revolution that brought Republican control of the Senate and a new, more conservative leadership to the House under the direction of Newt Gingrich. In 2006 the public rebuked the Republicans for supporting the president's policy in Iraq, for their ideological rigidity, and for the scandals that beset members of that party in the 109th Congress—bribery, ethical lapses, immoral and illegal actions, and the attempted cover-up of these activities by those in leadership positions. The ability to make a collective judgment enhances democratic government. When control of Congress shifts, however, particularly in an age of highly polarized parties, the consequence may be significant shifts in policy as well.

SUMMARY: PARTISAN DILEMMAS IN A NUTSHELL

Parties are important to a democratic selection process. They provide a critical link between candidates and voters and between elected officials and the people who elected them. Without such a link, it would be more difficult to hold elected officials collectively responsible for their actions.

Parties organize ideas, people, and institutions. The allegiances they engender, the attitudes they shape, and the electoral behavior they influence provide the electorate with a frame of reference for the campaign, a motivation for participating in it, an orientation that can be used to arrive at a voting decision, and criteria for evaluating the government.

The major parties have gone through cycles in which they have gained and lost adherents; their electoral coalitions have shifted over the years. The late 1960s ushered in an era in which partisan allegiances weakened, the number of self-declared independents grew, and voters began to split their tickets, voting more for the person or issue.

During that period, the candidates also became more independent in deciding whether to seek office and how to do so. They depended less on their party's organization and more on the campaign professionals they hired, experts skilled in the new computer-based technology, survey research, grassroots organizing, and media-oriented research and communications.

By the mid-1980s, the transition in politics had begun to run its course. Partisan ties strengthened, and partisan voting behavior increased. There was more partisan unity in government, and the parties began to rebuild their financial and grassroots bases. They also became more ideological, nominating and electing candidates with more consistent policy views. These changes divided the country and polarized the government. They led to long periods of divided government in the years from 1968 to 2008, during which domestic policymaking became more difficult. Trust and confidence in government declined.

Today, the parties continue to be distinctive in their policy orientations. Civility in political discourse has declined, as has comity within Congress as well as between it and the White House. Warring partisan coalitions contest policy publicly rather than deliberate it quietly behind closed doors. Reaching compromise has become more arduous, and serving constituency interests remains the key to reelection.

Is the current state of political affairs beneficial or harmful to a democratic electoral process? Candidates self-select but are dependent on political professionals for getting elected. Incumbents continue to be helped by the number of safe seats. As a consequence, it becomes more difficult for elections to reflect the popular mood of the moment. Democratic tendencies are undermined by a noncompetitive legislative election structure.

Is the voice of the people being heard more clearly? Is that voice being effectively and efficiently translated into public policy? Experts are divided. Some believe responsible parties have emerged and, as a result, collective accountability has increased; others see a decrease in the representation of people with moderate views and a continuing distinction between the influence of those in the majority and racial and ethnic minorities. They perceive government as being increasingly responsive to its core supporters instead of to the general public. They see it as making politically expedient decisions at the expense of longer-term policy solutions.

What should be done to enhance partisan representation and to make the parties more responsive and the government more effective? Imposing reforms on the parties is neither wise nor feasible. The parties need to reform themselves. They need to better reflect the diverse character of American society. But if they do so, can they still be internally cohesive, externally distinctive, and held collectively responsible?

Now It's Your Turn

Discussion Questions

1. Why did partisan loyalties decline in intensity during the transitional period, beginning in the late 1960s and continuing into the 1980s? Why have these loyalties gotten stronger today?
2. Has the realignment of the major parties along ideological lines strengthened or weakened their capacity to represent the American public? Has it improved or reduced their capacity to govern effectively?
3. Is it better in a democracy to vote for the best candidate regardless of that candidate's partisan affiliation or to vote for the candidate of the party that best represents a voter's political beliefs?
4. Are political parties the key to collective responsibility in government? If not, how can government be held accountable for its public policy decisions and actions?
5. Does having only two major parties facilitate or impede the representation of American voters, the conduct of elections, and the operation of government?

6. Does having two major parties make it more or less likely that public policy reflects the views and interests of the majority of people in the United States?
7. What type of electoral system most effectively represents the views of all the people? What type of electoral system results in the most effective government?

Topics for Debate

Challenge or defend the following statements:

1. All candidates who run on a party label should be required to promise that they will support the principal tenets of their party, as stated in the party platform, or be removed from the party line on the ballot.
2. Partisanship is undesirable; thus all candidates for office should run in nonpartisan elections.
3. Political parties are unnecessary and undesirable for a democratic government.
4. A two-party system is more efficient but may be less effective in representing the views of society.
5. A new third party should be created that speaks for the average American voter.
6. American political parties can represent public opinion or they can govern effectively, but they cannot do both simultaneously.

Exercises

1. Design a strategic memorandum for a new political party that addresses the needs and desires of your generation. In your memorandum, indicate the following:
   a. the key issues and the new party's position on them,
   b. the campaign appeals that your party should make, not only to your generation but also to others,
   c. likely sources of income for the party and its nominees, and the methods you would use to raise the money,
   d. other nonparty or party groups to which you might appeal for funds and votes in an election, and
   e. your first order of business if your party were to win control of the legislative or executive branch.
2. The major parties in the United States have been criticized for being too ideological by catering to the views of their most active partisans. Do you think this criticism is valid? Answer this question by comparing the major parties today on the basis of the following:
   a. their demographic and regional composition,

b. their positions on the major issues before Congress and the president today, and

c. their political philosophies.

INTERNET RESOURCES

- Democratic National Committee: www.democrats.org
  Main Web site of the national Democratic Party, with links to other Democratic organizations as well as to state Democratic parties.
- Democratic Congressional Campaign Committee: www.dccc.org
  Raises money and identifies Democratic candidates for elections to the House of Representatives.
- Democratic Senatorial Campaign Committee: www.dscc.org
  Raises money and identifies Democratic candidates for elections to the Senate.
- Republican National Committee: www.rnc.org
  Main Web site of the national Republican Party, with links to other Republican organizations as well as to Republican state parties.
- National Republican Congressional Committee: www.nrcc.org
  Raises money and identifies Republican candidates for elections to the House of Representatives.
- National Republican Senatorial Committee: www.nrsc.org
  Raises money and identifies Republican candidates for elections to the Senate.
- Other political parties:
  Communist Party of the United States: www.cpusa.org
  Democratic Socialists of America: www.dsausa.org
  Green Party: www.gp.org
  Libertarian Party: www.lp.org
  Reform Party: www.reformparty.org
  Socialist Labor Party: www.slp.org
  Socialist Party: www.sp-usa.org

SELECTED READINGS

Aldrich, John H. *Why Parties? The Origin and Transformation of Political Parties in America.* Chicago: University of Chicago Press, 1995.

Ansolabehere, Stephen, and James M. Synder Jr. "The Incumbency Advantage in U.S. Elections: An Analysis of State and Federal Offices, 1942–2000." *Election Law Journal* 1, no. 3 (2002): 315–338.

Bibby, John F., and L. Sandy Maisel. *Two Parties—or More?* Boulder, Colo.: Westview, 1998.

Black, Earl, and Merle Black. *The Rise of the Southern Republicans.* Cambridge: Harvard University Press, 2002.

Bond, Jon R., and Richard Fleisher, eds. *Polarized Politics: Congress and the President in a Partisan Era.* Washington, D.C.: CQ Press, 2000.

Fiorina, Morris P., with Samuel J. Abrams and Jeremy C. Pope. *Culture War? The Myth of a Polarized America.* New York: Pearson/Longman, 2005.

Gerring, John. *Party Ideologies in America: 1828–1996.* New York: Cambridge University Press, 1998.

Green, Donald P., Bradley Palmquist, and Eric Schickler. *Partisan Hearts and Minds: Political Parties and the Social Identities of Voters.* New Haven: Yale University Press, 2002.

Hetherington, Marc J. "Resurgent Mass Partisanship: The Role of Elite Polarization." *American Political Science Review 95* (September 2001): 619–632.

Hirano, Shigeo, and James M. Synder Jr. "The Decline of Third Party Voting in the United States." *Journal of Politics 69* (February 2007): 1–16.

MacKuen, Michael B., and George Rabinowitz, eds. *Electoral Democracy.* Ann Arbor: University of Michigan Press, 2003.

Schattschneider, E. E. *Party Government.* New York: Rinehart, 1942.

Stonecash, Jeffrey M. *Political Parties Matter: Realignment and the Return of Partisan Voting.* Boulder, Colo.: Lynne Rienner, 2006.

Wattenberg, Martin P. *The Decline of American Political Parties,* 6th ed. Cambridge: Harvard University Press, 1998.

White, John K. *The Values Divide: American Politics and Culture in Transition.* New York: Chatham House, 2003.

NOTES

1. E. E. Schattschneider, *Party Government* (New York: Rinehart, 1942), 1.
2. These party functions are presented and discussed in Samuel J. Eldersfeld, *Political Parties: A Behavioral Analysis* (Chicago: Rand McNally, 1964).
3. John H. Aldrich, *Why Parties? The Origin and Transformation of Political Parties in America* (Chicago: University of Chicago Press, 1995), 18–27, 277–296.
4. When David Duke, a former Nazi sympathizer and member of the Ku Klux Klan, announced that he would run for governor of Louisiana as a Republican, the party denounced his candidacy although it could not prevent him from running or claiming he was a Republican. The Democrats have had similar problems with Lyndon LaRouche, who has run for the Democratic nomination for president many times, even from jail.
5. To be eligible for funding, third parties have to have received at least 5 percent of the vote in the previous election. If they do, they receive funding equal to their percentage of the total

vote. Until they receive the 5 percent threshold, however, the funding is retroactive; they receive it after the election is over.

6. For an excellent article on this phenomenon, see Shigeo Hirano and James M. Snyder Jr., "The Decline of Third-Party Voting in the United States," *Journal of Politics* 69 (February 2007): 1–16.

7. Aldrich, *Why Parties?* 118–135.

8. They did so as a consequence of new laws designed to improve the honesty and integrity of federal elections. The laws, which were enacted by the states, required citizens to register in order to vote. Some also imposed a poll tax to pay for the conduct of elections and a literacy test to ensure that voters could read and had a basic understanding of the Constitution.

9. Frances Fox Piven and Richard A. Cloward, *Why Americans Don't Vote* (New York: Pantheon, 1988), 64–95.

10. The Democrats' success in the second decade of the twentieth century came as a result of a split within the Republican Party at the national level between those supporting William Howard Taft and those backing Theodore Roosevelt for the presidency in 1912.

11. Angus Campbell et al., *The American Voter* (New York: Wiley, 1960), 133–136.

12. See Lynda Lee Kaid and Anne Johnston, "Negative versus Positive Television Advertising in U.S. Presidential Campaigns, 1960–1988," *Journal of Communication* 41 (Summer 1991): 53–64; and John G. Geer, *In Defense of Negativity: Attack Ads in Presidential Campaigns* (Chicago: University of Chicago Press, 2006).

13. Thomas E. Patterson, *Out of Order* (New York: Knopf, 1993).

14. Pew Research Center for the People and the Press, "Independents Take Center Stage in Obama Era: Trends in Political Values and Core Attitudes: 1987–2009," May 21, 2009, http://people-press.org/report/517/political-values-and-core-attitudes.

15. According to Gallup polls conducted in the spring of 2009, the United States is becoming more conservative. Almost twice as many people identify themselves as conservative (40 percent) than as liberal (21 percent). About 35 percent consider themselves moderate. Gallup Poll, "Special Report: Ideologically, Where is the U.S. Moving?" July 6, 2009, www.gallup.com/poll/121403/Special-Report-Ideologically-Moving.aspx; see also Gallup Poll, "'Conservatives' Are Single Largest Ideological Group," June 15, 2009, www.gallup.com/poll/120857/Conservatives-Single-Largest-Ideological-Group.aspx. The General Social Survey of the National Opinion Center at the University of Chicago, the large national exit poll following the 2008 elections, and surveys conducted by the Pew Research Center for the People and the Press in 2008 and 2009 also found much higher percentages of self-declared moderates and conservatives than liberals.

16. Since 1992, Gallup polls have consistently indicated that more people think the government is doing too much rather than not enough. The only exception was in the first Gallup poll taken after the terrorist attacks of September 11, 2001; see Gallup Poll, "Topics from A to Z: Government," www.gallup.com/poll/27286/Government.aspx.

17. Ibid. Since the early 1970s, there have been very few instances in which a majority of people expressed a "great deal" or "quite a lot" of confidence in the major institutions of government: Congress, the presidency, and the Supreme Court.

18. Gallup Poll, "Topics A to Z: Congress and the Public," www.gallup.com/poll/1600/Congress-Public.aspx.

chapter 7

The Nomination Process
Whose Is It Anyway?

Did you know that . . .

- the goal of improving representation at the national nominating conventions has resulted in the selection of delegates who are more representative demographically but may be less representative ideologically of mainstream partisans?
- the changes in party rules to open the nomination process to more diverse candidates continue to favor candidates who are nationally known and well funded?
- despite the length of the nomination campaign and the extensive coverage of it by local and national news media, a majority of the electorate still does not vote in it?
- it is unclear which candidate, Barack Obama or Hillary Rodham Clinton, won the most popular votes during the 2008 Democratic nomination process?
- aspirants to a party's presidential nomination usually take more extreme policy positions in their quest for the nomination than they do in their general election campaign?
- more than 60 percent of the Democratic and Republican delegates to their party's 2008 national nominating convention held at the end of August and beginning of September were selected by the first Tuesday in February?
- the last time a presidential nominee did not personally select his running mate was in 1956, when the Democratic convention—not nominee Adlai Stevenson—chose Estes Kefauver over John F. Kennedy as the party's vice presidential candidate?
- the amount of broadcast network television coverage of the national nominating conventions has decreased as the parties' attempts to orchestrate that coverage have increased?
- the incumbency advantage is greater in the nomination process than in the general election?
- the increasing front-loading of presidential primaries works to benefit front-running candidates?
- the race for money has become in effect the first presidential primary?

Is this any way to run a democratic election?

No aspect of the electoral process has changed more fundamentally and more quickly since the 1970s than the way in which the major political parties choose their candidates for office. In the past, when party organizations were stronger, the leaders of those organizations shaped the process by which nominees were selected. Although the actual mechanisms varied from state to state, most nominations were controlled by party organizations, and party leadership dictated the results.

In exercising that control, the leadership had three goals in mind in addition to its primary objective of winning the election. First, party leaders wanted to reward the faithful who had worked for their candidates in previous elections. Next, they sought to choose experienced people who had worked their way up the ladder of elective office, who understood the rules and practices, and who, above all, were willing to abide by them. Finally, party leaders wanted to select partisans whose primary loyalty was to the party, its positions, its programs, and especially its leadership.

The merit of such a nomination system was that it fostered and maintained strong party organizations and loyalties. The organizations, in turn, provided continuity in programs, policies, and personnel. The loyalties gave a party a cadre of workers and voters on whom it could depend.

The main disadvantage of such a system was that it was a top-down rather than a bottom-up system. It was less participatory, less democratic. It kept party bosses, even corrupt ones, in power. It facilitated an old-boys' network. People had to play by the rules to get ahead. Rank-and-file partisans had little influence on the selection of the nominees and their policy positions.

THE MOVEMENT FROM AN ELITE TO A MORE POPULAR SYSTEM

The Progressive movement began in the early years of the twentieth century as a reaction to the closed and seemingly elitist character of American political parties. Progressives wanted to reform the political system to encourage greater public participation in the nomination and election processes. Conducting primary elections in which partisans could select the candidates they preferred for public office was one of their most touted political reforms.

The movement prospered for more than two decades. From 1900 to 1916, twenty-five states enacted laws to permit or require primary elections. After World War I, however, low turnout, higher election costs, and unhappy party leaders persuaded state officials to return to the older ways of selecting nominees.

Not until after World War II did democratizing tendencies begin to reemerge, along with a communication technology in the form of television that could bring candidates into full public view in American living rooms. The rapid expansion of television programming, the purchase of television sets by most American households, and people's addiction to this new entertainment and news medium provided incentives for candidates, particularly for those unable or unwilling to obtain positions of power within the traditional party hierarchy, to take to the airwaves to gain public support and start a new era in democratic political activity.

The catalyst behind the shift from a party leadership–dominated nomination system to one in which there was greater public participation was the rule changes that first occurred in the Democratic Party after its raucous 1968 presidential nominating convention. At that time, the successful nominee, Vice President Hubert H. Humphrey, won without campaigning in any of the party's primary elections. As a unifying gesture to those who had participated in the primaries and were frustrated by their failure to affect the choice of nominees, the Democratic convention approved the establishment of a commission to review and suggest changes to its presidential nominating procedures.

In making its recommendations, the commission's primary charge was to make the selection process more open to rank-and-file partisans and, in this sense, more democratic. A set of rules designed to facilitate rank-and-file involvement in the nomination process and greater diversity in the composition of convention delegates was enacted. The rules established selection criteria that state parties had to meet to ensure that their delegates would be certified as official delegates to the national convention. Delegates not chosen in conformity with these rules could be challenged and even prevented from representing their state parties at the convention.[1]

The Democratic Party in the 1970s and early 1980s was in a strong position to impose its new rules on the states. As the plurality party, the Democrats controlled about three-quarters of the state legislatures, and they were able to convince elected officials in the states that had Democratic legislators to enact laws that put them in compliance with the new party rules.

The changes affected the Republican Party's selection process as well. Although the GOP did not initially mandate rule changes for its state parties in the presidential nomination process as the Democrats had done, the new laws enacted by the states were applicable to them as well, forcing their state affiliates to conduct or giving the option of conducting primary elections.[2] Most of them did so, not wanting to be seen as opposing popular reforms.[3]

The new system rapidly took hold. Today, all states conduct primaries for nominations for federal and state offices. More than half use them exclusively; others employ a combination of primaries, state caucuses, and conventions.[4]

In effect, the national parties opened up their nomination process. They decentralized power that had already been decentralized by virtue of the federal system of government. Power flowed to those who participated. The parties hoped that increased participation in the nomination process would broaden their base of support, energize their electorate, enhance the representative character of the parties, and make them more responsive to the interests of their partisans. It seemed like a win-win situation for the party organization and its partisans. In practice, however, it has not been.

THE DEMOCRATIZATION OF NOMINATIONS: REPRESENTATIVE OR UNREPRESENTATIVE?

The Good News

The rule changes have contributed to the democratization of the nomination processes in both parties. By opening up the nomination process, the parties have involved more people in the selection of nominees. There are more primaries, and an increasing number of delegates are being selected in them. Table 7.1 indicates the number of primaries and the percentage of delegates selected in primaries from 1912 to 2008.

A second consequence of more open nominations has been broader representation of each party's electoral coalition at its national conventions. Delegates who attend these conventions are demographically more representative of rank-and-file party voters than they were prior to the rule changes. There are more women, more minorities, and more young people.

A third result, which also has improved the democratic character of the system, has been to tie candidates closer to the desires and interests of their electoral supporters. To gain the nomination, candidates have to take positions on salient issues, and keep them if elected, because their renomination is always open to challenge.

A fourth consequence has been to increase the pool of potential candidates. The number of people vying for their party's nomination at all levels of government has increased, especially when incumbents decide not to run for reelection.[5] The range of challengers is also greater. Anyone with access to the mass media, by virtue of a personal career or financial base, can mount a campaign and, in some cases, even win. George McGovern, Jimmy Carter, Michael Dukakis, Bill Clinton, and Barack Obama would not have been likely presidential nominees under the old system in which state party leaders chose the candidate. Al Gore, George W. Bush, John Kerry, and John McCain might have been, however.

Another more democratic aspect of the new nomination process is that it enlarges the arena of debate by allowing candidates to use the process as a vehicle to promote their ideas—be they the liberal economic and social programs that Jesse Jackson trumpeted in his quest for the 1984 and 1988 Democratic presidential nominations; the traditional, more conservative Christian values that Pat Robertson (1988), Pat Buchanan (1992 and 2000), and Alan Keyes and Gary Bauer (1996 and 2000) advocated when they ran for the Republican presidential nomination; or the antiwar views of Democrats Howard Dean, Dennis Kucinich, and Al Sharpton in 2004. Millionaire Steve Forbes's campaign for the 1996 and 2000 Republican nominations on the

TABLE 7.1 Number of Presidential Primaries and the Percentage of Convention Delegates from Primary States, 1912–2008

Year	Democratic		Republican	
	Number of state primaries	Percentage of delegates from primary states	Number of state primaries	Percentage of delegates from primary states
1912	12	32.9	13	41.7
1916	20	53.5	20	58.9
1920	16	44.6	20	57.8
1924	14	35.5	17	45.3
1928	16	42.2	15	44.9
1932	16	40.0	14	37.7
1936	14	36.5	12	37.5
1940	13	35.8	13	38.8
1944	14	36.7	13	38.7
1948	14	36.3	12	36.0
1952	16	38.7	13	39.0
1956	19	42.7	19	44.8
1960	16	38.3	15	38.6
1964	16	45.7	16	45.6
1968	15	40.2	15	38.1
1972	21	65.3	20	56.8
1976	27	76.0	26	71.0
1980	34	71.8	34	76.0
1984	29	52.4	25	71.0
1988	36	66.6	36	76.9
1992	39	66.9	38	83.9
1996	35	65.3	42	84.6
2000	40	64.6	43	83.8
2004	40	67.5	26[a]	55.5
2008	39	67.4	42	82.2

[a]Five Republican primaries, with a total of 309 delegates, were cancelled because only George W. Bush qualified as a candidate.

Source: Harold W. Stanley and Richard G. Niemi, *Vital Statistics on American Politics, 2009–2010* (Washington D.C.: CQ Press, 2009), 55.

promise of a flat income tax and socially conservative policy positions is but another example. Needless to add, in the process of running for the nomination, the candidates also promote themselves, thereby fostering their own political ambitions and satisfying their own psychological needs.

The number of candidates seeking the nomination, the range of issues being debated, and the diversity of the policy appeals have sensitized the parties to their base of supporters. The parties have given economic and social groups within them a chance to be heard, to pursue their interests, and even to put forth candidates who can win nominations. All of this has put the parties more in touch with themselves. That's the good news. The 2008 presidential nominations, particularly the Democratic one, illustrate the virtues of the system.

The Bad News

The bad news is that the reforms and changes in the nomination process have given states that hold their contests at the beginning of the process more influence. Candidates able to mobilize the rank-and-file partisans more effectively by virtue of their national standing, financial resources, and organizational support are also at an advantage. Cohesive groups within the party and partisans who participate more as a consequence of their more intense feelings and beliefs have benefited from this arrangement.

Uneven Influence of States. Although the presidential nomination process is open to all partisans, participation is uneven. It is higher at the beginning of the process and lower at the end, especially after the nominee has effectively been determined. Partisans in states that hold their contests early receive more attention. Candidates are encouraged to concentrate their efforts in the early states, spending their resources and addressing the issues of these states. Media attention follows.

As a result of these perceived benefits, states have been moving their nomination contests earlier and earlier, thereby front-loading the schedule. In 1972, 17 percent of the delegates had been chosen by mid-April; by 1976 that percentage had increased to 33. Since then, the front-loading has increased dramatically. In 2008, both parties moved the official opening of their primary calendar to the first Tuesday in February. By the end of that day, February 5, more than 60 percent of the delegates to each party's national convention had been chosen.

Front-loading has very serious and undemocratic consequences for the parties and their partisans, for the candidates, and for the public at large. For the parties, it gives greater benefit to the states that hold their contests first. To the extent that partisans in these states are not representative of the party's rank and file, their electoral choices can skew the outcome. The winning candidate may not be the first choice of most party voters or even the most acceptable compromise candidate.

Take Iowa and New Hampshire, for example. Both have legislation that requires them to go first—Iowa with a caucus selection process and New Hampshire with a primary. These states are certainly not representative of the country or the parties, particularly the Democrats. Together they account for less than 1.5 percent of the country's total population. Moreover, they lack ethnic and racial diversity. African Americans constitute only 4 percent of Iowa's population and less than 1 percent of New Hampshire's, compared with about 13 percent of the country as a whole and between 20 to 25 percent of the total Democratic vote in recent elections; similarly, Hispanics comprise only 3.7 percent of Iowa's population and 1.7 percent of New Hampshire's, yet Hispanics make up about 15 percent of the country's population and a growing proportion of the Democratic Party's electoral coalition.[6] How fair is that?

Moreover, a front-loaded contest may be decided before all the election issues become evident, before all relevant background information on the candidates becomes public, and before events that may influence the electorate's determination of the most relevant qualifications for the candidates to have may occur.

From a democratic perspective, a very serious consequence of having early caucuses and primaries determine the outcome is that the nomination is decided before most people are paying attention to the election. By the time the party's electorate tunes in, many of the candidates may have dropped out. Six of the twelve Republican contenders for the 2000 nomination withdrew even before the first state voted in that nomination process; two of the ten Democratic candidates did so as well in 2004. In 2008, it was more of the same. Of the nine Democrats who officially declared their candidacies in 2006 or 2007, all but two had dropped out before February 5, 2008, Super Tuesday; of the eleven Republicans who began the contest, three remained after February 7. When Mitt Romney dropped out on March 4, the Republican nomination was effectively settled. The Democratic nomination, however, continued until the final Democratic primaries in June.

The Democratic nominations proved to be more representative at the beginning of the process in 2008 because of the decision of several of the larger states, such as California, New York, and Illinois, to hold their primaries on the first day the party permitted them to do so. These states are demographically more reflective of the party's electoral coalition. The impact for the Republicans was just the reverse. The front-loading of these large states combined with their winner-take-all system of voting gave a moderate Republican, such as John McCain, more influence than he otherwise would have had if the smaller, more conservative states had dominated early voting as they usually do in the Republican nomination process.

The other equality issue for the states is the delegate allocation system. Both parties allocate delegates on the basis of state size and partisan loyalty. Democrats reward loyalty on the basis of the party vote in electoral districts in the last three presidential elections; Republicans reward it on the basis of the number of elected Republican officials, with a bonus for states that voted Republican at the presidential level in the last election. The system favors the large states for the Democrats and the most Republican states for the GOP. Is this a fair and equitable way to award delegates?

Unequal Opportunities for Candidates. For the candidates, front-loading moves their campaign forward into the year preceding the election, lengthening the nomination period but shortening its competitive phase. A front-loaded schedule forces candidates to devote more time and resources to early fund-raising since a compressed calendar leaves little time to parlay a strong showing in Iowa, New Hampshire, or one of the other early contests into a successful fund-raising campaign, as George McGovern was able to do in 1972 and Jimmy Carter in 1976.[7]

Under the current system, lesser-known candidates face a dilemma. They need to raise money to compete but have difficulty doing so because they cannot establish their electability until the caucuses and primaries are actually held. Moreover, if they are not perceived as viable by the news media, they get less coverage than the front-runners. Under the circumstances they usually raise less money, which increases their competitive disadvantage.

Nor do federal matching grants level the playing field as they did in the past. As noted in Chapter 4, the increase in campaign costs greatly exceeds the increase in spending limits that apply if candidates accept matching funds, while the increase in the amount individuals can contribute to presidential candidates has made private funding a much more desirable option than accepting public funds. In 2008, neither of the principal candidates in either party accepted federal funds during the nominations because it would have disadvantaged them to do so. The only piece of good news for candidates unable to raise sufficient money in the year before the election is that the two candidates who had the largest war chests at the end of 2007, Mitt Romney and Hillary Clinton, did not win their party's nomination.

Giving advantage to nationally recognized candidates is not necessarily undesirable or undemocratic. Political experience normally is considered a valuable prerequisite for higher office. However, when national recognition and political experience combine to create unequal campaign resources, then outsiders without these resources are penalized. Personal wealth alone does not suffice. Ross Perot, Steve Forbes, and Mitt Romney could buy the recognition they needed by spending millions of their own money on advertisements, but they couldn't buy experience or obtain the votes they needed to win.

Finally, front-loading normally creates a down period of three to four months after a winner has emerged but before the national nominating conventions are held. Naturally, public interest declines during this period, forcing the parties and candidates to engage in expensive advertising to remain in the public spotlight and to keep their base energized. McCain had trouble staying in the news as long as the Democratic contest continued in 2008. By not accepting federal matching grants, however, he was able to raise more private money and use it to gain visibility for himself, his party, and his policy positions.

Unequal Representation of the Partisan Electorate. A front-loaded schedule is not the only problem. Winner-take-all voting, which the Republican Party permits on a state or district basis, gives those who vote for losing candidates no representation in the state's convention delegation.

Some states allow independents to vote in party primaries and caucuses, which dilutes the vote of partisans and could potentially affect the outcome of the nomination. Polls taken during the 2008 Democratic nomination contest indicated that the party's rank-and-file preferred Clinton, but independents preferred Obama. The relatively early victory of McCain in the Republican nomination thus worked to Obama's advantage because it eliminated the other principal candidate who attracted the most independent votes in open state primaries. Was such a situation fair for Democratic partisans?

In 1980, the Democrats created superdelegates to ensure that party and elected officials could attend their national conventions, provide the decisive votes if the convention was deadlocked, and promote closer cooperation among its presidential candidate, Democratic members of Congress, and state and national party officials. Since the caucuses and primaries have been decisive, the superdelegates have played no major role in the selection of the nominee, but they potentially could have done so in 2008. With the elected delegates divided, and Obama without a majority of all convention delegates until Clinton conceded in June, the superdelegates held the balance of power.

Superdelegates tend to support the front-runner, which was Clinton throughout 2007. She had contributed more money than Obama to the 2006 reelection campaigns of Democratic members of Congress who are automatically superdelegates. She was better known among the Democratic leadership and was viewed as the "inevitable" nominee by most party regulars, with the result that more party leaders and members of Congress jumped on her bandwagon initially and pledged their support than for any other candidate.

When the race got closer, with Obama in the delegate lead, increasing pressure was exerted by both campaigns on the superdelegates who constituted 19 percent of the total number of delegate votes at the Democratic convention. The possibility that the superdelegates could reverse the caucus and primary results by disproportionately supporting Clinton raised the ire of Obama's supporters, who cried foul and pointed to the undemocratic consequences that such a reversal would produce for the party, its nominee, and its electorate. In the end, the superdelegates proved that they were politicians, and most backed the judgment made by the people of their states. But the controversy pointed to another potential unrepresentative feature of the Democratic nomination process, the fact that a relatively small proportion of non-elected delegates could reverse the choice of the electorate that participated in the Democratic caucuses and primaries.

It must be remembered, however, that the people who have participated in the nomination process over the years have not been representative of average partisan voters, much less the electorate as a whole. Primary voters and caucus participants tend to overrepresent people who are in higher income and education brackets. Older people who have more information, time, and incentive also tend to be more involved than the under-thirty age cohort. The less representative the people who participate in the process are, the less likely that the party's standard-bearers and its platform will reflect the wishes of its rank-and-file voters.

The reforms, intended to increase the party electorate's role in choosing nominees, have not, for the most part, achieved that objective. The current system gives party elites—composed of interest group leaders, campaign professionals, and partisan activists, people and groups that tend to be more ideological and issue oriented than the average partisan—an advantage because of their activism, organizational skills, and the resources they can mobilize.

The elites control the process and usually affect the outcome. They did not do so during the 2008 Democratic nominations because of the effective campaign Obama waged, his organization's ability to identify and get out large numbers of voters, his appeal to independents who participated in the Democratic primaries, and his message of change that resonated with the 2008 Democratic electorate. Obama was also fortunate that organized groups within the party's electoral coalition were divided in their preferences between him and Hillary Clinton.

The success of the Obama campaign is the exception, however. Usually party elites agree on a candidate based in part on that candidate's national reputation, leadership endorsements, and performance in the early caucuses and primaries. The elites then join forces to help that candidate secure the nomination as soon as possible.[8] Most party leaders, including most of the elites, believe that long, divisive nominations hurt the chances of their party's nominee in the general election.

Interest groups, such as labor unions and women's groups for the Democrats and evangelical and fundamentalist Christian and other social groups for the Republicans, have become increasingly important during the nominations because of their capacity to commit resources to educating the public and to mobilizing their supporters. Their impact often is reinforced by their activities before and after elections in the form of public relations campaigns, lobbying, and fund-raising events that maintain the ties among these groups, the candidates, and the elected officials that are sympathetic to their cause.

By emphasizing the policy positions that these groups advocate, the candidates have become more ideological and issue oriented themselves. They believe they have to be so to get nominated and elected and renominated and reelected. Thus, the positions of the candidates for nomination on a range of policy issues do not usually deviate much from the well-known preferences of the party's base. And when they do, as Republicans did about Ron Paul's and

Mike Huckabee's opposition to the Bush administration's policy in Iraq and Rudolph Giuliani's position on abortion, same-sex marriage, and stem cell research, they are criticized and often vigorously opposed by partisan activists.

The influence of the activists in both parties is the principal reason why aspirants for the Republican nomination tend to move to the ideological right of their party and Democrats to the ideological left of theirs as they compete for their party's nomination. After they get the nomination, though, they frequently find that their initial positions alienate mainstream voters who have more moderate perspectives and more pragmatic views, so they move toward the center in the general election. The ideological influence exerted within both parties' nomination processes are also evident in the selection of convention delegates, who tend to be more ideological in their thinking and beliefs than rank-and-file party identifiers and much more so than the general public.[9]

What an irony! Parties have reformed their nomination processes to reflect more accurately the attitudes, opinions, and candidate choices of their rank-and-file supporters. They've adopted rules to tie the eventual selection of nominees more closely to the party electorate. That party electorate, however, has been disproportionately influenced by party elites who have the incentives, the resources, and the skills to affect the nomination process and whose discernible interests and ideological beliefs distinguish them not only from the general public but also from typical supporters of their own parties. Thus, as a consequence of opening the process to achieve better representation, the parties may not represent the moderate, mainstream electorate nearly as well as they did in the pre-reform era when party leaders chose candidates primarily on the basis of their electability, not their ideological preferences or detailed issue positions.

Nor do rank-and-file partisans exercise the influence they did in the period after the reforms were originally instituted in the 1970s, before high costs, front-loaded contests, and creation of superdelegates gave the elites their current advantage. In short, the democratization of the process has not produced the democratic outcome for which the reformers had hoped. In theory, the people have influence; they have the opportunity to participate in their party's nomination if they choose to do so. In practice, however, it is the elites who have the incentives and resources to exercise the most clout, and they usually do.

And that's not all. Not only have the parties' elected officials become less representative of their rank and file, they also may be less capable of governing. Ideologues are not good compromisers.

THE IMPACT OF NOMINATIONS ON GOVERNMENT

Taking more consistent ideological stands is just the first step toward pursuing these policy positions if elected. The growing ideologicalization of American parties has resulted in sharper partisan divisions within Congress. The old-boys' club that operated according to informal folkways and mores has given way to the new activist politics replete with ideological rhetoric and partisan confrontation. This partisan stridency is what closed down the government in the winter of 1995–1996 for almost a month; two years later it led to a presidential impeachment. It has impeded the enactment of legislation during periods of divided government.

The ideological gap between the two major parties has filtered down to the grassroots level. The partisan electorate is highly polarized, creating an explosive political environment in which deliberation gives way to oratory, compromise is made more difficult, and the public has become more cynical and less trusting of those who represent them than they were two or three decades ago.

All of the factors that have contributed to the deterioration of America's political culture and to its governing problems cannot be blamed on the nomination process alone. The causes are deep-seated and varied. They have taken place over a longer period of time than have nomination reforms. Moreover, they have been exacerbated by social, technological, and political change. Nonetheless, the democratization of the nomination process has had a discernible impact that many evaluate as negative.

IMPROVING THE NOMINATION SYSTEM

What can be done about this representational problem and its impact on government? A return to the good old days, when party bosses controlled the selection of party candidates and influenced the policy positions they took, seems both unlikely and undesirable. There would be little public support for making the selection process more elitist and for reducing the input of rank-and-file voters, despite the fact that so many party identifiers have chosen not to take part in the process.

Nor would there be much support for taking a party's internal politics out of the public arena or limiting the news media's access to it. Some might desire the press to exercise more self-constraint, particularly when reporting and assessing the personal traits and private behavior of candidates, but there is far from unanimity on this point.

Can and Should Nominations Be Made More Democratic?

If going back to the old system isn't a viable option, then what is? Perhaps the parties could level the playing field by getting a greater cross section of their partisans to participate. Because activists gain disproportionate influence from their political involvement, getting more people aware, interested, and involved in primaries could lessen this influence. Presumably, if a broader cross section of a party participated in nomination politics, the candidates would have more incentive to appeal to a wider range of interests and views. But how can more people be encouraged to get involved, given the cynicism and apathy so apparent at the end of the twentieth and beginning of the twenty-first centuries?

Contemporary campaigns have responded to this challenge by communicating with potential voters directly. In 2004, the Republican Party mounted a turnout campaign in which individuals were targeted, contacted personally by Republican volunteers who live in the community, and then recontacted to get them out to vote. The party also used ballot initiatives in several key states to maximize its turnout. In 2008, the Obama and Clinton campaigns used the Internet effectively to activate their supporters, involve them in the campaign, and get them out to vote. These activities, combined with the closeness of the Democratic contest, generated a much larger primary vote than in the past.

There are dangers, however, in massive outreach campaigns. They can be labor-intensive and can cause deep divisions within the party that are difficult to heal. One challenge, which Barack Obama faced after his victory over Hillary Clinton, was to gain the support of women who had backed her candidacy. Extended competition hardens preferences, making it more difficult to unify the party.

From the perspective of party leaders, divisive nominations are a problem. The greater the number of candidates and the longer they campaign, the more likely that the party will remain divided and, as a consequence, the higher the odds against winning the general election. In this situation, the nominee's image has probably been damaged by opponents during hard-fought primaries, and some supporters of the losing candidates remain on the sidelines.[10] Party leaders would like to reduce the negative effects that bitter internecine warfare produces, not exacerbate them.

Can Divisive Nominations within Parties Be Avoided in a Democratic Nomination Process?

Reducing divisive primaries and their impact is not achieved by leveling the playing field. It is accomplished by "unleveling" it even more, by giving advantage to the advantaged—to well-known, well-financed candidates and, frequently, to incumbents. In short, the parties are faced with a situation in which they can encourage more candidates and voters to participate, possibly factionalizing themselves even further in the process and hurting their chances for electoral victory, or they can discourage participation, possibly making the nominees less representative of the wishes of rank-and-file supporters; but they can't do both simultaneously.

The Democrats adjusted some of the rules in their presidential nominating process to give an advantage to their national leaders who have national reputations. They made two adjustments: creating unpledged superdelegates and tightening the nomination schedule. Both changes decreased the odds that outside candidates could parlay early caucus and primary victories into a bandwagon for the nomination. And both parties have imposed sanctions on states that do not comply with party rules. The most frequent violation of party rules thus far has been to hold nomination contests before the date that the party permits. In 2008, the delegates to the national party conventions of the states that violated calendar rules were reduced by one half. Such a reduction, however, can threaten party unity and general election support in the states that are penalized. To avoid that possibility, the Democratic National Committee heeded the request of the Obama campaign to eliminate the sanctions after Obama had wrapped up the nomination; the Republicans maintained the penalty. They had no choice since their nomination rules are set by the previous Republican convention, the one that occurred four years earlier. The bottom line, however, is that the threat of sanctions has not been sufficient to prevent some states from violating party rules by holding their contests before party rules allow them to do so.

Inequitable state representation, reduced rank-and-file participation, and the need to raise more money to keep their presumptive nominees on television have encouraged both major parties to propose additional changes to the nomination calendar. A Republican advisory committee in 2000 recommended a series of regional primaries and an incentive system to give states extra convention delegates if they held their nomination contests after April 15 during the year of the election,[11] but the presumptive nominee, George W. Bush, objected to the proposal on the grounds that it would extend the schedule, cost the candidates more money, reduce the influence of the large states, and lead to a divisive debate at the 2000 Republican National Convention, a debate he did not want. As a consequence, the Republican Rules Committee did not approve the advisory commission's recommendation much less introduce it to the 2000 Republican convention for approval.

A Democratic Party Commission on Nomination, Timing, and Scheduling approved by delegates at the 2004 Democratic National Convention also attempted to spread out the caucuses and primaries by increasing the number of convention delegates states would receive if they held their primaries and caucuses later in the year.[12] In addition, the commission proposed—and the party accepted—a rules change that added one caucus and one primary to the early part of the Democratic nomination calendar. Following the Iowa caucus, Nevada, a state with a rapidly growing Hispanic population, was authorized to hold its caucus. Following the New Hampshire primary, South Carolina, a state with a large African American population, was given permission to schedule its primary. Both did so in 2008.

Should the Parties Institute a National Primary?

The hodgepodge of primaries, scheduling issues, low turnout, and dissatisfaction with the candidates who have won their party's nomination has led some to recommend a national primary in which both major parties would choose their nominees in a direct popular vote. The simplicity of this suggestion, the promise of higher turnout, and the expectation that the prospective nominees would have to address national issues like those they would encounter in office have generated support for such a proposal as has the fact that it would eliminate front-loading and the disproportionate influence that early states currently have on the nomination process.[13]

Although proposals for a national primary vary, most advocate conducting the election in the early summer, preceding the national nominating conventions. Candidates who could demonstrate their popularity and electability,
perhaps by obtaining a certain number of signatures on petitions or receiving
a minimum percentage of support in the public opinion polls conducted in the
months before the primary, could enter. Anyone who received a majority in the
national primary would automatically become the nominee. In some plans, a
plurality would be sufficient, provided it was at least 40 percent. In the event
that no one received 40 percent, a runoff election could be held several weeks
later between the top two finishers, or the convention could choose the nominee from among the top vote-getters.

A national primary would be consistent with the democratic principle of
one person–one vote.[14] Moreover, the attention that such an election would
receive from the press and the candidates should provide greater incentives for
a higher voter turnout than currently exists, particularly in states that hold
their nomination contests after the apparent nominee has emerged. If more
people participated, the electorate would probably be more representative than
today's electorate that chooses the parties' nominees, and the winning candidate would have been tested in a national campaign. And, finally, the outcome
of the vote should be clear; no longer could members of the press interpret
winners and losers as they saw fit.

The flip side of a national primary, however, is that it would exacerbate the
advantages that front-runners have, particularly Washington-based insiders
and large-state governors, people who can raise the money for an expensive
and, at most, only partly subsidized national campaign. Lesser-known candidates, unless they were independently wealthy and willing to spend their own
fortune on a national campaign, would have little chance of competing on an
equal scale with better-funded candidates.

Another potential problem is that a national primary could increase divi-
siveness within the parties, contribute to the personification of politics, and
weaken the organizational base of the parties. A post-primary convention
could not be expected to tie the nominee to the party, although it might tie the
party to the nominee, at least through the general election.

Finally, would state party leaders support a national primary in which they
would probably have less influence? Would the same early states that benefit
from the current arrangement agree to hold their contests later in the spring or
summer and on the same day as others? Would those states that have caucuses
agree to a primary? And if federal legislation were needed, would representatives of the states that prefer to exercise their authority to conduct elections for
federal officials support this "loss" of state power?

Moreover, the cumulative impact of a national primary, followed by
national party conventions, followed by a national election might be too much
campaign and election in too short a period of time. It might be more than
the electorate is willing or able to absorb. Imagine the same themes and
appeals, statements and advertisements, debates and more debates echoing

across the land for a period of six months to a year. Voters might tune out; they might become even more cynical and distrustful of politicians, particularly if such a long national campaign produced a long list of promises that the winning candidate would be expected to fulfill and on which that candidate's presidency would be evaluated. Certainly, governing might prove to be more difficult if party leaders and members of Congress had little to do with the presidential nominees' victory and thus lacked an incentive to follow the new administration's lead.

Whether a national primary winner would be the party's strongest candidate is also open to question. With a large field of contenders, those with the most devoted supporters might do best. Candidates who don't arouse the passions of the diehards but who are more acceptable to the party's mainstream might not do as well. Everybody's second choice might not even finish second unless a system of approval or of cumulative voting were used, each of which is likely to be complex.[15] These potential negative consequences for the major parties have discouraged them from supporting such a plan, despite its general public appeal. And if there is little enthusiasm within the Democratic and Republican parties for a national primary, then it is very unlikely that Congress would ever impose it on them.

Some of the pros and cons of a national primary from the candidates' and states' perspectives were illustrated on February 5, 2008, when more than 50 percent of the elected Democratic delegates and more than 40 percent of the Republican delegates to the national conventions were chosen. The large number of contests forced the candidates to make strategic choices: where to campaign and how to spend their resources. Obama, in the strongest position with the largest war chest at that time and the most extensive ground operation, chose to campaign in both caucus and primary states. Hillary Rodham Clinton could not afford to do so; she neglected the smaller-state caucuses and primaries in favor of the large-state primaries. Although she won most of those primary states, she did not gain more delegates than Obama on February 5. His campaign continued; hers paused to raise more money and to patch internal dissension and staffing problems. It was during the next three weeks in February that Obama built the delegate lead that he never relinquished.

Should the Parties Establish and Schedule a Series of Regional or Grouped Primaries?

Before the 2008 election cycle, it looked as if a regional system would evolve as a consequence of voluntary agreements among the states in a region to hold their contests on or close to the same date. The southern states were the first to enter into such agreements in 1988; some of the states in the Midwest followed in 1992. But actual primary results, beginning in the mid-1990s and extending through the first two election cycles of the twenty-first century, worked against this trend. The victors won early in the process, prompting states to front-load their contests rather than adhere to a date for the entire region.

Subsequently, both parties created committees to study the calendar and recommend changes. Although several proposals have been made, the only change approved by both parties was to move the date when any state may hold its contest from the first Tuesday in March to the first Tuesday in February.

Nonetheless, disaffection with the front-loading of the schedule and the amount of early fund-raising that it requires has prompted leaders to explore additional options. One proposal that has gained some backing is the so-called American Plan that would set up a spring calendar divided into ten intervals during which nomination contests would be held. The first group holding caucuses or primaries would consist of randomly selected small states that totaled together no more than eight congressional districts—Iowa and New Hampshire combined currently have seven districts. Any state or group of states that has a combined total of eight congressional districts could be in the first round of primaries and caucuses. In the second round the group of states permitted to hold their elections would increase in size by an additional eight districts. In subsequent rounds, the size of each group would increase accordingly.

Proponents argue that such a system would be fairer than the current one. Front-loading would be prohibited; the large states could not exercise disproportionate influence. Because the groups would be chosen randomly by size, no state would have a permanent advantage such as Iowa and New Hampshire presently do. Not only would the states be treated more even-handedly, but more candidates would have greater opportunities to compete and for longer periods of time with the need for less money up front because the states that held the early contests would be small in size.[16] Candidates with regional recognition would have greater opportunities to demonstrate their qualifications than in a national primary.

Whether Iowa and New Hampshire and the large states would agree to such an arrangement is questionable. Whether the parties could and would try to impose it on recalcitrant states is also problematic, given the need for party unity to run a general election campaign, the opposition to extended nominations, and the money that such nominations would need. Moreover, such a system would require that other nomination contests within each state be held at the same time to avoid the cost of holding two separate election days to encompass all nominations. Would incumbents and challengers for elected offices support such a change? Moreover, any new system could not be initiated for the Republicans until 2016 at the earliest because the 2008 Republican National Convention approved the party's 2012 nomination rules and procedures.

NATIONAL NOMINATING CONVENTIONS: ANACHRONISM OR STILL RELEVANT?

At the presidential level, the changes in party rules have rendered national nominating conventions obsolete, at least as far as the selection of nominees is concerned. The identity of the likely candidate is known well in advance of the convention. Even the vice presidential selection isn't the convention's to make. By tradition, the presidential nominee chooses a running mate, and the convention ratifies the choice because a majority of the delegates are supporters of the presidential nominee.

So what's left for the convention to decide? Sometimes national nominating conventions debate and resolve platform issues, but most of the time they don't. They ratify the document, which is a combination of principles and policies that a party committee, most likely controlled by the candidate who has won the primaries and caucuses, has drafted.

If disputes do emerge, they often reveal real and deep-seated differences among rank-and-file partisans, but they come to light primarily because the mass media highlight them. In other words, news coverage is an incentive for some disgruntled delegates to publicize their disagreements, taking their fight to the convention floor even though their prospects for victory are slight. It is the national visibility that makes it worthwhile. The threat of embarrassing the nominee by taking an oppositional position to the floor may be enough for the leading candidate to concede some platform points in an effort to avoid the appearance of disunity.

Why hold conventions? If the delegates are chosen in accordance with party rules and are unlikely to change the pledges they have made to support particular candidates, if the convention rules are decided in advance, if the successful candidate for the presidential nomination is preordained by the primaries and caucuses, if that candidate can choose a running mate, and if the platform is hammered out in advance, then why hold conventions at all? This is a question that the broadcast news media are asking with increasing frequency.

From the press's perspective, there's little news. In fact, correspondents and commentators often have to manufacture news by highlighting disagreements, no matter how small, by engaging in seemingly endless and often trivial commentary, and by suggesting potential conflicts, which may or may not exist or come to pass.

From the perspectives of the candidates, the parties, and the interest groups, however, the conventions remain an important political tradition that they wish to continue. The assembled delegates constitute an anointing body that legitimizes the selection of the nominees and a responsive audience that demonstrates enthusiasm for what the party has to offer. The convention provides a national podium from which the candidates can launch their campaigns and from which other leaders can gain recognition. Governor Sarah Palin's speech at the 2008 Republican National Convention energized Republican convention delegates as well as rank-and-file supporters who watched it on television, thereby giving the national ticket a boost of enthusiasm reflected in the post-convention polls. Senator Obama's acceptance speech at the Democratic National Convention that year put an exclamation point on his campaign, showed his rhetorical skills, and set out his themes for the general election while the large audience that filled a football stadium demonstrated its excitement with his candidacy.

From the party's perspective, conventions provide a unifying mechanism, one that can help heal the divisions of the nomination process. They're a reward to the delegates for their past participation and an inducement for them to continue to work in the party's political campaigns, particularly the one that is just beginning. And, finally, they are publicity for the party, its positions, its candidates, and its supporters. But there is a problem.

Naturally, the party wishes to present itself in the best possible light: unified, enthusiastic, optimistic, confident, with a clear sense of purpose, direction, and demonstrated governing abilities. Its leaders orchestrate the proceedings so that they will have this desired effect. The news media, in contrast, are interested in news (naturally, as they define it—new, unexpected, dramatic, and of human interest). They're also concerned with their public responsibility and their profitability, with their bottom lines measured in terms of audience size and the number of readers, subscribers, and listeners.

The objectives of the party and the news media are in conflict. Parties need media coverage of their conventions far more than the news media need to report them, particularly if conventions are boring and predictable, as most of them have been in the last three decades. Presented with this dilemma, the parties stage their meetings; there are daily themes, scripts, films, celebrities, and politicians—all made available to live cameras and microphones. But the parties' elaborate public relations extravaganzas seem to reinforce the news media's contention that the conventions have become almost all pomp and ceremony, with little or no substance. Broadcast network coverage of the major-party conventions, which has declined substantially, may soon be eliminated entirely, with only cable news and public affairs networks covering parts of the proceedings.

Third-party conventions receive practically no live coverage on the major broadcast networks. H. Ross Perot's acceptance speech at his Reform Party convention in 1996 and Ralph Nader's at the Green Party convention in 2000 were aired only by cable news networks and C-SPAN. Nader held news conferences in 2004 and 2008 to announce his candidacy, and they amounted to just sound bites on the evening news.

If the major networks no longer cover convention proceedings live, then are conventions still necessary? Will they survive? The parties hope so. Beginning in 2000, they launched interactive Web sites to provide information for and gain input from those who accessed their sites.

If conventions are abolished, then how will parties unify themselves after a divisive nomination struggle? How will they decide on and approve a platform on the critical issues? How will they engage and energize the public, particularly independent voters who tend to be less interested, less informed, and less involved? When will the general election campaign officially begin, or will it be an endless campaign cycle from pre-candidacy to nomination to election and then to pre-candidacy again?

If regional or grouped primaries were to be established by voluntary agreements among states, by national rules mandated by the parties, or by an act of Congress, a national nominating convention could still serve as a potential decision maker in the event that the primaries were not decisive. It could act as a body to choose or ratify the vice presidential nominee and as a platform maker for the candidates in the general election. The cheerleader and launch-pad functions also would continue to be important for the convention.

Similarly, if a national primary were instituted and the leading candidate did not receive the required percentage of the vote, the convention could then choose the nominee from among the top candidates. It also could serve as the decisive body to approve a platform for the winning candidate.

THE INCUMBENCY ADVANTAGE

Despite all the hoopla about how open the nomination process has become, incumbents who run for reelection usually win. The deck is stacked even more against challengers in nominations than it is in general elections. Take Congress, for example. For the period from the end of World War II through the 2008 election, 208 House incumbents out of 12,738 were defeated in their quest for renomination (less than 2 percent), and 42 senators lost renomination out of 920 who sought it (less than 5 percent). At the presidential level, the last incumbent to lose a presidential nomination was Chester Arthur in 1884 although Gerald Ford came close to losing to Ronald Reagan in 1976. Two Democratic presidents, Harry Truman and Lyndon Johnson, chose not to compete for renomination in part because of the opposition and competition within their own party. Table 7.2 indicates incumbency success in renomination for Congress between 1946 and 2008.

Why do incumbents do so well? The system gives them important built-in benefits. These include greater name recognition, superior fund-raising skills, and more campaign experience, coupled with access to more experienced campaign aides. Incumbents frequently have grassroots organizations and the ability to give help to and get help from other party leaders. These benefits translate into great odds for most incumbents seeking renomination.

The incumbency advantage is enhanced by the absence of competition. For the obvious reason that it is so difficult to defeat them, incumbents face fewer challengers than do candidates who run for open seats (seats for which an incumbent isn't running); and when incumbents are challenged, it is often by candidates who cannot raise sufficient funds to mount an effective campaign against them. Besides, voters tend to be risk averse, preferring a known candidate to an unknown one, unless the known candidate allegedly engaged in immoral, unethical, or criminal activities.

TABLE 7.2 Congressional Incumbents Seeking Renomination, 1946–2008

Year	Senate			House of Representatives		
	Total seeking renomination	Number defeated	Percentage defeated	Total seeking renomination	Number defeated	Percentage defeated
1946	30	6	20	398	18	5
1948	25	2	8	400	15	4
1950	32	5	16	400	6	2
1952	31	2	6	389	9	2
1954	32	2	6	407	6	1
1956	29	0	0	411	6	1
1958	28	0	0	396	3	1
1960	29	0	0	405	5	1
1962	35	1	3	402	12	3
1964	33	1	3	397	8	2
1966	32	3	9	411	8	2
1968	28	4	14	408	4	1
1970	31	1	3	401	10	2
1972	27	2	7	392	14	1
1974	27	2	7	391	8	2
1976	25	0	0	384	3	1
1978	25	3	12	382	5	1
1980	29	4	14	398	6	2
1982	30	0	0	387	4	1
1984	29	0	0	411	3	1
1986	28	0	0	394	3	1
1988	27	0	0	409	1	—
1990	32	0	0	407	1	—
1992	28	1	4	368	19	5
1994	26	0	0	387	4	1
1996	21	1*	5	384	2	1
1998	29	0	0	402	1	—
2000	29	0	0	403	3	1
2002	28	1	4	398	8	2
2004	26	0	0	404	2	—
2006	29	1	3	404	2	—
2008	30	0	0	403	4	1

*Sheila Frahm, appointed to fill Robert Dole's term, is counted as an incumbent seat.

Source: Harold W. Stanley and Richard G. Niemi, Vital Statistics in American Politics, 2009–2010 (Washington, D.C.: CQ Press, 2009), 43–44.

Is the incumbency advantage good or bad for a democratic election process and for a democratic government? On the positive side, it provides the party with continuity in its candidacies. Because incumbents have an advantage in the general election, the advantage enables the party to maintain its elective positions and the constituents to keep their representative. The more senior a representative is, the greater that person's influence within the legislative body is likely to be and the more that representative is able to accomplish for constituents.

On the negative side, though, the incumbent's renomination advantage translates into more independence from the party. There's little a party's leaders can do to a popular incumbent who chooses to deviate from the party's position on the issues.

SUMMARY: NOMINATION DILEMMAS IN A NUTSHELL

In theory, the movement to a nomination process in which more people have the opportunity to participate has opened the parties and theoretically expanded their base. From a democratic perspective, that's good. In practice, however, only a portion of the major parties' rank and file actually has gotten involved regularly and voted—the 2008 nominations, particularly the Democratic one, being the exception. From a democratic perspective, low participation is unhealthy. It contributes to the control of the process and its product—the nominee—by party elites. Front-loading, delegate allocation, open primaries, winner-take-all voting, and the designation of non-elected superdelegates by the Democrats all detract from a democratic nomination process.

That the states that hold the early caucuses and primaries are not representative of the party as a whole, that the people who do participate in the caucuses and primaries tend to have the strongest ideological orientations, and that the candidates who benefit from the current system tend to be those with the greatest name recognition, the most money, and the most organizational support all undercut the democratic character of the nomination process. This environment probably also contributes to the public's cynicism and distrust of politicians and their parties.

Various proposals for reforming the nomination process at the presidential level have been advanced. The goal of these proposals—democratizing the presidential selection process even more by getting more of the party's rank and file to participate—is laudable. The result, however, may be to advantage further the front-runners, particularly incumbents, to create more division within the parties and to make the parties more subject to the influence of those who win their nominations rather than the other way around. The parties are faced with a representational dilemma. Can they simultaneously reflect the wishes of their diverse base and also provide strong partisan, national leadership? What do you think?

Now It's Your Turn

Discussion Questions

1. Why did the major political parties reform their nomination processes in the 1970s, and did the reforms achieve their desired goals?
2. From the perspectives of the parties, candidates, and partisan supporters, what are the main advantages and disadvantages of the current nomination processes for president and members of Congress?
3. How would you reform the parties' current nomination rules to mitigate the disadvantages to the parties, candidates, and partisan supporters? Do you support or oppose the changes in party rules that recent party committees and outside groups have proposed? What effect, if any, do you think these rule changes would have on the democratic character of the presidential nominating process?
4. Does the advantage that incumbents have in securing renomination undercut the equity principle inherent in a democratic electoral system?
5. What impact, if any, does the process of nomination have on the structure of the parties and their ability to govern if elected?

Topics for Debate

Challenge or defend the following statements:

1. The reforms in the major parties' presidential nominating processes have not worked and should be reversed.
2. Congress should enact a law that establishes a national primary for selecting the major parties' presidential nominees.
3. Because Iowa and New Hampshire are not representative of the entire country, they should be prevented from automatically holding the first caucus and primary election.
4. Aspirants for their party's presidential nomination should not be allowed to campaign before the year of the election.
5. National nominating conventions are irrelevant and should be abolished.

Exercises

1. You've been asked to head a committee to reform the way your party chooses its nominees. The primary goals that the party wants you to consider when you propose your reforms are, in order of importance, to:
   a. select the strongest and most qualified candidate to run in the general election,
   b. give all partisans an opportunity to participate in some way in the nominating process,

    c. increase the likelihood that the views of the winning candidate will reflect the views of the rank and file, and

    d. have a nominating process that is open to all well-qualified candidates.

In your plan, indicate:

    a. when and how the nominees for national office will be selected,

    b. the rules for determining who can run and who can vote,

    c. the penalties, if any, that you would impose on states that threaten to disregard party rules,

    d. the method for approving or amending your reforms, and

    e. an explanation of how and why your proposed reforms will be an improvement on the present system.

2. Critique one of the proposals mentioned in the text for changing the nomination process. Indicate whether you believe the change would positively or negatively affect the parties, the candidates, and the partisan electorate. Give examples, hypothetical or real, to support your argument.

INTERNET RESOURCES

- *Congressional Quarterly:* www.cq.com
  Publishes a variety of journals on politics and government and is an excellent source of information on campaign strategy and tactics; site includes *Campaigns and Elections,* which can be accessed through the general site or directly at www.camelect.com.
- *National Journal:* www.nationaljournal.com
  Excellent magazine for studying politics and government, with numerous links to its own and other publications.
- U.S. Department of Defense Federal Voting Assistance Program: www.fvap.gov
  Provides information on absentee voting.
- United States Election Assistance Commission: www.eac.gov
  Established by the Help America Vote Act of 2002; central to its role, the commission serves as a national clearinghouse and resource for information on the administration of federal elections.

SELECTED READINGS

Altschuler, Bruce. "Selecting the Presidential Nominee by National Primary: An Idea Whose Time has Come." *The Forum* 5, no. 4 (2008): article 5.

Atkeson, Lonna Rae. "Divisive Primaries and General Election Outcomes: Another Look at Presidential Campaigns." *American Journal of Political Science* 42 (1998): 256–271.

Bartels, Larry M. *Presidential Primaries and the Dynamics of Public Choice.* Princeton: Princeton University Press, 1988.

Burden, Barry C. "The Nominations: Technology, Money, and Transferable Momentum." In *The Elections of 2004,* edited by Michael Nelson. Washington, D.C.: CQ Press, 2005.

Cook, Rhodes. *The Presidential Nominating Process: A Place for Us?* Lanham, Md.: Rowman and Littlefield, 2004.

Day, Christine L., Charles D. Hadley, and Harold W. Stanley. "The Inevitable Unanticipated Consequences of Political Reform: The 2004 Presidential Nomination Process." In *A Defining Moment,* edited by William Crotty, 74–86. Armonk, N.Y.: M. E. Sharpe, 2005.

Geer, John G. *Nominating Presidents: An Evaluation of Voters and Primaries.* Westport, Conn.: Greenwood Press, 1989.

Mayer, William G., and Andrew E. Busch, eds. *The Front-Loading Problem in Presidential Nominations.* Washington, D.C.: Brookings Institution Press, 2004.

Norrander, Barbara. "The Attribution Game: Initial Resources, Initial Contest, and the Exit of Candidates during the U.S. Presidential Primary Season." *British Journal of Political Science* 36 (2006): 478–502.

Polsby, Nelson W. *The Consequences of Party Reform.* New York: Oxford University Press, 1983.

Shafer, Byron E. *Bifurcated Politics: Evolution and Reform in the National Party Convention.* Cambridge: Harvard University Press, 1988.

Smith, Larry David, and Dan Nimmo. *Cordial Concurrence: Orchestrating National Party Conventions in the Telepolitical Age.* New York: Praeger, 1991.

Task Force on Campaign Reform. *Campaign Reform: Insights and Evidence.* Princeton: Princeton University Press, 1998.

Tolbert, Caroline, and Peverill Squire. "Reforming the Presidential Nomination Process." *PS: Political Science and Politics* 42 (January 2009): 27–79.

NOTES

1. The Supreme Court gave the parties this power in its 1975 landmark decision in *Cousins v. Wigoda* (419 U.S. 477). The Court held that political parties were private organizations with rights of association protected by the Constitution. Parties could compel state affiliates to abide by their rules of delegate selection for the national nominating convention unless there were compelling constitutional reasons for not doing so. The burden of proving these reasons was placed on the state that deviated from the party's rules. Although in theory the party has the power to enforce its national rules, in practice this has been difficult to do because states have the authority to conduct elections, including primary elections, for federal officials. State affiliates of the national parties are thus subject to the election laws of the state. To reject these laws and conduct their own selection process is difficult and costly.

2. Although Republicans profess the same broad goals, they mandated only one national rule for their state parties: that they not discriminate in the selection of delegates on the basis of race, creed, color, national origin, or gender. In other aspects of delegate selection, the GOP enforces whatever rules a state party observes.

3. The principal difference is that Republicans permit winner-take-all voting on a district or statewide basis, and the Democrats do not.

4. Paul Allen Beck and Frank J. Sorauf, *Party Politics in America,* 7th ed. (New York: HarperCollins, 1992), 234–235.

5. There are more challengers in a nomination contest to run against an incumbent of the opposition party in the general election than there are in the incumbent's party when that incumbent is seeking renomination. The more open system, however, keeps incumbents more attuned to their constituents' interests and needs, in part because of the threat of being embarrassed, much less being beaten by a challenger.

6. United States Census Bureau, "2005 American Community Survey: Data Highlights," 2006, http://factfinder.census.gov; updated by author.

7. In addition to front-loading, there also has been a regionalization of the presidential nomination contests, with states in similar regions of the country agreeing to hold their primaries and caucuses during the same period, often on the same day. This movement, which began in 1988 with a southern regional primary, has continued and even expanded in each subsequent nomination cycle. It too gives advantage to candidates with established national and regional reputations—those who are well known, well funded, and well organized—and hurts those without such reputations and resources. Engaging in multistate campaigning and using extensive media require substantial resources, which front-runners usually have and outsiders usually lack.

8. John Aldrich, "The Invisible Primary and Its Effects on Democratic Choice," *PS: Political Science and Politics* 42 (January 2009): 33–38; Marty Cohen, David Carol, Hans Noel, and John Zaller, *The Party Decides: Presidential Nominations before and after Reform* (Chicago: University of Chicago Press, 2008).

9. This phenomenon was first identified by Herbert McClosky, "Consensus and Ideology in American Politics," *American Political Science Review* 58 (1964): 361–382; see also Jeane J. Kirkpatrick, *The New Presidential Elite* (New York: Russell Sage, 1976). The phenomenon appears in the surveys of delegates since then.

10. Divisive primaries, however, if they encourage turnout, can have the beneficial effect of mobilizing the party's electorate for the general election and subsequent contests. See Walter J. Stone, Lonna Rae Atkeson, and Ronald B. Rapoport, "Turning On or Turning Off? Mobilization and Demobilization Effects of Participation in Presidential Nomination Campaigns," *American Journal of Political Science* 36 (August 1992): 665–691.

11. The proposal would have grouped states according to population and forced them to hold their caucuses and primaries on the same day. Primaries for each of the population groups would be scheduled about a month apart, beginning in early March, with the least populous states going first.

12. The Democratic Party's commission recommended that the calendar be divided into four stages. The states that held their nomination contest during the first stage, the two-week period beginning with the first Tuesday in March, would receive additional delegates equal to 15 percent of their total number of pledged delegates. If they held their election during stage two, the three-week period beginning the third Tuesday in March, they would receive an additional 20 percent. If their selection date was in the third stage, the three-week period that begins on the second Tuesday in April, they would be allocated an additional 30 percent, and

if they held it after that and before the end of the Democratic nomination process on the second Tuesday in June, they would be entitled to an additional 40 percent of their total number of delegates.

13. Several surveys conducted over the years indicate public support for a direct primary nomination system. A poll by the *New York Times* and CBS News conducted in July 2007 found 72 percent favoring such a system. A Gallup poll conducted nine years earlier also found a majority in support of a national primary election. Gallup Poll, "Electoral Reforms," April 10, 1988, as reported in *The Gallup Poll: Public Opinion 1988* (Wilmington, Del.: Scholarly Resources, 1989), 60–61.

14. For an extended discussion in favor of a national primary, see Bruce Altschuler, "Selecting the Presidential Nominee by National Primary: An Idea Whose Time has Come," *The Forum* 5, no. 4 (2008): article 5, www.bepress.com/forum/v015/iss4/art5.

15. Approval voting allows the electorate to vote to approve or disapprove each candidate who is running. The candidate with the most approval votes is elected. In a system of cumulative voting, candidates are ordered by rank, and the ranks may be averaged to determine the winner.

16. For an extended discussion of this plan, see www.fairvote.org.

chapter 8

Campaign Communications
How Much Do They Matter?

Did you know that . . .

- the Republican stereotype of Democrats as big-government, liberal do-gooders and the Democratic stereotype of Republicans as big-business, mean-spirited conservatives have existed for almost eighty years?
- most people believe that personality issues are relevant and important even though they also believe that the news media place too much emphasis on them?
- political advertising in presidential elections began in 1952, and the first negative presidential ad was run in 1964?
- political consultants believe that they perform an essential role in the democratic electoral process, and more than 80 percent of them find negative advertising perfectly acceptable?
- recent checks into the content of political advertisements in presidential elections consistently found exaggeration, misleading statements, and factual errors?
- Obama spent more than three times as much money on advertising as McCain in the final weeks of the 2008 campaign?
- the Internet now contains more campaign information (and also probably more unreliable information) than any other single media source?
- the Obama 2008 campaign collected more than 13 million e-mail addresses and had one million people sign up for its text messaging program?
- incumbents use the imagery of their public office to maximize their already large reelection advantages?
- the most influential negative ads in recent presidential election campaigns—the Willie Horton ad (1988) and the Swift Boat Veterans for Truth commercials (2004)—were sponsored by outside groups, not by the official candidate and party campaign committees?

Is this any way to run a democratic election?

CAMPAIGN COMMUNICATIONS AND DEMOCRATIC ELECTIONS

Campaigns matter! They determine who wins. They highlight the principal issues with which the public is concerned and that newly elected officials must address. They influence the electorate: who votes, for whom, and why. They test the adequacy of the principal components of a democratic political system: free speech, public participation, group advocacy, meaningful choice, informed judgment, and, ultimately, responsive and accountable government.

Although political campaigns are not the only factor that determines an election's outcome, its salient issues, turnout and voting behavior of the citizenry, and responsive government, they are a principal one that affects these aspects of electoral politics. They can also be a vehicle for educating and engaging the public. In this sense, they can and do contribute to participatory democracy.

However, campaigns often fall short of achieving their democratic goals. Instead of clarifying the issues for the electorate, they can obscure them; instead of turning out voters, they can turn them off; and instead of providing a realistic agenda for the new government, they can create unrealistic expectations that newly elected officials may not be able to meet. And as previously argued, they also can be an instrument by which the advantaged, those with superior resources—money, organization, and leadership—maintain or extend their political influence. In short, campaigns can strengthen or weaken the democratic system, depending on how they are conducted and what impact they have.

The key question is not whether campaigns are necessary. Of course they are. Rather, the issue explored in this chapter is: how well do contemporary campaigns meet the goals of informing and motivating voters? To answer this question the chapter examines campaign communication from the candidates to the electorate. The discussion begins by exploring the kinds of information that should be most helpful to the electorate in making an informed voting decision. Then it turns to the type of information candidates usually convey in their basic appeals to voters and how their modes of communication can intentionally or unintentionally distort the message the electorate receives. Finally, the text looks at the impact on voters of campaigning, particularly the Obama campaign's innovative use of the Internet.

The Need To Know

Campaigning is obviously an integral part of the electoral process. Candidates need campaigns to accomplish their principal objective of winning elective office. Candidates also need campaigns to learn about public concerns and to convince voters that they will address those concerns satisfactorily. The electorate needs the campaign for similar reasons: to voice its needs, espouse its interests, and gain the information necessary to decide which of the candidates (and parties) are more likely to benefit it in the years ahead.

What does the electorate need to know to make informed voting decisions? At the very least the voting public needs to be able to identify the candidates, anticipate the policies they will pursue and the judgments they are likely to make if elected, and make an overall evaluation of how successful they are likely to be in comparison with the others who are running. The promises candidates make, the positions they take, and the priorities they articulate should be reasonable guides to their performance in office. If they are, then voters can hold incumbents and, to a lesser extent, their party accountable in the next election. If they are not, then voters can evaluate the performance of public officials who seek reelection on the basis of how well their policies worked and what their consequences were for society.

Knowing what the candidates have to say is only part of the information needed to make enlightened voting decisions. Voters also need to know about the candidates themselves: their experience, their qualifications, and their personal strengths and weaknesses. This is where character fits in.

Elected officials may not be able to fulfill their promises even if they try to do so. New issues may arise; unexpected events will occur; and the economic, social, and political environment may change. Moreover, the knowledge they accumulate in office should be deeper and broader than it was when they were candidates.[1] Thus, it is important to anticipate how candidates will adapt to change. Character provides an insight into work style, adaptability, and the capacity to handle new challenges.[2]

In addition to knowing about the candidates, their philosophy, policy positions, and character, the electorate also needs to know whether they stand a good, fair, or poor chance of winning. It would be nice to vote for a person who thinks as we do and in whom we have confidence, but it might prove to be meaningless if that individual has little or no chance of being elected. An intelligent voting decision may include the component of not wasting your vote.[3] For the vast majority of people, voting for someone who has little or no chance is not a smart vote, unless it is to prevent one of the other candidates from winning.

The Information Game

Given the importance of an issue debate to a democratic electoral process, how much information should candidates provide? Should they present a general map that indicates the policy directions they hope to pursue, and should they also fill in the details?

The Policy Perspective: Generalities v. Detail. If the amount of information most people have or are interested in knowing is any indication of what the public desires or is capable of learning, then candidates should be more general than specific. They should talk about their philosophies, their basic goals, and their priorities. But being too general also can be a disadvantage if a candidate is perceived as purposefully vague. That was the case when Republican Thomas E. Dewey ran for president in 1948. Because he had a large lead in the polls and also did not want to alienate a predominantly Democratic electorate, Dewey spoke in platitudes and generalities that seemed empty and directionless when compared with President Harry S Truman's straight talk, specific promises, and Democratic imagery. Truman energized the Democratic faithful sufficiently by the time of the election to win a surprising victory.

The same criticism—being vague and talking in generalities—was directed at George W. Bush during his 2000 nomination and election campaigns by opponents who claimed that he lacked a detailed knowledge of the issues.[4] Barack Obama was also accused by his Democratic nomination opponent, Hillary Rodham Clinton, of being all style and no substance. Obama responded to the criticism by detailing his policy positions on his Web site and in debates he had with the other Democratic candidates.

There is another problem with being too general. Wrong impressions can be created and unrealistic expectations can result. Candidates who are relatively new on the political scene, as Ronald Reagan and Barack Obama were when they ran for president, have to contend with the problem that supporters often delude themselves by seeing what they want to see and believing what they want to believe in a candidate. It was this perception that led Obama to try to lower expectations immediately after he won the 2008 presidential election.[5]

Being too specific, in contrast, can turn off voters who do not care and alienate those who disagree. It can put the candidate and, if that candidate is successful, the elected official in a position from which compromise on public policy is made more difficult, not a desirable outcome (except perhaps to true believers) in a governmental system that divides power and requires compromise most of the time.

The Republicans' Contract with America, the platform on which House Republicans ran in 1994, is a case in point. The contract listed ten proposals that Republican candidates pledged to support if elected. The congressional party's refusal to compromise on these issues, particularly those that pertained to cuts in taxes and domestic spending, was a major cause of the government shutdown in the winter of 1995–1996, a shutdown that reverberated to the congressional Republicans' political detriment. Similarly, Bill Clinton's promise to end discrimination against gays in the military is another illustration of a specific policy proposal that got the newly elected president into trouble at the very beginning of his administration; it was a promise he could not keep.

The generality versus specificity dilemma often places candidates in a "dammed if you do, dammed if you don't" situation. To win their party's nomination and build their electoral coalitions, they need to make specific promises to specific groups. The members of these groups are frequently the most ideologically oriented party identifiers. Then in the general election the candidates usually have to broaden their appeal; most adopt a strategy of moving toward the center of the political spectrum in order to attract independent voters and supporters of the other party. These candidates face a difficult juggling act, made even harder by the fact that any adjustment they make has to be done in full public view. Promises are recorded by the news media, inconsistencies are highlighted, and contrasts in emphases are noted.

The alternative strategy of maintaining consistency in policy positions and priorities was the strategy George W. Bush pursued in 2004. This strategy energizes the base but does not necessarily broaden it. For candidates who adhere to this strategy, the key to success is maximizing partisan turnout by reinforcing the attitudes and opinions of people already inclined to support a particular party. Thus, the GOP mounted a turnout drive in 2004 that targeted "lazy Republicans," people likely to vote for Bush if they voted at all. In a highly polarized and equally divided electorate, "motivation becomes as important as persuasion," according to Matthew Dowd, chief strategist for the Bush-Cheney 2004 campaign.[6] In a diverse but nonpolarized environment, it may not be.

From the perspective of the electorate, information needs vary considerably. Within their own areas of interest and expertise people demand and digest much more information than they do in areas in which they have less knowledge and interest. Business executives may want detailed information on tax policy, investment incentives, and labor-management issues, but they may be much less interested in policy that does not have a discernible economic impact on them, perhaps a program to put one hundred thousand more teachers into classrooms or one that extends prescription drug benefits to people on Medicare. Others, for example, homemakers with young children or older relatives living with them, are probably more interested in these educational and health benefits and less in tax and management issues.

Even if the public is not particularly informed about a policy, there still is reason to demand that candidates discuss their proposals in some detail. Such a discussion tells the electorate a lot about the candidates themselves: their competence, their consistency, their communication skills, and, to some extent, their candor. These traits have become increasingly important in candidate-oriented elections. Here is an example: in his 1972 presidential campaign George McGovern proposed a $1,000 grant to all poor Americans, those whose annual income was less than $12,000. But McGovern could not tell how much his plan would cost the taxpayers, which led many to question his understanding of these matters, much less the viability of the specific proposal he had made. Similarly, replying to criticism that he opposed supplementary appropriations for the military in Iraq, John Kerry said, "I actually did vote for the $87 billion dollars before I voted against it." Kerry's statement reinforced Republican criticism of him as a flip-flopper. In September 2008 when real estate prices were falling, mortgages defaulting, and the credit market in serious difficulty, John McCain said, "the American economy is basically sound,"[7] a statement that contrasted with the faltering economic conditions but reinforced the view that McCain's expertise was not in the economic arena. In short, the promises candidates make and the arguments they use to support their positions indicate their knowledge, experience, and potential for making good policy judgments and governing successfully.

The Character Issue: Public v. Private Behavior. In recent elections, character issues have received much more attention; in some cases character issues have even dominated coverage. In the 1996 presidential election, for example, only two policy issues, the economy and taxation, were mentioned more than Clinton's character by the anchors of the evening news on the major broadcast television networks.[8]

Electing the right people and having confidence in them is nothing new. What is different today is the emphasis placed on personal behavior outside the public arena, which in the past was considered to be irrelevant and, hence, was not reported as news. Are character in general and personal behavior in particular legitimate issues for the electorate to debate? Most observers, pointing to numerous contemporary examples in which character has affected performance in office, think that they are. Richard Nixon's cover-up of the Watergate break-in and his disregard for the civil rights of others, Jimmy Carter's reluctance to deal with the Washington political establishment or even to call members of Congress on the phone to ask them to support his programs, Ronald Reagan's penchant for delegation and unwillingness or inability to supervise his aides closely, Bill Clinton's lack of integrity and candor when responding to allegations about his political dealings as governor of Arkansas and sexual improprieties, and George W. Bush's unwillingness to admit mistakes in the war and occupation of Iraq are all character-based problems that adversely affected their performances in office. It was no coincidence that much attention in 2004 was devoted to George W. Bush's service in the Alabama National Guard and John Kerry's Vietnam War experience and in 2008 to Barack Obama's relationships with his pastor (Jeremiah Wright), a former 1960s and 1970s militant (William Ayers), and a Chicago developer (Tony Rezko) who was indicted for conspiracy and influence peddling.

Assessing candidates' character is important for several reasons. It provides an indication of how they may react to unforeseen events and situations, how flexible they are, how they make decisions, and how they interact with others. It tells the electorate something about their work style, energy and confidence, empathy, honesty and candor, personal integrity, and leadership skills.[9]

Overemphasizing character, however, can be harmful as well. It draws attention away from policy issues. It leads people to draw inferences about behavior that may have little or nothing to do with job performance. It attributes too much influence to personality as a driving force and not enough to other factors that can affect what people say and do—from the information they receive to the goals they wish to attain to the procedures and precedents they are expected to follow. Character-based judgments also encourage flippant, often superficial, assessments by those not trained in psychological analysis and even sometimes by those who are.[10]

A preoccupation with personality also can lead to unrealistic expectations, both good and bad, of what a single person can do in a political system that decentralizes power and responsibilities. Liberals feared Ronald Reagan's strong anticommunist views and George W. Bush's antiterrorism crusade combined with their shoot-from-the-hip speaking styles could plunge the country into more military encounters, whereas conservatives feared that Bill Clinton's penchant to please combined with his promises to end discrimination against homosexuals in the military, support affirmative action, provide a comprehensive health care program with universal coverage for all Americans, and stimulate the economy with more federal spending would result in an even bigger and more intrusive national government, fears that were also expressed about Barack Obama's health care proposals. The fears about Reagan and Clinton were not realized, in part because institutional and political checks within the system prevented these presidents from dominating the government so as to dictate public policy outcomes. However, the war in Iraq seemed to confirm the worst fears about Bush.

Spin: Positive v. Negative. Candidates obviously need to make their own cases. They have to provide reasons for voting for them and against their opponents. To do so, they must state their policy positions, personal qualifications, and experience and somehow get their opponents' negatives onto the public record. They do so by leaking the negatives to the news media, mentioning them in their own campaign advertising, or referring to them in speeches, press conferences, and debates.

The electorate does need to know some of this information. People have to evaluate the strengths and shortcomings of a candidate in order to make an informed judgment about that candidate's suitability for the office. And as we know, the candidates themselves are not the best source for information about their own shortcomings. Most campaigns maintain an active opposition research operation on the belief that if they do not find the dirt on their opponents, it's possible no one will. They justify this research on the grounds that their opponents also engage in it.

How much negativism is desirable? Too much can lead to public cynicism toward all of the candidates. It can lead to a perception that the voting choice is about the lesser of two (or more) evils. Too much negativism also can have a boomerang effect on those who resort to it too heavily. Both Steve Forbes and Robert Dole saw their poll numbers decline as they began to air negative ads against their opponents in the 1996 campaign, as did Richard Gephardt and Howard Dean in 2004. The fear of a negative public reaction to attacking Barack Obama led Hillary Clinton to reject the advice of her senior strategist, Mark Penn, to "target Obama's lack of American roots."[11] Deep fissures within the Clinton organization resulted, forcing the candidate to change her advisers in the midst of her campaign. Finding the right balance that appropriately trumpets one's own strengths and an opponent's weaknesses is often a difficult task.

CAMPAIGN IMAGERY

Campaign appeals can distort or clarify. In articulating their messages, candidates usually use partisan imagery. They do so to rouse the faithful, their core supporters. They also do so to stereotype their opponents negatively, particularly when they cannot find other policy or character issues that resonate with the electorate.

Partisan Stereotyping

Sounding a partisan refrain conjures up familiar images about the parties, past and present, both positive and negative. For Democratic candidates, the positive images are economic; they stem from the roots of the Roosevelt realignment. This is why Democratic candidates tend to emphasize bread-and-butter issues such as jobs, wages, education, and social benefits for the working and middle classes. They contrast their empathy for the plight of the average American with Republicans' ties to the rich and the GOP's indifference, even hostility, toward the less fortunate.

From the Republicans' perspective the economic images are very different. Republicans see themselves as defending the free enterprise, capitalist system against their liberal-leaning Democratic opponents, the so-called tax-and-spend liberals, who favor big government and what Republicans call its give-away programs.

Social images are more complex. The Democrats stress equal opportunity and political liberty, whereas the Republicans point to individual initiative in the economic arena and law and order within the domestic sphere. In the national security area, the stereotypes are less distinct, although Republicans have been associated with a more ideological approach that emphasizes American exceptionalism, values, interests abroad, and the use of force as an instrument of diplomacy while the Democrats have stressed negotiation, multilateralism, and realism in their approach to national security issues.

Partisan stereotyping can be dangerous and misleading because it puts everyone in the same box. All Democrats become liberal, pacifist do-gooders and all Republicans turn into wealthy, law-and-order, mean-spirited conservatives. Such images cloud significant differences among candidates of both parties.

Stereotyping also is used to explain current positions and past actions. In 1988, Democratic presidential candidate Michael Dukakis was characterized by his partisan opponents as a knee-jerk liberal who released hardened criminals from jail. To support this accusation, a group opposing Dukakis aired a commercial about a Massachusetts prisoner, Willie Horton, who raped, pistol-whipped, and knifed his victims while on parole. The Bush campaign then reinforced the distinction between Bush's tough approach to criminals and Dukakis's leniency.[12]

To offset being stereotyped as a liberal in 1992, Bill Clinton called himself a "New Democrat" and took pains to differentiate his moderate policy orientation from his liberal Democratic predecessors. Similarly, in 2000, George W. Bush emphasized his "compassionate" conservatism to shown the human dimension of his conservative policy views. In 2008, both candidates ran against their party stereotypes, McCain as a Republican maverick and Obama as a change-oriented Democrat.

In addition to partisan stereotyping, candidates may resort to "wedge issues," those issues that energize particular groups in their electoral coalitions. Robert Dole attempted to use immigration as such an issue in the 1996 election campaign when he appealed to Californians beset with problems stemming from the settlement of so many new immigrants in their state. In 2004, George W. Bush reiterated his support for a constitutional amendment that would have defined marriage as a heterosexual relationship; in the 2008 election, the war in Iraq began as the wedge issue that distinguished the candidates and parties but faded in importance as the economic meltdown became of overriding concern to voters.

If an issue is very controversial and on some level socially unacceptable to raise directly in a campaign, "code words" such as right to life, family values, affirmative action, and same-sex marriage may be used to alert those for whom these words have great and often emotional meaning to engender predictable reactions.

Partisan stereotyping can get in the way of meaningful debate. It can substitute for information, and it can unfairly typecast individuals in a manner that does not accurately reflect their values, priorities, positions, or what they would do if elected to office. Stereotyping does not educate as much as it reinforces preconceptions, dispositions, and biases.

Experience and Incumbency

"Experience is the best teacher" is a maxim that incumbents would like voters to believe. They use their "official" imagery to compare their qualifications with those of their opponents, reminding voters what they have done for them and how they can use their influence to continue to work on their constituents' behalf.

As noted previously, being an incumbent is usually a great advantage. What incumbency imagery does is reinforce and extend the advantages that incumbents already have in running for reelection. The numbers speak for themselves. Table 8.1 notes the reelection rates for members of Congress since 1946.

Although incumbent presidents have not fared as well in reelections because they are subjected to closer and more critical press scrutiny and a more competitive electoral environment, they still have won more than they have lost. Of the eighteen presidents who sought reelection in the twentieth century, only five (Taft in 1912, Hoover in 1932, Ford in 1976, Carter in 1980, and Bush in 1992) were defeated, but it also should be noted that several avoided possible defeat by choosing not to run again. In his study of the incumbency advantage for presidents, Professor David Mayhew found that the party in power kept the presidency about two-thirds of the time when it ran an incumbent but only half the time when an incumbent was not running.[13]

Why do incumbents win more than they lose? A lot has to do with their name recognition and the relatively low level of public knowledge about challengers who seek political office. Name recognition conveys a "known" quality. In general, people would rather vote for someone they have heard of than for someone about whom they know little or nothing.

Incumbents tend to be disadvantaged in only two types of situations: when bad times or multiple grievances hurt those in power, and when incumbents say or do something their constituents find very objectionable.

The incumbency advantage unlevels the playing field. It puts the burden on the challengers to make the case for change. Unless challengers can make that case, they are unlikely to win. To defeat an incumbent requires resources, but, as previously noted, unless challengers are independently wealthy or have considerable backing from their party, they usually are not able to raise as much money as their incumbent opponents. This is why those who desire an elective office try to wait until a seat is open before they seek that office, unless they calculate that the recognition they gain by running against an incumbent (and losing) will put them in real contention the next time around.

COMMUNICATION DISTORTIONS

Accentuating the Positive

Political advertising on radio, television, and, more recently, the Internet has become a primary means of projecting images and conveying information about the candidates. The ads are a big part of the distortion problem in part because they are so effective.

Candidates and their political consultants believe they need to advertise to reach voters. They may be right, although the emphasis on personal contact and grassroots organizing has reduced the influence of political commercials. Technology, such as TiVo, DVDs, and direct-dial movies and movie channels, has also had an impact because it allows people to avoid advertising when they record and watch their favorite programs.

Nonetheless, candidates for national office still spend the bulk of their money on political advertising, and 2008 was no exception. More than $200 million was spent on the presidential nominations alone.[14] At the presidential level, 42 percent of the expenditures went into advertising of one type or another.[15] More than $620 million was spent on television advertising by or on

TABLE 8.1 **Congressional Reelection Rates, 1946–2008**

Year	House of Representatives			Senate		
	Total seeking reelection who were renominated	Defeated in general election	Percentage reelected	Total seeking reelection who were renominated	Defeated in general election	Percentage reelected
1946	370	52	88.6	24	7	70.1
1948	385	68	82.3	23	8	65.2
1950	394	32	91.9	27	5	81.5
1952	380	26	93.2	29	9	69.0
1954	401	22	94.5	30	6	80.0
1956	405	16	96.0	29	4	86.2
1958	393	37	90.6	28	10	64.3
1960	399	25	93.7	29	1	96.6
1962	390	22	94.4	34	5	85.3
1964	389	45	88.4	32	4	87.5
1966	403	41	89.8	29	1	96.6
1968	404	9	97.8	24	4	83.3
1970	391	12	96.9	30	6	80.0
1972	378	13	96.6	25	5	80.0
1974	383	40	89.6	25	2	92.0
1976	381	13	96.6	25	9	64.0

1978	377	19	95.0	22	7	68.2
1980	392	31	92.1	25	9	64.0
1982	383	29	92.4	30	2	93.3
1984	408	16	96.1	29	3	89.7
1986	391	6	98.5	28	7	75.0
1988	408	6	98.5	27	4	85.2
1990	406	15	96.3	32	1	96.9
1992	349	24	93.1	27	4	85.2
1994	383	34	91.2	26	2	92.3
1996	382	21	94.5	20	1	95.0
1998	401	6	98.5	29	3	89.7
2000	400	6	98.5	29	6	79.3
2002	390	8	98.0	27	3	88.9
2004	402	7	98.3	26	1	96.2
2006	402	22	94.5	29*	6	79.3
2008	399	19	95.2	30	5	83.3

*Includes Joseph Lieberman, who was not renominated by the Democrats but ran as an independent and won.

Source: Basic data from Harold W. Stanley and Richard G. Niemi, Vital Statistics in American Politics, 2009–2010 (Washington, D.C.: CQ Press, 2009), 43–44.

behalf of the major-party candidates in 2004; more than $700 million was spent in 2008.[16] For members of Congress the proportions and the media vary, but the need for and use of political advertising do not.

Why do candidates and their consultants believe that advertising is so important and presumably so effective? The answer is that advertisements provide critical information that people need and may not get through their normal sources for news. Ads are repeated frequently, whereas news stories are not.[17] Moreover, political advertisements can be dramatic, startling, and even funny in contrast with the news that is supposed to be presented seriously, in a matter-of-fact manner.

Almost all advertising scripts have been pretested to find out which words and pictures best evoke the desired response. And ads target their audience more than broadcast journalists can. Most ads have a simple message. There is little subtlety, and the point is usually hammered home.[18]

The impact of advertising often is reinforced because the advertising directs attention to items that already may be in the news. The ads themselves can become news if they are controversial enough. Studies have shown that people actually obtain and recall more substantive information about the candidates and their policy stands from advertisements than they do from news reports.[19]

All advertising is obviously not beneficial to a democratic electoral process, such as those ads that make their point by exaggeration, imbalance, and unsupported allegations or those that tread lightly or distort truth. In its continuing study of the accuracy of political advertising, the Annenberg Public Policy Center at the University of Pennsylvania has operated a "fact check" in which it identifies misleading statements, inferences, and factual errors. The Center has found that most campaign ads contain some exaggerations, half-truths, and innuendos designed to create favorable impressions of the candidate supported by the ad and unfavorable impressions of that candidate's opponent.[20]

Excessive Negativity

One criticism of contemporary campaign commercials is that they have become increasingly personalized and negative (see Table 8.2). The conventional wisdom, supported by empirical data, is that the proportion of negative advertising is increasing with each subsequent election.[21] The 2008 presidential nominations were no exception. A study by Darrell M. West found " . . . 61 percent of the 2008 Democratic ads were negative, compared to 43 percent of the Republican ads. Both rates are higher than the average ad negativity of 31 percent for Democrats and 36 percent for Republicans in nominating contests from 1972–2008." [22]

From the perspective of news media consultants, the people who design, market, and profit from the ads, there are more negative advertisements because they work. Political consultants generally subscribe to the proposition that the more negatives a candidates has, the less likely that candidate is to win.[23]

TABLE 8.2	**Public Perceptions of Negativity in Presidential Elections**

Question: Compared to past presidential elections, would you say there was MORE mudslinging or negative campaigning in this campaign or LESS mudslinging or negative campaigning in this campaign?

	1992	1996	2000	2004	2008
More	68	49	34	72	54
Less	16	36	46	14	27
Same (volunteered response)	14	12	16	12	16
Don't know/refused	2	3	4	2	3

Source: Pew Research Center for the People and the Press, "High Marks for the Campaign; a High Bar for Obama," November 13, 2008, http://people-press.org/report/471/high-bar-for-obama.

Negative advertising can have a boomerang effect, however. The George H. W. Bush campaign was reluctant to use negative advertising early in its 1992 campaign because it feared a "there-you-go-again response" from the press and public after its successful negative advertising campaign four years earlier. Campaign insiders were correct; voters were more leery of the negative ads in 1992.[24] When Robert Dole raised character issues about Clinton in his 1996 election advertising, Dole's poll ratings actually declined. The public reacted negatively to his negativism. However, President Clinton's negative ads in 1996 did not produce a similar reaction because they focused on Dole's policy positions, not his personal failings.

What is the impact of negative advertising on voters? Studies based on experimental research indicate that negative messages can turn off voters, thereby decreasing turnout and increasing cynicism.[25] Other studies based on empirical research have reached a very different conclusion, however; these studies suggest that while negative ads may turn off some voters, they turn on others, specifically strong partisans who are energized by the criticism of the other party's candidate.[26]

Not surprisingly, the public claims that advertising does not help them make their voting decisions.[27] Everyone seems to agree that false, inaccurate, and deceptive ads, positive or negative, are unfair and run counter to a democratic electoral process.[28] That so many of these negative spots have been sponsored by party and nonparty groups prompted the reformers who designed the BCRA in 2002 to include a "stand by your ad" provision that requires candidates to assert that they take responsibility for the ad. The framers of the law assumed that the provision would result in less negative advertising, but it has not done so.

Ad Monitors

If advertisements mislead the public, which many scholars claim that they do, should they be monitored and, if so, by whom? Some countries do not allow political advertising. Whether such a prohibition is good or bad is probably immaterial in the United States because the First Amendment to the U.S. Constitution protects a candidate's right to advertise as that candidate sees fit. But it does not necessarily follow that candidates should be free to say or claim anything they want under the banner of free speech. Just as obscenity is not protected by the First Amendment, neither is libel or slander. However, the Supreme Court has also made it extremely difficult for public officials to demonstrate that they have been libeled or slandered by the news media. Falsehood alone is not sufficient evidence. Malice also has to be proved.[29]

Short of suing for libel and slander, what else can be done to promote and police truth in advertising? Perhaps the regulations for commercial advertising, which make advertisers liable for the false claims of their products and give an independent regulatory body, the Federal Trade Commission, authority to prescribe penalties, could be applied to politics. However, it might be very difficult to prove an ad false if it presents only one side of the story.

What about the private sector? Should the news media monitor the political advertising they print or air? They have already begun to do so, although the amount of advertising in national campaigns greatly exceeds the attention and space the press has devoted to advertising scrutiny. Moreover, media monitors may not be the most expert or impartial judges.

Nonetheless, "ad watches," as they have been called, serve a useful purpose by calling attention to false claims and charges and helping to correct perceptions that the public may develop about the candidates and their issue positions. On one hand, the knowledge that ads may be subject to close examination by the news media and public interest groups also encourages those who design them to be more careful about what they say and show.[30] On the other hand, ad watches often reinforce ads by making them into news items.

The first commercial that the Swift Boat Veterans for Truth produced and aired following John Kerry's speech at the Democratic National Convention is a case in point. Kerry spoke with pride about his military service in Vietnam and presented it as evidence that he was qualified to be president during the time of a national security crisis. The Swift Boat ad contradicted Kerry's claims. Featuring men who said that they had served with Kerry in Vietnam, the ad disputed Kerry's acts of heroism; the veterans in the ad also minimized the injuries Kerry suffered, injuries that earned him two Purple Hearts.

Almost immediately, the ad, which was shown only in small media markets in three states, became a news item on the around-the-clock cable news channels and a hot topic on talk radio. The veterans who criticized Kerry were interviewed. The attention they received generated unsolicited donations to the group sponsoring the ad. The money enabled the swift boat veterans to design and run additional commercials criticizing Kerry's conduct during and after the war. Despite challenges to the veracity of the ads and to the veterans' contentions that they had served with Kerry, the ads effectively undermined Kerry's claim that his war record qualified him as a strong and courageous leader.

Checks on advertising also come from opposition candidates, public interest organizations, and even prominent people. Nancy Reagan strongly objected to footage from the assassination attempt on her husband that was included in a 1996 Clinton ad on gun control. After Mrs. Reagan's complaint, the Clinton campaign removed the objectionable footage, but not before the ad had been shown many times and had become a news item and point of controversy.

A similar controversy erupted in March 2004 when an ad for George W. Bush contained two seconds of footage from ground zero at New York City's World Trade Center in which fire personnel were seen carrying a stretcher, presumably of human remains, draped in an American flag. Some families of the victims protested the "political exploitation" of the tragedy. Although subsequent Bush commercials omitted the scene, Bush's media consultants concluded that references to 9/11 evoked a very powerful and positive image of the president, and they continued to show in their commercials footage of ground zero and the president's actions after the terrorist attacks.[31]

THE NEW TECHNOLOGY OF POLLING, TARGETING, AND MESSAGING: BETTER COMMUNICATION OR MORE EFFECTIVE MANIPULATION?

One of the major changes in political campaigns today is its professionalization. Run by experts at discerning public attitudes, designing public appeals, and directing them to the most receptive audiences, these political consultants who operate profit-making businesses have replaced the party pros and their precinct captains as the new handlers of contemporary political campaigns.

Today, every aspect of the campaign—from the public opinion polling to the focus group reactions to the pretested speech, from the orchestrated events to the guests invited to them, and from the cameras that record the action to the spinmeisters who echo the theme and fax the sound bite—has been planned, staged, and recorded by and for the mass media markets. Campaigns have become made-for-TV productions. It's a big show, with the candidates front and center and their aides working hard behind the scenes to make sure everything comes out all right or, if it doesn't, to fix it as soon as possible. Little is left to chance.

The bookends of the campaign are frequently public opinion polls. Surveys are used to find out what is on the public's mind; the initial perceptions of the candidates, parties, and issues; and the salient issues for groups within and outside the party's electoral coalition. Armed with this knowledge, organizers can develop the broad outlines of a campaign, including the strategic approach, the issue appeals, and the references to candidate traits both positive and negative.

The basic rule of thumb is to be careful. Winging it is viewed as dumb and dangerous. Spontaneity is out. Major ideas, promises, and most words are pretested in focus groups to gauge reactions and see which provide the most positive response. After the message is designed and tested, it is targeted to specific groups. There used to be four principal targeting mechanisms: telephone solicitation, direct mail, radio, and cable and local television. Now with the Internet there are five.

The targeting mechanism is used in conjunction with large databases that the parties and various political consultants have assembled over the years. Without knowing it, people become part of these mammoth data sets when they make a contribution to a candidate running for office or to a group supporting a particular issue or if they subscribe to a particular publication or give their cell phone number or e-mail address to a candidate or party.

Armed with the list and the special code words that turn on particular groups of people, the campaign targets its messages toward those groups. In this way, people get the issues that directly affect them the most from the candidate; they are also likely to receive those policy stands of the candidate that most closely accord with their own views. What they do not get is the rest of that candidate's positions. The reason is that campaign handlers believe that the targeted group would not be as interested in these positions, or worse yet, might be opposed to them. Besides, the greater the number of positions a candidate takes, the more likely voters will become confused about the candidate's policy priorities—which is most important and will get the greatest attention and resources if that candidate is elected.

To make matters worse, people may not realize the limited scope and content of the information they do receive. The press does not cover the advertising campaigns on radio, television, or the Internet with the same scrutiny that it reports on "real events."

Have these new marketing tactics contributed to a democratic election process? Some critics believe that the new marketing techniques have made candidates into composites of their consultants' professional imagery, that the negative advertising has turned qualified candidates into caricatures of themselves.

The way in which advertisements are compartmentalized and directed toward those who are most likely to approve them has transformed a broad range of ideological and issue appeals into a narrow set of messages. The image that is presented is not that of an informed electorate grappling with the issues as presented by the candidates, but an electorate composed of almost inert objects of opportunity that candidates manipulate at their will—not a very pretty picture, but also fortunately only one side of the story. The other side is of a more sophisticated public, one that sees through the ads or discounts them because they are ads, puts them in perspective, gains information from more objective media sources, and uses that information to reach an informed judgment—but, more often than not, a judgment that coincides with preexisting attitudes and opinions as well as perceptions of current conditions.

CAMPAIGNING ON THE INTERNET

The use of the Internet as a communication vehicle began in the 1990s. The Clinton-Gore campaign communicated internally via e-mail. Once in office, the administration continued to use e-mails to keep its staff informed on policy and political matters. In 1993, the White House launched its own Web site, as did Congress. By 1994 some candidates running in the midterm elections and most major news outlets had Web sites on which they presented videos of the campaign and poll data as well as news and informational items.

What followed was a rush to get online. In the ensuing years having a Web site evolved from occasional outreach efforts designed to gain attention and reach a relatively small number of voters into a necessity to get the message out, raise money, recruit volunteers, build crowds for campaign events, mobilize supporters, and turn out voters.

The increase in campaign-related information available on the Web paralleled the growth of Internet users. Within a relatively short period of time, the number of users grew by leaps and bounds, as did the number of people who go online for news or information about politics and elections. The Pew Internet and American Life Project reported that in 1996 only 4 percent of all adults went online for political and election-related news; by 2000 that percentage had risen to 18; by 2004 it was 29; and in 2008 it reached 44 percent.[32] For those younger than thirty years of age, the figure is even higher: 58 percent of eighteen- to twenty-nine-year-olds went online for political news in 2008.[33]

Not only do more people go online, but they do so in a more proactive way than they did in the past. Many participate in active social networks in which they communicate with others about the campaign and the candidates they support. Table 8.3 indicates the percentage of social-networking-site users within various age groups and the political activities in which they engage.

John McCain was one of the first candidates to use the Internet to solicit contributions. In 2000, he raised $5 million on his Web site, most of it following his surprise victory over George W. Bush in the New Hampshire primary.[34] But McCain's effort paled in comparison with Howard Dean's campaign four years later.

Joe Trippi, Dean's campaign manager, created a campaign blog, which thousands accessed and on which Trippi and other campaign staff, including Dean, regularly commented and responded to suggestions. The objective was to create a virtual campaign that could be activated quickly. Dean raised $27 million online, much of it in small contributions.[35] The press took notice. More than five hundred thousand people signed up on Dean's site, but his campaign's failure to turn out these backers in Iowa and New Hampshire cast doubts on how effective the Internet could be as a strategic link between the organization and the electorate. In 2008, the Obama campaign erased those doubts.

From the perspective of the electoral process, the reach of the new technology—the Internet and its interactive potential and text messaging—has contributed to the democratic character of elections by informing and energizing

TABLE 8.3 **Political Social Networking, 2008 (in percentages)**

	Ages			
	18–24	25–34	35–44	45+
Groups with social-networking profiles	83	53	36	15
Political activities				
Get candidate or campaign information	26	24	19	19
Start or join a political group	20	15	16	11
Reveal own vote for presidential candidate	32	29	24	14
Discover for whom friend voted	54	51	30	17
Sign up as friend of any of the candidates	15	13	13	6
Did any of the above	65	56	41	36

Source: Pew Internet and American Life Project, "Post-Election Survey," November–December 2008, www.pewinternet.org/PPF/r/272/report_display.asp.

the electorate. The Internet extends the political debate to more people. It has brought the campaign home to millions, particularly to a generation that had not previously been heavily involved.

The Internet has the potential to reverse some of the distortion of campaign communication. The accessibility and variety of news outlets allow the online public to be as knowledgeable as it desires, to check the veracity of claims from impartial as well as partisan sources, and to reduce candidates' dependence on nonparty groups for the money, mobilization, and material support.

There are, of course, potential hazards as well. Security can be breached, and campaign sites can be invaded. Rumors spread rapidly, as does misinformation. Moreover, people can put on their own blinders by accessing sites that conform to their party, candidate, and issue preferences. Nor are Web hits the same as attending a caucus or voting in a primary election. Nonetheless, if the Internet facilitates communication; if it better informs the electorate; if it brings more people into the campaign; and if it provides additional opportunities for candidates, parties, and nonparty groups to discuss the issues at greater depth, then the democracy is being well served and the election process has been improved.

SUMMARY: CAMPAIGN COMMUNICATION DILEMMAS IN A NUTSHELL

Political campaigns are part and parcel of a democratic election process. They are important for several reasons. They enable candidates to interact with the

BOX 8.1   **Obama's Internet Revolution**

The Obama Web campaign began even before Obama declared his candidacy in February 2007. Moved by his keynote address to the 2004 Democratic National Convention, several college students had already set up their own Obama blogs to pass the word and drum up support for his presidential candidacy. Obama's Internet advisers took advantage of these blogs, encouraged others to start their own, and eventually incorporated the most successful ones into the organization's Internet campaign.

Obama's Internet team was headed by Chris Hughes, one of the cofounders of Facebook; Joe Rospars, who had worked on Howard Dean's campaign and then set up his own Internet fund-raising company; Kate Albright-Hanna, a former CNN producer and YouTube expert; Scott Goodstein, a text-messaging adviser; and Sam Graham-Felsen who helped design the campaign's principal blog. The operation, which employed a staff of ninety-five, was designed to take advantage of the new technology, the growing use of the Internet particularly by those younger than thirty, and the grassroots movements that were already under way.[1]

The official campaign site, my.barackobama.com, was intended to be multipurposed and user friendly, a social-networking site from which those who accessed it could participate in the campaign in any number of ways: they could start their own online discussion groups for friends; register to vote; donate money; and get information about the campaign and the candidate's positions, speeches, and advertisements. After Obama won the nomination, lists of phone numbers to call or addresses to visit were given to volunteers online so that they could campaign on behalf of Obama in or near their own homes and neighborhoods.

"Obamaites" made millions of calls during the primaries and general election, three million during the final four days alone. Jose Antonio Vargas reported in the *Washington Post* that the campaign sent more than 7,000 different messages.[2] Correspondence was targeted toward supporters who had entered their e-mail address on the campaign's Web site. In total, more than one billion e-mails landed in boxes.[3] The messages included solicitations for contributions; invitations to rallies; and appeals to make phone calls, knock on doors, and help with the registration and get-out-the-vote drives. Periodic campaign updates were also e-mailed, including a few Internet-first announcements, such as Obama's choice for vice president, Joe Biden.

The campaign also collected cell phone numbers to which text messages could be sent and received. A million people participated in the text-messaging program, which was keyed to major campaign events. Vargas reported that, on the night Obama received the Democratic nomination, "more than 30,000 phones among the crowd of 75,000 were used to text into the program." The text messaging continued through election day when volunteers in the key states received at least three text messages. The campaign sent people in the program ". . . five to 20 text messages per month, depending on where they lived—the program was divided by states, regions, zip codes and colleges—and what kind of messages they had opted to receive."[4]

The point was to make people feel that they were part of the campaign, that their communication with friends, and their help in contacting others would make a difference. And it did! During the course of his two-year quest, Obama was profiled in more than fifteen online communities, including BlackPlanet; MySpace; AsianAve; and Eons, a Facebook type of site for baby boomers. On Facebook alone he had 3.2 million friends and more than five million on other social-networking sites.

(continued on next page)

BOX 8.1   **Obama's Internet Revolution**   *(continued)*

The campaign also took advantage of YouTube for what amounted to free advertising and repeat showings of Obama's speeches. When Obama made his address on race after the incendiary remarks of his pastor, the Reverend Jeremiah Wright, the speech was seen on television by 4 million viewers, but it was viewed on YouTube by 6.7 million people for an estimated 14.5 million hours.[5]

By the end of the campaign almost 40 percent of registered voters said that they had seen campaign videos online.[6] Obama had stockpiled thirteen million e-mail addresses compared with three million for Kerry in 2004 and six hundred thousand for Dean in 2000. The campaign created more than thirty-five thousand voluntary groups and received more than $500 million in online donations, twelve times as much as Kerry received online four years earlier. The campaign reported that 6.5 million people donated to the campaign, most of them more than once. The average online contribution was $80.[7]

Obama created a groundswell of support, particularly among younger voters. More important, he activated them in a political campaign, making them feel a part of his yes-we-can message. In doing so, he revolutionized campaigning, created an organization for governing (as well as reelection), and invigorated participatory politics at the national level.

1. Jose Antonio Vargas, "Obama's Wide Web," *Washington Post,* August 20, 2008, sec. C.
2. Jose Antonio Vargas, "Obama Raised Half a Billion Online," *Washington Post,* November 20, 2008.
3. Ibid.
4. Ibid.
5. Claire Cain Miller, "How Obama's Internet Campaign Changed Politics," *New York Times,* November 7, 2008, http://bits.blogs.nytimes.com/2008/11/07/how-obamas-internet-campaign-changed-politics.
6. YouTube videos featuring the major presidential candidates were viewed 3.2 billion times, according to the measurement firm, TubeMogul; see David Carr and Brian Stelter, "Campaign in a Web 2.0 World," *New York Times,* November 2, 2008, www.nytimes.com/2008/11/03/business/media/03media.html?_r=1&pagewanted=2.
7. Steven Hill, "World Wide Webbed: The Obama Campaign's Masterful Use of the Internet," *Social Europe Journal,* April 8, 2009.

electorate and hear the people's concerns. They also give candidates a podium from which to express their views, demonstrate their knowledge, respond to policy and personal inquires, and appeal to voters. For the electorate, campaigns are equally important as a source of information and an opportunity to question the candidates or at least to evaluate their views and their qualifications for office.

The communication dilemma stems from conflicting candidate and voter needs and goals. The candidate's primary goal to win creates an incentive to shape the scope, content, and spin of the information provided to voters. Candidates stress their best issues, not necessarily the country's most important ones. They present a partial perspective, not a comprehensive one. The voters are left with an incomplete picture, and one in which the negatives often outweigh the positives. Is it any wonder that people are suspicious of politicians and disappointed with elected officials?

Campaigns distort information in other ways, too. Partisan appeals conjure up familiar stereotypes by which individuals and parties are categorized, sometimes unfairly and almost always too simplistically. Incumbent imagery is used to buttress the resources and recognition that already give those in office an immense advantage when they run for reelection. Symbols, code words, and sound bites often substitute for argument and debate. Messages are more effectively targeted with modern computer-based marketing techniques to rally the faithful, convince the undecided, and frequently inform less-attentive and less-knowledgeable voters.

Personality issues are stressed, and character traits are highlighted. Whether these traits are relevant depends on varying conceptions of the job. For those who see election to high public office as a position of trust, respect, and great moral and ethical responsibility, having the proper virtues and leading the exemplary life are essential qualifications. For those who have a results-oriented view of public service and who are more interested in policymaking than personal modeling, political skills such as flexibility, persuasiveness, and pragmatism; communicative skills; and leadership abilities are the most relevant traits for the job.

All of the hype and hoopla and all of the promises and images can create unrealistic expectations that, if not met, can contribute to mistrust of politicians, apathy in the elective process, and cynicism about government. Nonetheless, there have been some hopeful developments.

During recent political campaigns, campaign communications were evaluated for their truthfulness by partisan and nonpartisan public interest groups and the news media. Now candidates have to acknowledge that they approve their campaign's ads that make claims on their behalf. More sources of information are available to more people, who can then find more ways to get involved in campaigns. Candidates are using the Internet to reach a broader electorate, which may lessen their dependence on party and nonparty organizations. The combination of the Obama campaign's success in enlarging and engaging its electorate through online social networking and its masterful use of a variety of communication devices from e-mails to text messaging, from television ads to YouTube videos, from telephone calls from a virtual phone bank to cell-phone alerts from the campaign has breathed new life into campaigning and new energy into the electorate; and the Obama administration is now poised to use some of the same techniques for governing. Elections have become more democratic by the use of these newer, quicker, cheaper, and more direct methods of communication.

Moreover, more information is available to more people. The electorate continues to believe that it has sufficient knowledge about the candidates, parties, and issues to make an informed judgment when voting. If this belief accords with reality, then campaigns are serving some of their principal functions: to inform, to energize, to provide opportunities for public choice, and to guide government officials in the agendas they pursue and the decisions they make.

Now It's Your Turn

Discussion Questions

1. Is information about personal behavior outside of public office a relevant consideration for election to public office?
2. Does partisan stereotyping add to or detract from an informed voting decision, particularly for voters who are less attentive to the candidates, their parties, and their policy positions?
3. Has the growth of issue advocacy and the activities of nonparty groups in political campaigns resulted in a more informed electorate or one that is more subject to manipulation by special interests?
4. Should the federal government regulate truth in political advertising as it does in commercial advertising?
5. Is the incumbency advantage undemocratic? Does it facilitate or impede the operation of government?
6. Has the Internet on balance had a positive or negative impact on electioneering, the electorate, and election outcomes?

Topics for Debate

Challenge or defend the following statements:

- Candidates should be required to tell the truth in their political advertisements and on their Web sites and be disqualified if they do not do so.
- The government should establish a nonpartisan, independent regulatory agency to monitor and regulate all political communications.
- Candidates who are the object of negative ads should be allowed to respond to them at the expense of the candidate, party, or groups that sponsored the negative ad.
- All polling should be conducted online so everyone has a better opportunity to participate.
- The country's truth-in-advertising law should be applied to political communications.
- The incumbent advantage is harmful to a democratic electoral process and should be modified in some way.

Exercises

1. A new federal agency has been established to monitor and regulate political communications. You have been asked to develop the mission statement for this agency. In your statement indicate the principal goals of the agency, the methods you suggest for monitoring communications,

the kinds of activities that should be regulated, and the penalties that should be imposed on violators.

2. Assume that you have just been assigned by your local newspaper to be its ad monitor. Over the course of an election campaign in progress, monitor the advertising on local television and in the local newspaper for one week. In the story that you write for the paper indicate the scope and content of the ads, the relevancy and veracity of claims that were made in them, the groups to whom the advertisements were targeted, and your general evaluation of the effectiveness of this advertising on the electorate. Do you think that the advertising made a difference?

3. You have just been appointed Internet coordinator for your candidate's campaign. Write a memo to your candidate indicating the various ways in which the Internet could be used to benefit the campaign. Also warn the candidate of any potential dangers.

INTERNET RESOURCES

Most of the sites for Chapter 7 will be applicable for campaign communications as well. In addition, the offices of incumbents running for reelection should be useful for monitoring their activities or linking to their campaign Web sites. For federal officials, begin with their institution:

- House of Representatives: www.house.gov
- Senate: www.senate.gov
- White House: www.whitehouse.gov

All candidates and their campaigns should be accessible through their parties.

Listed below are a few additional sites on the media:
- Accuracy in Media: www.aim.org
  Conservative organization that monitors liberal bias in the press.
- Center for Media and Public Affairs: www.cmpa.com
  The best single source for evaluating the content and spin of news stories on the three major broadcast networks.
- Factcheck: www.factcheck.org
  Monitors campaign statements and advertisements; site run by the Annenberg Public Policy Center at the University of Pennsylvania.
- Pew Research Center for the People and the Press: http://people-press.org/
  Independent opinion research group that surveys attitudes toward the press, politics, and public policy issues.
- Project for Excellent in Journalism: www.journalism.org
  Analyzes campaign coverage from print and electronic sources and evaluates that coverage on the basis of its content, themes, spin, and strengths and weaknesses; part of the Pew Research Center.

SELECTED READINGS

Cornfield, Michael. *Politics Moves Online: Campaigning and the Internet.* New York: Century Foundation Press, 2004.

Denton, Robert E., ed. *The 2004 Presidential Campaign: A Communication Perspective.* Lanham, Md.: Rowman and Littlefield, 2005.

Devlin, L. Patrick. "Contrasts in Presidential Campaign Commercials of 2004." *American Behavioral Scientist* 49 (2005): 279–313.

Geer, John G. *In Defense of Negativity: Attack Ads in Presidential Campaigns.* Chicago: University of Chicago Press, 2006.

Haynes, Audrey A., and Brian Pitts. "Making an Impression: New Media in 2008 Presidential Nomination Campaigns." *PS: Political Science and Politics* 42 (January 2009): 53–58.

Jamieson, Kathleen Hall. *Dirty Politics: Deception, Distraction, and Democracy.* New York: Oxford University Press, 1996.

———. *Packaging the Presidency: A History and Criticism of Presidential Campaign Advertising.* New York: Oxford University Press, 1996.

Kaid, Lynda Lee. "Political Advertising." In *Handbook of Political Communication Research,* edited by Lynda Lee Kaid, 155–202. Mahwah, N.Y.: Lawrence Erlbaum Associates, 2004.

Lawson-Borders, Gracie, and Rita Kirk. "Blogs in Campaign Communication." *American Behavioral Scientist* 49 (2005): 548–559.

Miller, Claire Cain. "How Obama's Internet Campaign Changed Politics." *New York Times,* November 7, 2008. http://bits.blogs.nytimes.com/2008/11/07/how-obamas-internet-campaign-changed-politics.

Morris, Dick. *Behind the Oval Office.* New York: Random House, 1997.

Semiatin, Richard J. *Campaigns in the Twenty-First Century.* New York: McGraw Hill, 2005.

Smith, Aaron. "The Internet's Role in Campaign 2008." Pew Internet and American Life Project, April 15, 2009. http://pewresearch.org/pubs/1192/internet-politics-campaign-2008.

Tedesco, John. "Changing the Channel: Use of the Internet for Communication about Politics." In *Handbook of Political Communication Research,* edited by Lynda Lee Kaid, 507–532. Mahwah, N.Y.: Lawrence Erlbaum Associates, 2004.

Trippi, Joe. *The Revolution Will Not Be Televised: Democracy, the Internet, and the Overthrow of Everything.* New York: Harper Collins, 2004.

Troy, Gil. *See How They Ran: The Changing Role of the Presidential Candidate.* New York: Free Press, 1991.

Vargas, Jose Antonio. "Obama Raised Half a Billion Online." *Washington Post,* November 20, 2008. http://voices.washingtonpost.com/44/2008/11/20/obama_raised_half_a_billion_on.html.

West, Darrell M. *Air Wars,* 5th ed. Washington D.C.: CQ Press, 2009.

———. "A Report on the 2008 Presidential Nomination Ads: Ads More Negative than Previous Years." Brookings Institution, October 18, 2009. www.brookings.edu/papers/2008/0630_campaignads_west.aspx.

NOTES

1. When asked what surprised him the most after he became president, John F. Kennedy quipped: "that things were as bad as I said they were during the campaign."

2. There is no one right way to adapt to change. From the perspective of those who hold certain policy positions paramount, the candidates' consistency and their determination to pursue their policy goals despite situational changes may be critical criteria in their evaluation. George W. Bush's conservative views and his antiterrorism policies, especially the war in Iraq, were seen by those of a similar political persuasion as strength. Others less happy with Bush's policies and his unwillingness to change them despite the human and material costs of the war saw his actions as weakness, an inflexibility to adjust to changing times. In contrast, Bill Clinton's adaptability, his willingness to compromise in the light of opposition to many of his domestic policy proposals, was seen as a strength by those who wanted results, the half-a-loaf is better than no-loaf crowd, but a weakness by those who didn't know where he stood, what he believed, and what he would do next. These critics found him unprincipled, and they found that unnerving.

3. For others, candidate viability is less important than registering discontent by the act of voting itself or, sometimes, by not voting. Some people wish to use their vote as a protest. Republicans in New Hampshire in 1992 were unhappy with President George H. W. Bush. About one-third of them demonstrated their unhappiness by voting for Pat Buchanan in the Republican primary. Realistically, Buchanan had little chance of replacing the incumbent president for the Republican nomination, but angry New Hampshire voters did not care. They were more interested in registering their discontent with Bush and his policies. Similarly, in 1996, 8.4 percent of those who voted cast ballots for H. Ross Perot, even though most of them must have known that it was very unlikely that Perot would win. In fact, some people may have voted for Perot because he had little or no chance of winning. Thus, there would be no danger in exercising this protest vote.

4. This claim was reinforced by an incident early in the campaign when Bush was asked by a reporter to name four foreign leaders who were recently in the news. He was unable to do so.

5. "The road ahead will be long. Our climb will be steep. We may not get there in one year or even one term, but America—I have never been more hopeful than I am tonight that we will get there." See "President-elect Obama's Grant Park speech," *Chicago Sun-Times,* November 5, 2008, http://blogs.suntimes.com/sweet/2008/11/obamas_grant_park_speech.html.

6. Matthew Dowd as quoted in Institute of Politics, Harvard University, ed., *Campaign for President: The Managers Look at 2004* (Lanham, Md.: Rowman and Littlefield, 2006), 100.

7. "Our economy, I think, still, the fundamentals of our economy are strong." John McCain, speech in Jacksonville, Florida, September 15, 2008.

8. "Campaign '96 Final: How TV News Covered the General Election," *Media Monitor* 10 (November/December 1996): 3.

9. Which of these traits is most relevant to the voting decision varies, however. Some are endemic to the job, whereas others are important because of the times or the frailties of the previous president.

10. Perhaps the most flagrant so-called personality analysis of a candidate occurred during the 1964 presidential election. *FACT* magazine sent a letter and survey to the more than twelve thousand members of the American Psychiatric Association, asking them whether Republican Barry Goldwater was psychologically fit to serve as president. Approximately 19 percent of the psychiatrists responded, with two out of three saying no. The magazine not only cited the psychiatrists' responses as evidence of Goldwater's unfitness for the presidency, but it also published parts of their comments, editing out some of the qualifying statements that the psychiatrists had included in their responses. Groups such as the American Medical Association and journals such as the *American Journal of Psychiatry* quickly criticized the study as bogus medicine that lacked scientific credibility and validity. Warren Boroson, "What Psychiatrists Say about Goldwater," *FACT* 4 (September/October 1964): 24–64.

11. In a memo to Clinton, Penn wrote:

> All of these articles about his boyhood in Indonesia and his life in Hawaii are geared towards showing his background is diverse, multicultural and putting that in a new light.
>
> Save it for 2050.
>
> It also exposes a very strong weakness for him—his roots to basic American values and culture are at best limited. I cannot imagine America electing a president during a time of war who is not at his center fundamentally American in his thinking and in his values.
>
> "Penn Strategy Memo," March 19, 2007, in Joshua Green, "The Front-Runner's Fall," TheAtlantic.com (September 2008), www.theatlantic.com/doc/200809/hillary-clinton-campaign.

12. The most potent of the George H. W. Bush crime ads was entitled "Revolving Door." As prisoners were seen walking through a revolving door, an announcer said: "As governor, Michael Dukakis vetoed mandatory sentences for drug dealers. He vetoed the death penalty. His revolving-door policy gave weekend furloughs to first-degree murderers not eligible for parole. While out, many committed other crimes like kidnapping and rape. And many are still at large. Now Michael Dukakis says he wants to do for America what he's done for Massachusetts. America can't afford the risk." L. Patrick Devlin, "Contrasts in Presidential Campaign Commercials of 1988," *American Behavioral Scientist* 32 (March/April 1989): 389.

13. David R. Mayhew, "Incumbency Advantage in U.S. Presidential Elections: The Historical Record," *Political Science Quarterly* 123 (Summer 2008): 201–228.

14. Wisconsin Advertising Project, "Nearly $200 Million spent on Presidential Campaign TV Ads to Date," June 2, 2008; Center for Responsive Politics, "2008 Presidential Expenditures," July 16, 2009, www.opensecrets.org/pres08/expenditures.php?cycle=2008.

15. Center for Responsive Politics, "2008 Presidential Expenditures."

16. L. Patrick Devlin, "Contrasts in Presidential Campaign Commercials of 2004," *American Behavioral Scientist* 49 (2005): 279. See also Michael M. Franz, Joel Rivlin, and Kenneth

Goldstein, "Much More of the Same: Television Advertising Pre- and Post-BCRA," in *The Election after Reform: Money, Politics and the Bipartisan Campaign Reform*, ed. Michael J. Malbin (Lanham, Md.: Rowman and Littlefield, 2006), 142; Center for Responsive Politics, "2008 Presidential Expenditures."

17. The principal exceptions are the twenty-four-hour news stations and channels that inevitably repeat their top stories.

18. There are exceptions, such as the "Wolves" ad produced by the George W. Bush campaign in 2004, which showed a pack of wolves circling for the kill. With ominous music sounding in the background, an announcer talked about the cuts in intelligence and defense spending that Kerry and liberal Democrats supported prior to the terrorist attacks of September 11, 2001. The relationship between the wolves and the budget cuts was not made clear, however. Were the wolves the terrorists, just a general threat, or an endangered species?

19. Thomas E. Patterson and Robert McClure, *The Unseeing Eye* (New York: Putnam, 1976), 58; and Craig Leonard Brians and Martin P. Wattenberg, "Comparing Issue Knowledge and Salience: Comparing Reception from TV Commercials, TV News, and Newspapers," *American Journal of Political Science* (February 1996): 172–193.

20. Annenberg Public Policy Center, University of Pennsylvania, www.factcheck.org; for empirical data on campaign negativity, see Franz, Rivlin, and Goldstein, "Much More of the Same," 149.

21. The political consultants who design the negative ads place more of the blame for increased negativity and the cynicism that goes along with it on the news media coverage than they do on themselves. Although journalists admit to being too cynical, they do not think that they are too adversarial. Pew Research Center for the People and the Press, "Don't Blame Us: The Views of Political Consultants," June 17, 1998, www.people-press.org/reports/display.php3?ReportID=86.

22. Darrell M. West, "A Report on the 2008 Presidential Nomination Ads: Ads More Negative than Previous Years," Brookings Institution, July 2, 2008, www.brookings.edu/papers/2008/0630_campaignads_west.aspx.

23. The proposition that the greater the negatives about a candidate, the less likely that candidate is to win was pioneered by Republican strategist Lee Atwater, who directed the George H. W. Bush campaign in 1988; see Thomas B. Edsall, "Why Bush Accentuates the Negative," *Washington Post*, October 2, 1988, sec. C.

24. Stephen J. Wayne, *The Road to the White House 1996: Postelection Edition* (New York: St. Martin's Press, 1997), 269.

25. Stephen Ansolabehere and Shanto Iyengar, *Going Negative: How Political Advertisements Shrink and Polarize the Electorate* (New York: Free Press, 1995), 141–142.

26. Brians and Wattenberg, "Comparing Issue Knowledge and Salience." See also Stephen Ansolabehere, Shanto Iyengar, and Adam Simon, "Replicating Experiments Using Aggregate and Survey Data: The Case of Negative Advertising and Turnout," *American Political Science Review* 93 (December 1999): 901–909.

27. Surveys conducted after recent elections by the Pew Research Center for the People and the Press have asked the following question: "How helpful were the candidates' commercials to you in deciding which candidate to vote for?" In each survey, a majority of voters found them not too helpful or not helpful at all. Pew Research Center for the People and the Press, "High Marks for the Campaign, a High Bar for Obama," November 13, 2008, http://people-press.org/report/471/high-bar-for-obama.

28. Darrell M. West, L. Sandy Maisel, and Brett M. Clifton, "The Impact of Campaign Reform on Political Discourse," *Political Science Quarterly* 120 (Winter 2005–2006): 642.

29. To demonstrate libel or slander, government officials and others deemed public figures must not only prove that the news item or advertising was false but also that it was published with malicious intent. The latter is very difficult to prove. See *New York Times Co. v. Sullivan,* 376 U.S. 254 (1964).

30. Of the political consultants surveyed, 56 percent indicated that they believed ad watches have made campaigns more careful about the content of their ads. Pew Research Center for the People and the Press, "Don't Blame Us," June 17, 1998, question 17, http://people-press.org/report/86/.

31. Devlin, "Contrasts in Presidential Campaign Commercials of 2004," 282.

32. Aaron Smith, "The Internet's Role in Campaign 2008," Pew Internet and American Life Project, April 15, 2009, 48, http://pewresearch.org/pubs/1192/internet-politics-campaign-2008.

33. Ibid., 50.

34. Anthony Corrado, "Financing the 2000 Elections," in *The Election of 2000,* ed. Gerald Pomper et al. (New York: Chatham House, 2001), 102.

35. Joshua Green, "The Amazing Money Machine," TheAtlantic.com, June 2008, www.theatlantic.com/doc/200806/obama-finance.

Elections and Government
A Tenuous Connection

Did you know that . . .

- divided partisan control of the national government has been the rule, not the exception, from 1968 through 2008?
- in almost half of the states, the governor's party does not control both houses of the state legislature?
- in 2006 there was a total of 205 ballot issues in thirty-seven states on which voters could register their policy preferences, and in 2008 there were 153 in thirty-six states?
- between 1904 and 2008, there were 2,305 state ballot initiatives, of which 41 percent were approved?
- Americans favor a smaller national government with fewer services than a larger one with more services? They also oppose a decrease in government spending for Social Security, Medicare, education, the environment, health, and defense.
- it is difficult to convert an electoral coalition into a governing coalition and keep that governing coalition together for an extended period of time?
- the distinctions between campaigning and governing have become blurred in recent years as elected officials engage in constant campaigning to maintain public support and position themselves for the next election?
- election mandates rarely occur, even when one party dominates the outcome, as in 1994, 2006, and 2008?
- exit polls taken after people vote explain more about the public opinion on election day than do the actual returns themselves?

Is this any way to run a democratic election?

Who governs, and how prepared are they to do so? What priorities and policy positions should newly elected officials pursue, and which party and candidates are more likely to be successful in pursuing them? How can those in power be simultaneously kept attuned to popular sentiment, responsive to public needs, and accountable for their actions in office?

We hold elections to answer these questions. Elections determine the personnel for government and provide policy guidance for the new administration. They help forge and reinforce the coalitions that enable a government of shared powers and divided authority to make and implement public policy. Finally, elections are the principal enforcement mechanism by which citizens keep those in power responsive to their needs and interests and accountable for their collective actions and individual behavior in office.

This chapter explores how well American elections serve these purposes. Do they make governing easier or harder? Do they provide direction and legitimacy for the public policies that ensue, or do they present mixed signals, undefined mandates, and conflicting claims upon those in positions of authority? Do they tie government decisions and actions more closely to the popular will, or do they more often reveal the absence of such a will? Do they encourage responsiveness in government or provide a nearly blank check for public officials?

The discussion begins by looking at the link between who wins, who governs, and how they govern. Then it moves to the policy mandate—what the election means and how the interpretation of that meaning affects the policy decisions of newly elected officials. From the mandate and its impact the text turns to the tie between electoral and governing coalitions, the transference or maintenance of power by groups within the American polity. Finally, the chapter ends by completing the circle from public choice to government responsiveness, examining the extent to which elections hold public officials accountable for their decisions and behavior in office.

WHO GOVERNS?

The Compatibility of the Winners

The election determines the winners, but those winners are not always compatible with one another. They may not know one another, may disagree on the priorities and issues, and may have different perceptions of how to do their job in government. Yet they all come with an electoral mandate to represent their constituency and act in its interests. One issue that directly affects government's ability to function efficiently is how to enhance the compatibility of newly elected officials in an electoral system designed to mirror the diversity of the population and the character of the federal system more than reflect a national consensus or even mood.

The compatibility problem is largely systemic, the product of a constitutional framework designed to brake rather than promote the dominant opinions of the moment by creating differing but overlapping electoral constituencies and terms of office. It also is rooted in the political environment, in the self-selection process for running for office, in the unequal resources that the candidates possess, and in the decentralized party structure. Given the systemic problem, achieving compatibility in outlook, goals, and policy priorities requires stronger, more cohesive national parties; an overriding national threat; or some issue that unifies the population and helps produce a consensus for action, such as the terrorist attacks of September 2001 or the economic crisis of 2008–2009.

A related issue pertains to the compatibility of those elected with those already in office—other elected officials, those who serve for fixed terms of office or at the pleasure of the top executive officials, and civil servants. Rarely do the personnel of an entire governmental body change. And even though a complete turnover is theoretically possible in the House of Representatives and in many state legislatures, in practice, turnover tends to be very limited because of the incumbency advantages and the lack of competitive legislative districts. The fewer new people chosen for government in any one election, the less likely the election will redirect what government does or how it does it. The absence of turnover limits the impact of those who wanted and voted for change.

From the perspective of a participatory democracy, muting the latest expression of the popular will is an unfortunate consequence of overlapping terms of office. The trade-off is more experience, savvy, and continuity in government—all of which may produce better public policy over the long run and more legislative independence. With the limited knowledge that the public has on most issues, braking the emotion of the moment actually may result in a more considered judgment later on as "cooler heads" prevail and more information becomes available to more people who begin to understand the complexities of the issue and the consequences of various policy options.

Obtaining a considered judgment in the public interest but not becoming prisoner to the passion of the moment was part of the original rationale for dividing powers and for overlapping constituencies and terms of office. Leery of an aroused majority, particularly if that majority tried to deny minorities their rights, the framers of the U.S. Constitution wanted to place hurdles on the road to policymaking. Their system of internal checks and balances requires sustained support over time, across electoral constituencies, and within and among institutions of government to formulate new public policy.

That system, artfully designed in 1787, remains alive and well today. However, public expectations of the role of government have increased enormously. These expectations have been fueled in large part by the needs of an industrial and, later, technological society; by governmental responses to those needs, such as the New Deal and Great Society programs; and by politicians' promises made in their quest for elective office. How to overcome what the

Constitution divides is the political challenge public officials face today, a challenge made more difficult by the autonomy of federal elections; competing policy agendas within and between the major parties and their elected officials; and, more often than not, divided partisan control of government since 1968.

Voting for the best person regardless of party reinforces the separation of powers. Add to this Americans' distrust of big and distant government and their more contemporary fear of ideologically driven party activists' imposing their policy priorities on the country, and one quickly arrives at a justification for split-ticket voting and divided government.

The point here is that the current electoral system, with its propensity to focus on the candidates and their policy positions, can result in a government of virtual strangers whose ties to their electoral constituency are stronger than their ties to one another.[1] To repeat this chapter's theme, contemporary elections mirror America's diversity more than they reflect a national consensus, a consensus that could serve as a guide for action as well as the foundation on which a governing coalition could be built.

The Qualifications of New Hires

Not only does an election determine those who will serve, it also influences those who will help them in office. Except for professional campaign consultants, who continue to provide elected officials with such for-profit services as polling, media consulting, computing, and Internet expertise, the people most likely to accompany the newly elected into public service are those who worked long and hard on their campaigns. They are unified by their loyalty to the winning candidate, but they may lack the analytical skills and substantive knowledge necessary for a staff job in government. Many of these aides lack governing experience, magnifying the initial adjustment problem for those elected to office, especially for the first time.

There are several reasons why newly elected officials turn to their campaign aides when choosing their advisory and support staffs. They owe them a lot, and undoubtedly some of the aides have ambitions of their own, which may include moving to the capital and working with the person they helped elect. Moreover, campaign workers have demonstrated their loyalty and industry, two important qualifications for good staffing. That they are not part of the previous team, which might have been rejected at the polls, is also seen as an asset by the winners. And, finally, those who have just won election to a new office do not usually have the contacts and acquaintances that incumbents possess, but they are familiar with their campaign staff. They know what they can do. So why not hire them?

Actually, there are plenty of reasons for not doing so. The principal ones are that campaigning differs from governing, and the skills and attitudes required for each also differ, although there's some overlap between campaigning and the public relations dimension of government.[2]

THE RELATIONSHIP BETWEEN CAMPAIGNING AND GOVERNING

Do contemporary campaigns facilitate or impede governing? Do they provide the skills necessary for elected officials to perform representative and policy-making functions, or do they divert their focus, harden their positions, and convert governing into constant campaigning? In truth, they do both.

Similarities: The Constant Campaign

Governing is becoming more campaign oriented than ever before. Increasingly it is conducted in the public arena and is poll driven, with mass-marketing techniques used to gain support and promote the results. A principal motivation for elected officials making public policy decisions is how those decisions will affect their own reelection. Campaign skills may be useful for achieving these aspects of governing.

In campaigns, candidates and their entourages have to sell themselves and their policies to the electorate. They continue doing so once elected. Executive and legislative leaders in particular have to build public pressure for their proposals outside of government in order to gain the enactment of their policy priorities within government. They also must be concerned with their own popularity because it is thought to contribute to their political influence and subsequent policy success.

Although both candidates and government officials appeal to the public, they do so in slightly different ways. In campaigns, the candidates try to lead the media, respond quickly to their opponents' charges and to press allegations, and continuously spin campaign-related issues. In government, elected officials announce their plans, explain how those plans will remedy major policy problems, and use the prestige of their office to enhance the credibility of their remarks and the success of their policymaking efforts. As public officials responsible for the formulation and execution of policy, they have to respond to critical media that tend to highlight disagreement more than consensus and focus on the potential or actual negative consequences that follow from governmental decisions and actions. Moreover, they also have to contend with more investigative reporting, reporting that is more difficult during the limited time frame of a campaign. Candidates may be moving targets, but elected officials are sitting ducks, especially when term limits stop them from running for reelection.

In both campaigns and government, the press imputes the political motives of the subjects they cover. During the campaign, having a political motive is expected; political motives are what campaigns are all about. Not so in government; in that arena, political motives may be viewed as petty, partisan, even personal. Government officials have to defend the reasons for and merits of their actions and do so in terms of the public interest. Thus, candidate Bill

Clinton could criticize Bob Dole's policy positions during the 1996 campaign even though his motive was political, but the congressional Republicans' focus on Clinton's behavior in office and the impeachment trial that followed were seen by many as blatant partisan politics.

Once elected, incumbents keep their eyes on the next election and do their best to ready themselves for it by raising money, performing services, and staying in the news. The representative role—servicing constituency needs, representing constituency views, and satisfying constituency interests in the short run—has become more important and less difficult. In contrast, legislating longer-term national policy has become less important but more difficult for individual legislators. Executive oversight has received more emphasis, particularly during periods of divided government. It contributes to partisan positioning for the next election and spotlights the watchdog activities of members of Congress.

That more and more governing functions are subject to media scrutiny and take place within the public arena has both positive and negative consequences for democratic government. It benefits democracy in that elected officials are motivated to stay closely tied to their electoral bases and more responsive to their constituency's needs. The cost of maintaining such ties, however, has been a growing public perception, fueled by the press, that elected officials follow, not lead, and do what is best for themselves (that is, get reelected), and not necessarily what is best for the country.

A second problem that stems from the campaign-oriented environment in government is the hardening of policy positions. If candidates for office are increasingly defined by and held accountable for the promises they made and the positions they took during the campaign, it will be harder for them as elected officials to make the compromises necessary to govern, particularly if those compromises have to be negotiated in full public view. Strong ideological beliefs today contribute to this problem as well.

The difficulties that a campaign-style atmosphere creates for government suggest that there are fundamental differences between campaigning and governing. Unless and until these differences are understood, the constant campaigning will continue to impede rather than facilitate the operation of democratic government.

Differences: Pace, Mentality, Orientation, and Experience

Pace—Hectic v. Deliberative. A campaign has to keep up with events and presumably stay ahead of them or face defeat on election day. It is frantic almost by definition. In a competitive electoral environment, a campaign exists in a state of perpetual motion; often, a crisis atmosphere prevails, and most have war rooms to deal with these perpetual crises. But all of this motion and activity ends on a certain day, the same day that most of the campaign's personnel are out of jobs and are jockeying for new positions, many of them in government if their candidate wins.

Not so with government. It cannot operate in a perpetual crisis for extended periods without sacrificing the deliberation and cooperation needed to reach solutions to pending issues. Elected officials of the opposing parties still have to interact with one another after a major policy decision has been made. Whereas campaigns are a single battle with a definable end, government is a multiple set of political skirmishes fought before and after elections among many of the same combatants. The relationships within government and the problems with which it deals persist over time, across institutions, even over the course of several administrations.

Mentality—Win at All Costs v. Give and Take. A campaign is what political scientists like to call a zero-sum game. If one candidate wins, the other loses and the game's over. The winners no longer have to consider the losers, who may fade quickly from the public spotlight. Government is not a zero-sum game. For one thing, the losers on a particular issue do not disappear after a battle has been lost. They stay to fight for their next issue. The history of the clashes between environmental and economic interests, between secular and sectarian groups, labor and management, and producers and consumers are good examples of continual conflicts that occur and recur within the political arena.

Campaigns need to be run efficiently. Their organization and operation are geared to one goal: winning the election. In government, although efficiency is desirable, other goals are equally important. A legislative body has to deliberate on issues of public policy. In doing so, it must conduct hearings to permit outside groups to be heard, forge compromise among the contending parties, and then oversee the executive branch's execution of the law. All of this takes time and involves different people with different constituencies in different parts of the government. The legislative process may not be efficient, but it must be representative and should be deliberative.

Similarly, there is also tension between efficiency and effectiveness within the executive branch. The Clinton administration tried to reduce the costs of government by downsizing the number of federal employees, whereas the administration of George W. Bush focused on competition between public and private sectors, known as "competitive sourcing," to improve the operation of government and make it more efficient—a stimulant, not a restraint, on the capitalist system.

Orientation—Consistency v. Compromise. Candidates are judged by their potential for office. In demonstrating their qualifications, particularly if they aren't incumbents, they need to show that they have a grasp of the issues, have good ideas, and will keep their promises if elected. More often than not, keeping promises means adhering to the policy positions they articulated and highlighted during the campaign and trying to get them enacted into law.

Officeholders are judged by their performance as well as by conditions. They need to show results or at least be in a position to claim achievements.

Adhering to policy positions and not compromising on them can jeopardize a record of achievement. Moreover, elected officials are subject to myriad pressures from within and outside of the government: the bureaucracy, the media, interest groups, and the legislature. Not only do these groups have different agendas, different constituencies, and different time frames, they also may have the clout to thwart new initiatives. These political forces cannot be ignored the way a minority group can be during a campaign.

Not only are campaigning and governing different, so is the permanency of the coalitions on which candidates and public officials depend. Electoral coalitions usually stay together for the duration of the political campaign. Governing alliances shift more with the issues. Today's opponent may be tomorrow's ally and vice versa. Unlike those in campaigns, the losers and winners in government should not become permanent enemies.

Experience—Outsiders v. Insiders. The distinction between running and governing has been exacerbated of late by two developments: the changes within the electoral process that have provided greater opportunities for those with limited experience to run for office and the public's mistrust of those in power and its desire for new faces not connected to the current political establishment. In an increasing number of elections, lack of experience, in particular the absence of a connection to the "mess in government," is regarded as a virtue, not a liability. This was evident in 2006 when Democratic challengers defeated twenty-two Republican incumbents in the House and six in the Senate to gain control of Congress, and in 2008 when a candidate in national office for fewer than four years defeated several senior senators and a former first lady for the Democratic nomination and a well-known senior senator and war hero for the presidency.

Not only are many challengers who win election neophytes to governing, but their campaign staffs most likely are neophytes as well. In the past, the political pros who ran the campaigns had experience in electioneering and governing. Today, the political pros have been largely replaced by the professional campaign technocrats—pollsters, media consultants, political strategists, fund-raisers, Internet and computer geeks, and grassroots organizers who sell their services to the highest bidders, some even without regard for partisanship.[3] These campaign technocrats usually have little if any governing experience and little desire to work in government; they do want to work for government, though, content to sell their services to those in power, especially to incumbents getting ready to run again.

The others who work on campaigns are the trusted soldiers, the people who perform the day-to-day, nitty-gritty grunt work of staging events, writing speeches, doing research, dealing with the press, setting up phone banks, responding to critics, and blogging with supporters. They work long and hard for low salaries or for free; many are young, in or recently out of college, with little government experience. They may be involved because they believe in the candidate, enjoy the excitement of the campaign, or want a job once the campaign is over. They may even be doing it for social reasons, such as meeting like-minded people.[4] Whatever their motivation, they are not likely to have the inside information that a newly elected public official needs the most: knowing how things work and which people have the power to get things done.

The presidential transitions of Carter and Clinton suffered from many of these staffing inadequacies. The people they appointed to their White House staffs came from their campaigns and had little or no experience in Washington politics or in dealing with the national press corps, the congressional leadership, and, in Clinton's case, the military establishment. Moreover, these newly appointed aides suffered from another malady that frequently afflicts the newly elected and their staffs: they came to power with chips on their shoulders. They assumed, probably correctly, that they had won because people had grievances against those in power. Because Carter and Clinton were outsiders, even within their own party, they were suspicious of all those in the establishment, Democrats and Republicans alike. Initially, they tried to have as little to do with them as possible—with disastrous results.[5] Their legislative initiatives failed, their White Houses became embroiled in controversy, and they lacked a consistent policy message. By the time they got on their feet, they had lost much of the enthusiasm that accompanies a new administration into office and the political capital that it brings.

George W. Bush in 2000 and Barack Obama in 2008 ran against the strident partisan tone of Washington politics, promising to return civility to political discourse and a bipartisan dimension to governing. Although both lacked much Washington experience, they surrounded themselves with experienced Washington hands. As a consequence, they got off to better starts than did the administrations of Carter and Clinton.

Running against the Washington establishment may be an effective campaign strategy, particularly if the public is unhappy with the way it perceives the government to be working, but it's not an effective governing strategy, especially if the goal is to bridge institutional divide in order to make and implement new public policy. Understanding how government works is a prerequisite for getting it to work.

The Impact of Campaigning on Governing

Contemporary campaigning has made contemporary governing more difficult. Campaigns raise public expectations about public policy and public officials at the same time that they feed into distrust of politicians and the politics in which they engage. They emphasize personal accomplishments in a system designed to curb the exercise of institutional and political power. They harden policy positions in a governmental structure that depends on compromise. They have increasingly brought partisan and ideological rhetoric into the policymaking arena, where a pragmatic approach and quiet diplomacy is often needed to get things done. And the candidates have developed a public persona that they continue to project once in office, a persona that can get in the way of behind-the-scenes compromises on major issues on which they have articulated their policy positions and thus in which they have a stake.

A second impact of campaigning on governing, especially since the 1970s, has been the increasing number of winning candidates who have not come up through the ranks and lack governing experience. These candidates may overestimate their ability to make a difference and underestimate the views and legitimacy of others who are part of the governing establishment. "Reinventing the wheel" wastes time and energy and increases the start-up costs of government.

To make matters worse, candidates who are not incumbents usually do not have regular access to the information and expertise that government officials have. What they do have access to, however, are poll results that indicate political attitudes, salient issues, and the public's opinions on the issues. Armed with this information, it is relatively easy to craft a position popular with a specific group. Campaigning by public opinion polls is just a short step away from governing by public opinion polls. An increasing number of public officials seems to have taken this step.

Directions for Reforms

If contemporary campaigning has contributed to the difficulty of governing, what changes might reverse this pattern and make governing easier? More party control over the electoral process might reduce the number of free agents elected to government and impose more discipline on those who are elected. But how can this be accomplished in light of the reforms to the nomination process? Those who regularly participate in primaries and caucuses are not likely to voluntarily give up their right to vote on their party's nominees.

If terms of office were longer and if voters were more nationally focused and less interested in the short-term impact, then elected officials would have more opportunities to make decisions in what they believed were the country's long-term interests rather than their constituency's short-term interests. But then the ties between government and the governed also would be looser, responsiveness might suffer, and incumbents might be even more advantaged than they are today. Term limits could reduce this advantage, forcing greater turnover in office, but term limits also would result in the election of less experienced and knowledgeable public officials who would need time to acquire expertise or would be more dependent on civil servants and professional legislative staff for support. Besides, term limits are undemocratic and unconstitutional for members of Congress.[6]

THE ELECTION AND PUBLIC POLICY

In addition to choosing who governs—which candidates, parties, and staffs— elections should provide policy guidance for government: what issues to address, what approaches to take, and even what specific proposals to make.

Except for policy initiatives, which appear on state ballots, elections refract rather than reflect public opinion on most issues. The reason they do so is because they are primarily designed to choose people, not policies.

The Movement toward Policy Initiatives

Voting on state constitutional amendments, policy initiatives, and other substantive measures has become an increasingly popular vehicle for individuals and, especially, for organized groups to pursue their policy agendas when they are unable to do so successfully through the legislative process. A majority of the states, primarily those in the West and Midwest, provide for voting on substantive policy issues. These votes illustrate direct democracy at work.[7]

But they usually also require substantial resources to be successful. Just getting on the ballot requires that the signatures of a certain percentage of the state's eligible voters be obtained within a specified period of time. The higher the percentage of signatures required and the shorter the time frame, the more difficult and expensive ballot access becomes. If an organization lacks enough of its own volunteers, including the foot soldiers who gather these signatures, it will have to engage an outside firm to collect them and pay several dollars per name. The total cost can run into the millions, and that is just the first step.

A public relations campaign for the initiative also must be waged during the election period. If successful, it still may be challenged in the courts, as was California's Proposition 187, a ballot initiative approved by the voters that denied such state benefits as education and health care to illegal aliens and their families.[8] The legal charges can be substantial.

Interest groups have become adept at using the ballot initiative process to their own economic, ideological, or political advantage. The gambling industry; sports promoters; the Humane Society; and groups that want to impose legislative term limits, make English the official U.S. language, legalize the sale of marijuana for medical purposes, permit doctor-assisted suicides, issue school vouchers, increase taxes for education, and prevent same-sex marriage all have used the initiative process to circumvent or pressure recalcitrant state legislatures.

State executive and legislative leaders have also used referendums to avoid making tough, unpopular decisions, but they have not always been successful in doing so. Take the case of Governor Arnold Schwarzenegger of California. Faced with a huge budget deficit in 2008 and not wanting to raise taxes or cut spending, the governor and state legislative leaders agreed to put six budget-related measures on the ballot. Voters rejected five of them, however, forcing the governor and legislature to do the cutting themselves and accept the political consequences.[9]

A few wealthy, public-interested individuals also have tried to use this process to achieve what they consider to be desirable public policy. Billionaire financier George Soros has spent millions in support of initiatives that would legalize the medical use of marijuana and provide for forfeiture of assets and rehabilitation rather than lengthy jail terms for convicted drug offenders. Paul

Allen, the cofounder of Microsoft, contributed $3 million to a group that was supporting an initiative to establish charter schools in the state of Washington. Businessman Tim Draper spent $23 million of his own money on an initiative to provide school vouchers to children in California. The list goes on.[10]

Others have turned to initiatives to change policy, gain recognition, and even make money. Bill Sizemore has used the initiative process in Oregon probably more than any other state resident. He placed five initiatives on the 2008 ballot alone, one for the third time, which was again defeated by Oregon voters.[11] Sizemore runs a business that collects signatures for ballot initiatives, so he makes money and tries to affect public policy at the same time. He also used his visibility in the state to run for governor in 1998, but he was defeated.[12]

The amount of money that it takes to mount a successful initiative drive and the fact that much of it may come from outside the state have led some states to try to limit the number of ballot initiatives and the influence of outside groups and people who do not live in that state. Colorado enacted legislation that permitted only its registered voters to circulate initiative petitions. It required those who circulate petitions to wear badges identifying themselves and their affiliation and that the costs of initiative drives be made part of the public record. In 1999, however, the U.S. Supreme Court found that these restrictions violated the First Amendment by inhibiting communications with voters.[13]

In addition to the financial issue, there are other problems with the widespread use of these public referenda. Some are extremely complicated and difficult for the average person to understand, much less appreciate, all the implications and costs. Just reading these ballot initiatives can take a considerable amount of time, which holds up voting for others. Moreover, initiatives circumvent the legislative process, thereby diminishing the role of those whose job it is to consider public policy issues, those who presumably have more time, knowledge, and skills to do so than the average person or voter.

According to political scientist Richard J. Ellis, an expert on the initiative process, there has been a steady increase in ballot initiatives since the 1970s. Whereas they averaged thirty-five per ballot in the 1970s and fifty in the 1980s, during the last two decades of the twentieth century the average number of state ballot initiatives was seventy-six per election, with the most (103) coming in 1996. Ellis reports that a little less than half of these initiatives have become law.[14] The numbers in the twenty-first century have been even higher. Table 9.1 lists the number of ballot measures in the twenty-first century.

Issue Voting in a Candidate-Oriented Environment

With the exception of voting on policy issues, most elections are imperfect mechanisms for determining public policy. People vote for a variety of candidates for lots of different reasons. Partisan affiliation, candidate qualifications, and issue positions are some of the factors that affect voting behavior. Of these, issues are least likely to be the primary focus for most voters.[15]

TABLE 9.1	**State Ballot Measures, 2000–2009**		
Year	Number of states	Number of measures	Percentage approved
2000	42	204	63
2001	—	—	—
2002	40	202	62
2003	8	22	64
2004	34	162	67
2005	12	45	49
2006	37	205	67
2007	6	34	82
2008	36	153	59
2009	7	26	77

Source: Initiative and Referendum Institute, University of Southern California School of Law, www.iandrinstitute.org/ballotwatch.htm.

People also may be voting against candidates because they are unhappy with the job they have done, the conditions that occurred while they were in power, their behavior while in office, or even their personal traits or policy preferences that are revealed during the campaign. Such a negative vote, if discernible, may indicate what the electorate does not want but not what it does want, except perhaps by inference.

Another factor contributing to the difficulty of understanding the meaning of elections is that there are many candidates and many issues at many levels of government. People have different reasons for casting different votes. They may split their ballots, voting for candidates from different parties. This type of voting behavior produces mixed results from which a clear message is not always or easily discernible, despite political pundits' and exit pollsters' explanations to the contrary.

If a voting pattern were to emerge, if one party were to win or maintain control of the legislative and executive branches, then there might be some reason for believing that voters were sending a message—although the substance of the message itself would not necessarily be clear. At the national level, however, such a pattern was the exception, not the rule, between 1968 and 2008. During this forty-year period, the same party controlled the White House and both houses of Congress for a total of ten years. And even though there was one-party control at the beginning of George W. Bush's administration for about five months (until Senator James Jeffords defected from the Republican Party), the president could hardly claim an electoral mandate, having lost the popular vote. Under these circumstances, with mixed results in overlapping constituencies, what can the election returns tell us about the policy direction that newly elected officials should take? The answer is usually, not very much.

The Absence of Policy Mandates

The national electoral system is not structured in a way that facilitates policy voting. It has encouraged partisan voting, but the declining use of the party-column ballot and the candidate orientation of many voters make it more difficult to achieve partisan mandates today. Some do claim that the 1994 midterm elections produced such a mandate for the Republicans, as did the elections of 1932, 1964, and 2008 and the midterms of 1974 and 2006 for the Democrats.

To have a mandate for governing, a party's candidates must take discernible and compatible policy positions that are distinguishable from the opposition's, and the electorate must vote for them primarily because of those positions. Most elections do not meet these criteria. Candidates usually take a range of policy positions, often waffle on a few highly divisive and emotionally charged ones, and may differ from their party and its other candidates for national office in their priorities and their stands on other issues.

House Republican candidates did take consistent policy positions in 1994; all pledged to support the goals and proposals in their Contract with America. Other Republican candidates, however, didn't take such a pledge. Nonetheless, the results of the 1994 election, in which every Republican incumbent for Congress and governor won and the Republicans gained seats in most state legislatures, were interpreted as a partisan victory. What did such a victory mean? What policy goals did it imply?

Newly elected Speaker of the House Newt Gingrich chose to interpret the vote as an affirmation of the ten basic goals and legislative proposals in the House Republicans' Contract with America. Such an interpretation provided Gingrich with a legislative agenda to pursue and promote in the House of Representatives. But his interpretation also created performance expectations that the Republicans were unable to meet outside of the House.

Moreover, it was probably an incorrect interpretation. The vote in 1994 was a repudiation of the Clinton administration and the Democratic-controlled Congress; it was also a rejection of big government, big deficits, and big social programs such as universal health care for all Americans. Indirectly, it could be interpreted as a vote for less government, lower taxes, and a smaller deficit. It was not a vote for the Republicans' Contract with America. How do we know? Exit polls indicated that only 25 percent of the voters and 20 percent of the population had ever heard of the Contract with America, much less knew what was in it. How, then, could the 1994 election be a mandate for the policy proposals in that contract if such a small proportion of the population was aware of that contract, much less the proposals in it?

The presidential elections of 1988, 1996, and 2004 also were seen as referendums in support of the administration in power. Presidents who are reelected have received a vote of confidence for their past leadership; they have support to continue the policy actions that they initiated, but not necessarily to start something new. Beyond that, gleaning much meaning and guidance from an incumbent's reelection is problematic at best. Nonetheless, most presidents claim public support for their second-term goals, some of which they articulated during the reelection campaign.

Take George W. Bush following his 2004 election victory. Bush believed that his reelection ended Iraq as a political issue and gave him political capital to pursue his second-term domestic policy priorities: a national energy policy, the partial privatization of Social Security, tax reform, a new immigration policy, and an extension of his first-term tax cuts. Exit polls, however, offered little evidence that these priorities were on voters' minds on election day, much less were the primary reasons that Bush won reelection (see Table 9.2). Had the president not misread the meaning of the election, he might have saved himself the political embarrassment of failing to achieve most of these policy goals.

In contrast, the defeat of an incumbent president, such as Carter in 1980 and Bush in 1992, indicates a repudiation of the president's leadership and usually dissatisfaction with the conditions in the country in the election year and, frequently, before it. But other than improving that leadership and those conditions, the specific initiatives the electorate desires the new administration to take are often unclear. Under the circumstance the safest behavior for candidates who defeat incumbents is to do what they said they would, redeem their campaign promises, and thereby maintain their credibility. They assume that the voters support those promises because they won. That assumption, however, can get them into trouble.

Exit Polls and the Meaning of the Vote

The results of elections may not explain very much, other than who wins and who loses, but election day surveys that probe voters' opinions and preferences to discern why they voted as they did do provide more information. Such surveys enable analysts to correlate the opinions and preferences with voting behavior and the demographic and attitudinal characteristics of voters. In this way, it is possible to interpret the meaning of the election.

Election day exit polls interview voters after they have cast ballots at randomly selected voting precincts across the country.[16] A large number of people are questioned, usually between 13,000 and 17,000; in 2008, it was 17,836 plus 2,378 telephone interviews.[17] On the basis of their answers, analysts are able to discern the attitudes, opinions, and choices of groups of voters.

Exit polls are usually very accurate because of their large size (compared with about 1,000–1,200 for other national surveys) and because they are conducted at so many different voting precincts across the country over the course of election day. The principal limitation of this poll, however, is that it provides only a snapshot of the electorate on one particular day. It can't show how the campaign affected the public's attitudes and opinions or the impact of other

TABLE 9.2 **Portrait of the American Electorate, 2000–2008**

Percentage of total in 2008		2000			2004			2008		
		Bush	Gore	Nader	Bush	Kerry	Nader	Obama	McCain	Other
	Total Vote	48%	48%	3%	50%	49%	1%	53%	46%	1%
47	Men	53	42	3	54	45	1	49	48	3
53	Women	43	54	2	47	52	1	56	43	1
74	Whites	54	42	3	57	42	1	43	55	2
13	African Americans	9	90	1	11	89	0	95	4	1
9	Hispanics	35	62	2	42	55	2	67	31	2
2	Asians	41	55	3	41	59	—	62	35	3
3	Others							66	31	3
66	Married	53	44	2	56	43	1	47	52	3
34	Unmarried	38	57	4	40	59	1	65	33	2
18	18–29 years	46	48	5	44	54	1	66	32	2
29	30–44 years	49	48	2	51	47	1	52	46	2
37	45–64 years	49	48	2	50	49	1	50	49	1
16	65+ years	47	51	2	53	46	0	45	53	2
4	Not H.S. graduate	38	59	1	49	50	0	63	35	2
20	H.S. graduate	49	48	1	51	48	1	52	46	2
31	Some college	51	45	3	53	46	0	51	47	2
28	College graduate	51	45	3	51	47	1	50	48	2

Postgraduate	17	44	52	3	43	55	1	58	40	2
Protestant/other Christian	54	56	42	2	58	41	0	45	54	1
Catholic	27	47	50	2	51	48	1	54	45	1
Jewish	2	19	79	1	24	76	—	78	21	1
Something else	6							73	22	5
None	12							75	23	2
Attend religious activities more than once a week	12							43	55	1
Attend religious activities once a week	27							43	55	1
A few times a month	15							53	46	1
A few times a year	28							59	39	2
Never	16							67	30	3
Union household	21	37	59	3	39	60	1	59	31	2
Family income										
Less than $15,000	6	37	57	4	36	63	1	73	25	2
$15,000–$29,999	12	41	54	3	41	58	0	60	37	3
$30,000–$49,999	19	48	49	2	48	51	0	55	43	2
$50,000–$74,999	21	51	46	2	55	44	1	48	49	3
$75,000–$99,999	15	52	45	2	53	46	0	51	48	1
$100,000–150,000	4	54	43	2	56	43	1	48	51	1
$150–199,999	6							48	50	2
$200,000+	6							52	46	2

(continued on next page)

TABLE 9.2 **Portrait of the American Electorate, 2000–2008** (continued)

Percentage of total in 2008		2000			2004			2008		
		Bush	Gore	Nader	Bush	Kerry	Nader	Obama	McCain	Other
	Total Vote	48%	48%	3%	50%	49%	1%	53%	46%	1%
	Family's financial situation is									
24	Better today	36	61	2	79	20	0	37	60	2
34	Same today	60	35	3	48	50	1	45	53	2
42	Worse today	63	33	4	19	80	1	71	28	1
21	Northeast	39	56	3	43	56	1	59	40	1
24	Midwest	49	48	2	51	48	1	54	44	2
32	South	55	43	1	58	41	0	45	54	1
23	West	46	48	4	45	53	2	57	40	3
32	Republicans	91	8	1	93	7	0	9	90	1
29	Independents	47	45	6	47	50	2	52	44	4
39	Democrats	11	86	2	10	89	0	89	10	1
22	Liberals	13	80	6	13	86	1	89	10	1
44	Moderates	44	52	2	44	55	0	60	39	1
34	Conservatives	81	17	1	83	16	1	20	78	2
65	Employed*	48	49	2	52	46	1	55	44	1
35	Unemployed*	48	47	3	49	50	1	50	48	2
11	First-time voters	43	52	4	45	54	1	69	30	1

2008 – Most important issue for voting

	Taxes 2004	56	44	0			
7	Education 2004; Energy 2008	25	75	—	50	46	4
10	Iraq 2004–2008	25	74	0	59	39	2
9	Terrorism 2004–2008	84	14	0	13	86	1
63	Economy 2004–2008	18	80	1	53	44	3
	Moral values 2004	79	18	2	—	—	
9	Health care 2004–2008	78	—	73	26	2	—
22							

Question: Do you work full-time for pay? "Yes" answers were categorized as "employed," "no" answers as "unemployed."

Sources: 2000 general exit polls conducted by VNS for the National Election Pool, a consortium of the major news networks; 2004 and 2008 general exit polls conducted by Edison Mitofsky International and found on the Web sites of major news organizations (such as ABC News, CNN, Fox News, and MSNBC) following the election.

factors over the course of the election. To discern such information, election analysts depend on the American National Election Studies (ANES), a smaller survey conducted under the auspices of the universities of Michigan and Stanford. The survey data are made available to scholars. The ANES survey interviews many of the same people before and after the election, thereby allowing researchers to discern opinion change over the course of the campaign and the factors that contributed to that change.

Although exit polls of the 2000 and 2004 elections were not necessary to show that the electorate was evenly divided in the presidential contests, the polls did reveal patterns that helped explain why these elections were so close (see Table 9.2). The principal factor was partisanship. During these first two presidential election cycles of the twenty-first century, the major parties were at rough parity with each other, with partisans voting overwhelmingly for their party's nominees. Core groups within each party's traditional electoral coalition also voted along party lines: African Americans, Hispanics, and organized labor for the Democratic candidates, and the Christian Coalition and other religious groups for the Republicans. The independent vote was also closely divided.

Although the principal components of each party's electoral coalition have not changed, partisan parity has ended, at least for now, with the Republican base shrinking, the proportion of independents increasing, and the Democratic electorate slightly increasing its level of support. Table 9.2 presents a portrait of the electorate taken on the day people voted during the last three presidential elections.

The election of 2008, however, provided a very different outcome and partisan division. Barack Obama was the first Democratic candidate since Lyndon Johnson to receive a majority of the popular vote. More people identified with the Democrats than the Republicans. And the Democrats also took a larger share of the independent vote.

Obama also redrew the Electoral College map, winning states in the South, Southwest, and Midwest that had previously voted Republican at the presidential level. His effective grassroots operation also turned out record numbers of voters. Obama won traditional Democratic groups by large margins: African Americans (91 percent), Hispanics (36 percent), and labor union households (28 percent). He increased the sizes of the gender and age gaps that favor the Democrats.

The ideological and religious preferences reflected past voting patterns, although the Democrats picked up support from voters who identified themselves as moderates, thereby counterbalancing the advantage that the larger number of people who identify themselves as conservatives give to the Republicans. Traditional voting patterns continued among religious groups, with Protestants supporting McCain and Catholics and Jews voting Democratic. A sectarian-nonsectarian division was also evident. The more that people regularly attended religious services, the more likely they were to have voted Republican.

If the patterns evident in the 2008 election persist, the Republicans may be a permanent minority if voters under thirty; Hispanics, the fastest-growing group in the electorate; and women continue to vote so heavily Democratic. The gain in House and Senate seats for the Democrats suggests that the Republicans must broaden their coalitional base if they are to remain competitive.

In summary, the results of an election indicate who won, but not much else: not the reasons people voted as they did and not the mandate the winners usually claim. Elected officials who act as if they had a mandate usually are doing so to gain support within the government for the policy initiatives they wish to pursue. It is also important to understand that the more time that elapses after the election, the less important that election is as a guide to policy and an influence on those who make it.

POLICY AND PERFORMANCE: RESPONSIVENESS AND ACCOUNTABILITY

Government is based on the consent of the governed. That's the reason why public officials are so concerned about the meaning of the election and why they may even claim it to be a mandate from the voters. That meaning or claim ties elections to government in three ways:

- Elections provide direction for public officials.
- Elections help generate popular support for achieving election-based goals and more specific campaign promises.
- Elections reaffirm the legitimacy of government and, to a large extent, what that government does.

Providing Direction

Campaigns are full of promises, both substantive and stylistic. They provide a broad blueprint for those in power. They also create a climate of performance expectations. These expectations are often hyped by the emphasis the candidates themselves place on certain character skills and traits they claim to possess and promise to exercise if elected: strong and decisive leadership, high standards of moral and ethical behavior, and excellent management skills. Successful presidential candidates have pledged to "never tell a lie," create "a kinder and gentler America," exercise "compassionate conservatism," and initiate "policy and political change." But candidates have to be careful not to promise too much. If they set too high a bar for themselves, they may not be able to clear it, with the likely result that their popularity and probably the public's confidence in them will decline.

Normally, multiple campaign pledges and policy initiatives, low levels of information among voters, and most people's preoccupation with current conditions give public officials considerable leverage in designing policy, as long as they stay within the broad parameters of acceptability and have a beneficial short-term result. In this sense and on a collective level, the electoral process provides both opportunities and flexibility for those in power. What it often does not provide is the consensus necessary to convert promises into public policy. The task for legislative and executive leaders is to convert their election coalition into a governing coalition. And that task is not easy.

Take Obama's pledge on health care, for example. During the 2008 campaign, he promised to reform the nation's health care system, reducing costs and providing opportunities for everyone to get coverage. Although the economy was the major issue in the 2008 campaign, 9 percent said health care was the most important problem (see Table 9.2). As the economy worsened and people lost their jobs, the number of Americans without health insurance grew. After the enactment of the American Recovery and Reinvestment Act and the president's budget, the Obama administration turned its attention to health care.

Initially, the plan was to have the Democratic Congress take the lead in formulating the legislation. With large majorities in both houses and the public desiring reform, the administration assumed that health care reform would receive broad support and Congress could quickly reach agreement on the matter. Several different committees in the House and Senate debated and drafted proposals while the administration made deals with various parts of the health care community to gain their support. These deals, however, did not stop the industry from spending millions of dollars to lobby Congress for a bill that did not adversely affect them.

Meanwhile public support was shifting, a consequence of Republican criticism of Democratic proposals, the large budget deficit, and general suspicion that a government-run plan would reduce people's options, increase their health care costs and decrease their medical choices, and dig the government deeper into debt. A gap was developing between the idea of reform, which the public supported, and the specific proposals, on which there was disagreement. Fearful that a divided Congress would not reach an agreement, the president used his "bully pulpit" to launch a public relations campaign, addressed a joint session of Congress, and had his policy aides launch a full-court press to gain sufficient support for a health care reform bill.

Getting Results

The public's focus shifts after the election. Some people become disappointed when their expectations go unmet. Constituencies clash within as well as between parties. Well-financed interest groups continue to exercise power and spend millions lobbying for their policy goals. The result may be that the election determines the policymakers. What it does not usually provide is the coalition across institutions of government that is necessary to get results. The principal task for elected leaders is to build that coalition and do so as quickly as possible by using their victory and the goodwill that ritually follows an election outcome to enhance their base of electoral support.

Having a partisan majority helps, but it does not guarantee success, as George W. Bush found out at the beginning of his second term. To get results, constant campaigning is necessary priority by priority. Pollsters are used to determine policy parameters, and focus groups are employed to refine the language of messages and target each to the appropriate group or groups. Partisan and nonpartisan appeals are made, depending on the issue and the political configuration of public opinion. Interest group coalitions, organized by the White House or by the political parties, are used to promote the policy and mobilize support for it.

Ensuring Accountability: Individual and Collective

As a check on those in government, the electorate holds a trump card: rejection at the polls the next time around. The card isn't often played, however, for several reasons. The practical advantages of incumbency usually outweigh the theoretical option of voting someone out of office. With the exception of the president and other chief executives, it is difficult to assign individual responsibility for institutional action or inaction. It's even hard to assign individual responsibility for economic and social conditions, although chief executives (the president, state governors, and mayors) do tend to receive more credit and blame than their influence over these conditions merits.

Another reason why it is difficult for the public to assess responsibility for what government does is that people generally are not well informed about the actions of government. They don't become well informed until the news media focus on a particular issue for a sustained period. The war in Iraq is a case in point. Initial coverage was shaped by the administration's claim that Iraq's possession of weapons of mass destruction (WMDs) posed a threat to the United States. Removing the government of Saddam Hussein was presented as the only acceptable option. During the military buildup and conduct of the war, American news coverage was favorable to the administration's objectives.[18] Subsequent news coverage was not. It emphasized the chaos, the resistance, the absence of WMDs, the sectarian violence, and the costs to the United States in terms of lives and money. Over time, the perceptions of reality presented in the news media turned the American people against the administration's policy and in favor of the pullout of U.S. forces.

Assigning collective responsibility is even more difficult than holding individuals accountable for their own actions. When control of the government is divided, credit and blame are shared. Which institution and political party were to blame for the huge increase in the national debt that occurred during the Reagan years—the Republican president, the Republican Senate, or the Democratic House? And which institution should receive credit for the budget surpluses of the late 1990s—the Democratic president, the Republican Congress, or both? Which institution was responsible for the government bailout of Wall Street investment firms during 2008–2009—the president or Congress? One of the most negative consequences of divided government is the inability to hold one party collectively accountable for public policy outcomes.

For individual behavior, however, responsibility can be pinpointed, even though it does not usually result in electoral defeat. There are some exceptions to the nonrejection rule by the voters. Outrageous personal behavior in office is one of them. Illegal acts, such as the theft of government property, acceptance of bribes, lying under oath, failure to pay income taxes or child support, or even indulging regularly in a prohibited substance like cocaine or marijuana, would probably produce sufficient negative media and public concern to force an official to resign from office or face the strong possibility of defeat in the next nomination or election. Similarly, immoral or unethical behavior, such as sexual improprieties, the flagrant misuse of public property, abusing the perquisites of office, or making false claims about one's military service or educational qualifications, would also endanger an official's reelection prospects, if only to encourage a quality challenger.

Accountability in government is enhanced by the potential for election defeat, even if that potential is rarely achieved. In the increasingly public arena of government, under the eye of an investigative press, and with the public relations campaigns that one's partisan or ideological opponents can wage to highlight behavior and actions that might be viewed as objectionable by a sizable electoral constituency, public officials tend to behave as if they were in the spotlight most of the time. They probably perceive themselves as more visible to their constituencies than they actually are. As a result, responsiveness and accountability are fostered by the electorate's holding a trump card, even if it isn't played very often, and by a free and critical press.

SUMMARY: ELECTIONS AND GOVERNMENT DILEMMAS IN A NUTSHELL

Elections provide a critical link between the people and their government. That link is the very reason for having elections: to choose the people who will make the major public policy decisions, to provide them with policy direction and political support, to give their decisions legitimacy, and to hold them accountable.

Elections satisfy these democratic goals, but they do so imperfectly. They determine the winners, but the winners are not always compatible with each other, much less with those already in power. Elections choose the most popular candidates (with the obvious exception of the 2000 presidential contest), but popularity and governing ability are not synonymous and, in some cases, may not even be closely related.

Elections for different offices at different levels of government over different time periods more often than not yield mixed verdicts. Governing becomes more difficult when the differences among elected officials outweigh their commonalities. Adding to the problem is the public's perception that successful candidates are and will continue to be primarily beholden to themselves, to their contributors, and to their constituents for election and reelection, but not necessarily to their parties, to their president, or to some larger public interest.

Doing what makes political sense for the folks back home becomes a primary guide to legislative decision making. As a consequence, the electoral process seems to mirror the country's diversity much more effectively than it reflects majority sentiment. This parochialism is a problem for governing at the national level, a problem that can be magnified by electing inexperienced candidates who in turn select inexperienced staff for advisory and administrative positions. To a limited extent, however, public opinion polls that reflect national popular sentiment counter the constituency orientation of legislative bodies.

The differences between campaigning and governing remain significant. Campaigns have definite winners and losers; government does not. Campaigns are replete with political and ideological rhetoric. Such rhetoric is an impediment to compromise in policymaking. Campaigns generate a crisis atmosphere; such an atmosphere is not conducive to the deliberation and adjustments that must accompany sound policymaking.

Because governing is being conducted more and more in the public arena, however, the campaigning skills of going public, that is, of tailoring and targeting messages to special groups to build support and achieve a favorable impression, are becoming an increasingly important component of governing.

Elections are supposed to guide public officials in what they do and in when and how they do it, but their outcomes often present mixed verdicts and messages. Unless the electorate is voting directly on a policy initiative, it is difficult to cull the meaning of an election, much less translate that meaning into a policy agenda for government. Exit polls and other national surveys provide some guidance about voters' attitudes, opinions, and the most salient issues, but they aren't exact measures, and certainly not blueprints, for governing. Opinions change, as do conditions. As a consequence, public officials usually have considerable discretion when making policy judgments, as long as they do so within the broad parameters of mainstream politics.

The potential for election defeat, combined with negative publicity and a "thin skin" for criticism, keeps elected officials responsive to their constituencies, more so on an individual than on a collective basis. Accountability is enhanced by transparency in government, by an attentive media, and by an opposition that wishes to gain political advantage from the decisions and actions of their partisan opponents. It is made more difficult by divided partisan control of government.

Elections are also important for converting promises into performance. The key here is not only the composition of the majority, but also the ability of its elected leadership to convert a winning electoral coalition into a winning governing coalition. To be effective, that coalition has to cross constituency, institutional, and sometimes even partisan lines, which is why its composition may shift issue by issue.

Do elections serve government? Yes, they do. They renew and reinforce the link between the elected and the electorate. They contribute to policy direction, coalition building, and legitimacy for and accountability in government. But they do so imperfectly and often indirectly, and they sometimes impede rather than enhance governing.

Now It's Your Turn

Discussion Questions

1. Is the election of public officials who are more ideologically and politically compatible with one another a good or bad development for American democracy? Explain why or why not.
2. How would federal elections have to be changed if the electorate were given the opportunity to vote on the issues rather than just on the candidates running for office? Would the meaning of elections be clearer and governing made easier by issue voting?
3. Can the representative character of government and collective responsibility in government be enhanced at the same time?
4. How do elections affect the permanent government, what the bureaucracy does, and how it does it?
5. Now that you have completed this book, how would you answer the question posed by its title: "Is this any way to run a democratic election?" What are the principal strengths and weaknesses of the U.S. electoral system from a democratic perspective?

Topics for Debate
Challenge or defend the following statements:

1. To enhance responsiveness and accountability in government, all elected public officials should stand for reelection at the same time every four years.
2. The electorate should be given the opportunity to express its opinion on the ten most salient issues when voting in national elections.
3. No congressional impeachment and conviction of the president should take place unless approved in a special election by American voters.
4. All candidates for the presidency should be required to announce their cabinet choices at least one month before the election.
5. All new public officials should be required to take a course on the structure and operations of the institution to which they were elected or appointed.

Exercises

1. Upset by the gap between democratic theory and practice, a presidential commission has been studying ways to make American elections more compatible with the goals of a democratic political system. The commission has identified three objectives that it hopes any new electoral process will meet:
   a. Public preferences for individual candidates and the priorities they should pursue should be clearly identified.
   b. Public opinion on the most salient and controversial policy issues should be determined.
   c. The public's evaluation of how well those in power have performed in office should be indicated.

With those objectives in mind, suggest changes to make American elections more compatible with democratic goals. Also tell the commission how you would implement the changes you are suggesting and their likely impact on government.

2. List the campaign promises that Barack Obama made in his 2008 presidential campaign. You can find these promises on the Web site of most major news organizations or www.barackobama.com.
   Determine, if you can,
   a. how Obama prioritized these promises,
   b. which of them he has tried to achieve and which of them he actually has achieved, and
   c. which of his promises he has ignored, modified, or reversed.

On the basis of your analysis, how would you rate Obama's success in converting his campaign agenda into a governing agenda and then into public policy?

INTERNET RESOURCES

Most major media sources report the large election exit poll in detail. The Gallup Organization (www.gallup.com) as well as the Pew Research Center for the People and the Press (www.people-press.org) conduct preelection and postelection surveys and make the results available on their Web sites. For a longitudinal analysis, the preelection and postelection American National Election Surveys (www.electionstudies.org) are the source of data that most political scientists use when analyzing elections. These data are usually available about six months after the election. The Election Assistance Commission issues the official results of the national election on its Web site (www.eac.gov); however, the fastest listing of unofficial results is on the wire services, such as the Associated Press (www.ap.org).

SELECTED READINGS

Abramson, Paul R., John H. Aldrich, and David W. Rohde. *Change and Continuity in the 2008 Elections.* Washington, D.C.: CQ Press, 2010.

———. "The 2004 Presidential Election: The Emergence of a Permanent Majority?" *Political Science Quarterly* 120 (2005): 33–57.

Conley, Patricia Heidotting. *Presidential Mandates: How Elections Shape the National Agenda.* Chicago: University of Chicago Press, 2001.

Dahl, Robert A. "Myth of the Presidential Mandate." *Political Science Quarterly* 105 (1990): 355–372.

Fishel, Jeff. *Presidents and Promises.* Washington, D.C.: CQ Books, 1985.

Ginsberg, Benjamin, and Alan Stone, eds. *Do Elections Matter?* Armonk, N.Y.: M. E. Sharpe, 1996.

Jacobson, Gary C. "Polarized Politics and the 2004 Congressional and Presidential Elections." *Political Science Quarterly* 120 (2005): 199–218.

———. "The 2008 Presidential and Congressional Elections: Anti-Bush Referendum and Prospects for the Democratic Majority." *Political Science Quarterly* 124 (Spring 2009): 1–30.

Miller, Arthur H., and Martin P. Wattenberg. "Throwing the Rascals Out: Policy and Performance Evaluations of Presidential Candidates: 1952–1980." *American Political Science Review* 79 (1985): 359–372.

Popkin, Samuel L. *The Reasoning Voter.* Chicago: University of Chicago Press, 1991.

Wattenberg, Martin, ed. "2004 Presidential Election." *Presidential Studies Quarterly* 36 (2006): 141–296.

NOTES

1. The term "a government of strangers" was first suggested by Hugh Heclo in his book *A Government of Strangers* (Washington, D.C.: Brookings Institution, 1977).
2. For an excellent discussion of the differences between campaigning for and governing in the presidency, see Charles O. Jones, *Passages to the Presidency* (Washington, D.C.: Brookings Institution, 1998 Press).
3. A good example of the latter is Dick Morris, who came to President Clinton's aid after the Democrats' defeat in the 1994 midterm elections. Morris, who engineered Clinton's reelection victory, had previously worked as a political consultant for Clinton in his third campaign for the Arkansas governorship as well as for such conservative Republicans as Trent Lott, the Senate Republican leader, and Jesse Helms, a senator from North Carolina.
4. Like the candidate they supported, they also may have little executive experience and be unfamiliar with the formal and informal procedures of the institution to which their candidate has been elected and with the people who work there.

5. Although senior members of the Reagan administration did not fall into this morass with the political establishment, they did do so with civil servants who staffed the federal bureaucracy. Reagan and his supporters distrusted the national government, particularly the bureaucracy, and they tried to circumvent the permanent government when putting their priority proposals in place. The problem was that Reagan's newly appointed department heads and their aides lacked the expertise to get things done. Over time, most of Reagan's political appointees grew to depend on and respect the civil servants who worked for them.

6. *U.S. Term Limits, Inc. v. Thornton*, 514 U.S. 779 (1995).

7. In addition to policy initiatives, some states also have a procedure known as a referendum, which allows a state legislature to place items directly before the voters on an election ballot.

8. A federal district court in San Francisco found that many of these restrictions were unconstitutional.

9. The one measure that was approved prohibited certain state officials from getting salary increases when the budget was in deficit.

10. Richard J. Ellis, "The States: Direct Democracy," in *The Elections of 2000*, ed. Michael Nelson (Washington, D.C.: CQ Press, 2001), 143–145.

11. The measure that was defeated would have prevented the use of public resources for political purposes. Sizemore wanted to prohibit public unions from deducting funds to be used in political campaigns.

12. Ellis, "The States," 137.

13. *Buckley v. American Constitutional Law Foundation*, 97 U.S. 930 (1999).

14. Ellis, "The States," 134.

15. For issues to be an most important influence on voting behavior, voters must have an opinion about them, perceive differences in the candidates' positions, and then vote on the basis of these differences and in the direction of their own policy preferences.

16. The random selection is made within states in such a way that principal geographic units (cities, suburbs, and rural areas) and a precinct's size and past voting record are taken into account. Approximately 1,200 representatives of the polling organization administer the poll to voters who are chosen in a systematic way (for example, every fourth or fifth person) as they leave the voting booths. Voters are asked to complete a short questionnaire (thirty to forty items) designed to elicit information on voting choices, political attitudes, candidate evaluations and feelings, and the demographic characteristics of those who voted. Several times over the course of the day, the questionnaires are collected and tabulated, and the results are sent to a central computer bank. After most or all of the election polls in a state have been completed, the findings of the exit poll are made public. Over the course of the evening they are adjusted to reflect the actual results as they are tabulated.

17. "2008 Exit Polls," *New York Times*, November 5, 2008, http://elections.nytimes.com/2008/results/president/exit-polls.html.

18. Center for Media and Public Affairs, "TV News Turned Sour on Bush after Iraq War Ended," press release, December 17, 2003.

INDEX

Note: Figures, notes, and tables are indicated by f, n, and t following the page number.